BOOKED!

BOOKED!
THE GOSPEL
ACCORDING TO OUR
FOOTBALL HEROES

JOHN SMITH AND DAN TRELFER
FOREWORD BY LEE DIXON

First published by Pitch Publishing, 2018

Pitch Publishing
A2 Yeoman Gate
Yeoman Way
Worthing
Sussex
BN13 3QZ
www.pitchpublishing.co.uk
info@pitchpublishing.co.uk

A CIP catalogue record is available for this book
from the British Library.

ISBN 978-1-78531-393-6

Typesetting and origination by Pitch Publishing
Printed in the UK by TJ International, Padstow, Cornwall

Contents

Foreword
By Lee Dixon

All I can say is: it's about time. With so many autobiographies by footballers out there, it's difficult to keep up. Even with my natural curiosity about the lives of other players, I simply haven't had time to read all the books by my contemporaries, let alone those who came before me and those who came after. (I played with Paul Merson for ten years and still haven't bothered to read *both* of his books; sorry, Merse.) So thank goodness that John and Dan have done the legwork for us and present here the stories, opinions and best bits from well over a hundred stars of the game.

There are three things you need to know about '*Booked!*' Firstly, this has clearly been a passion project for the authors, and their love of the game and its many characters constantly shines through. Secondly, it's very, very funny, and you will laugh a lot. And thirdly, while footballers love to embellish things a little for the sake of spinning a good yarn, the stories contained within this book are authentic and enlightening, and take me back to the dressing room, the training ground and, of course, the pitch of my own playing days. I might have been there when some of this stuff happened, including Steve Bould's epic nine-dinner coach journey (you'll see), but certain parts of this book were eye-opening, even for me.

With the 2018 World Cup having been one of the best in living memory, maybe football fans are falling in love with the game all over again – and this book is a good place to start, either for the dedicated football fan who already has an in-depth knowledge of the game, or for the more casual supporter who just likes funny, interesting and occasionally outrageous stories.

It was nice to be asked to write at the front of this book, and I guarantee that by the time you reach the back of it, you will have a better understanding of some much-loved people in the game, you will have plenty of stories to share with mates and you might even have a new-found appetite for reading the books of footballers. But most of all, you will have laughed a lot. And you can't say fairer than that.

Enjoy yourselves.

Introduction

'I have never taken drugs, but I would imagine that the nearest thing to a psychedelic experience must be winning the FA Cup Final at Wembley.'

It begins, as all things should and must, with The Keegan.

Until the person who has both taken psychedelic drugs *and* won the FA Cup steps forward to either confirm or deny the above statement (we might be looking at you, Brian Kilcline), we are duty bound to take Kevin's word for it. We may have a list of other players that might potentially help with our enquiries in that area, but this book is not about speculation. Rather it's about the facts, and the first-hand accounts, and the nuggets of gold, like our opener from King Kev.

His statement is the very tip of the iceberg of profound truth, dubious wisdom, cod philosophy, eye-watering vitriol, troublesome muck-raking, wild speculation, infuriating inaccuracy, outright fibs, surprising vindictiveness and banter (oh, the endless banter) that can be found within that greatest of book genres – the footballer's autobiography.

This book is a sort of almanac of the funniest, strangest, stupidest and most brilliant things we have found in reading so many of these joyous memoirs, but it also serves as a portrait of the average footballer – and sometimes the above-average footballer.

Former (insert almost any Scottish football club outside the big ones here and it will likely work) midfielder Chic Charnley says, 'Hindsight is a wonderful thing. Unfortunately, it's absolutely bloody useless.' This book takes the opposite view. We bloody love the hindsight. And not just because Charnley goes on to tell us about the time his manager genuinely murdered a living creature and threw the carcass at a player as part of a motivational team talk.

In the modern world of football, we can see too much. Our newspapers, computers and chosen mobile devices can be saturated with football, from the tiniest morsel of speculative transfer gossip, to every possible stat you could want about every player or team you could want. In an era when we can access live Turkish second-tier football at the click of a mouse, who among us has time to keep up with it all?

As we drown under an avalanche of instant information and access it's easy to forget what's truly important in this game we love – the little things. Such as:

- Stuart Pearce claiming he can recognise every one of his team-mates just by their feet.
- That time Ian Marshall frightened the medical staff at Bolton by attaching his heart monitor to his dog without telling them.
- The manager who used a glove puppet as part of his unsuccessful cup final team talk.

Moments like these could be lost to us like tears in the rain if we don't stop for a moment, take stock and indulge in a sumptuous feast of hindsight. With this in mind, your authors have read and digested well in excess of one hundred footballer autobiographies, so you don't have to. And now we're ready to excrete the very best and, naturally, the very worst bits into this critical compendium. You're welcome, society. This book contains genuine moments of ...

Insight:

'Some people have suggested that I was able to see more than other players because my eyes are further apart than normal.'

– Pelé on why he was so very bloody good

Inspiration:

'He was the man that gave me the courage to wear ripped jeans.'

– Ashley Cole on Freddie Ljungberg

Hero-worship:

'If he'd have told me to stick my head in a bucket of shit I'd have done it without hesitation.'

– Roy McDonough on playing for Bobby Moore

And Outlandish Boasts:

'Not only did we introduce button-down collar shirts into the

West Riding which, until then, were unheard of, we also started the Wooly Bully dance craze too.'

– Frank Worthington on him and his trend-setting mate Glyn

And that's just the content. That's before we touch upon the colourful prose. Joseph Heller once responded to being asked why he had never written anything as good as *Catch-22* with a pithy 'Who has?' We can only assume that Heller has never come across the Barry Fry autobiography chapter entitled 'Play-offs, promotion and ponces'. And we suspect he's never soaked up the glory of a great chapter from the pen of Wally Downes called 'Bish, Bash, Bosh', where Downes asserts: 'The start of 1986 was, to put it lightly, shit.' And surely we can be certain that Joseph H has definitely not sat down in his comfiest armchair to lose himself in Alan Brazil's evocative opening to *There's an Awful Lot of Bubbly in Brazil*:

'It was the most beautiful evening you could imagine in the ski resort of Meribel. The sky was inky black, the snow was as white as a tin of Dulux paint.'

Stirring stuff, we're sure you agree. Not a crisp clean sheet, not a glistening, bejewelled blanket, not a fresh page on which to write the story of your day, but a tin of white paint. Specifically, Dulux paint. Strong enough to open with, Alan? Yeah, that'll probably do.

Every footballer is as unique and wonderful as a snowflake, each with their own unusual anecdotes and strange quirks. And yet, after devouring so many of these books, we've discovered that, in many ways, they're remarkably similar too. Regardless of the era in which they played, it seems that most footballers have been arrested, met Rod Stewart and/or witnessed the wanton destruction of shoes or socks in the name of team bonding. Managers will often be disparaged, even despised, but almost always simply because the man in question wasn't writing the name of our unreliable narrator on his team sheet every week. And we've found that just about every footballer has some kind of anecdote involving male genitalia. Perhaps it's a natural consequence of seeing your workmates naked every day, we're not really sure, but footballers genuinely do have a thing about their winkles and balls.

As time goes on, the footballer autobiography may become a lost art form. Current and future players will be earning enough money on a weekly basis to swim in it like Scrooge McDuck, so may decide they have no need to spill their guts in the hope of selling a few books and boosting the pension pot. Instead, they may choose to keep their thoughts and feelings private, meaning we may never know what makes the likes of Ruben Loftus-Cheek tick.

Players are more guarded now, and why wouldn't they be? Their every move off the pitch is documented by tabloid journalists for their papers and websites, or by Citizen Media with their arsenal of iPhones who are waiting to record every Shisha Pipe, balloon full of laughing gas, or sexual indiscretion before launching the outrage on to your Twitters, your Facebooks or your Instagrams of this world, where millions lie in wait to greedily inhale every crumb of information about them. The distance created between these multi-millionaires and the average fan will become a chasm, and it will all be because of our efforts to get closer to them.

But we're waffling here, and getting a bit bogged down early doors. Paul Merson put it far more succinctly in his cautionary tale, *How Not to Be a Professional Footballer*, when he said: 'We didn't have Facebook when I was crapping on Spunky's balcony or throwing Grovesy in the sea.'

Indeed.

One of the big complaints about players and managers today is that they are media-trained to within an inch of their lives. In post-match interviews, they give nothing away – humble to the point of parody after a big win; no more than a hint of disappointment after a heavy defeat. Fans sigh and say how boring they are and how there are no characters left in the game. And to some extent that is all true. Footballers are, generally speaking, meek and dull and predictable in TV or radio interviews. They go out of their way to not be controversial, to not give the press anything to write about, fearful of creating a feeding frenzy with a misplaced comment. But until the art form dies out, there is still one arena where they feel free to open up: the autobiography. And open up they do. In some cases, they open up far more than really anyone would expect or, perhaps, would even want. If they said some of the stuff on TV that they put in their books, it would be on the front page of every tabloid – every day.

So if it's all the juice and the marrow, the fun and the feuds you want, from well over a hundred lifetimes in football, without actually having to pore through tens of thousands of pages yourself, then read on.

We go again.

1

Title Contenders

Hoddledygook

As we've established, there are an awful lot of footballer autobiographies. As well as a lot of awful footballer autobiographies. In this crowded market it's important to try to make your book leap from the crowd like Sergio Ramos at a corner and demand attention. A catchy, interesting title can help significantly with that. On the other hand, if you're a footballer, you're already instantly recognisable to anybody who might buy and read it anyway, and you have access to a loyal fanbase that consistently proves itself willing to part with hard-earned money for any old rubbish they are served up (bad performances, third kits, club shop tat etc.), so why bother?

And not bothering is very much the watchword for many players who clearly think that a nice snap and a simple title will do. Hence the plethora of 'My Story', 'My Life in Football' or 'My Autobiography' efforts clogging up the shelves. Surely we can do better than that? We're not saying everyone needs to call their book *Snod This for a Laugh*,[1] but come on. 'My Autobiography' particularly rankles. Of course it's your autobiography if you wrote it about your life. Who else's autobiography is it going to be? Hats off then to those who get it right and call it 'The Autobiography', and hats even further aloft to the ones that call it 'An Autobiography' in the hope of milking their experiences for a sequel or two somewhere down the line.

One such chancer drip-feeding us his every thought is Harry Redknapp. His first book is called *My Autobiography*, the updated version

---

1   It's by Ian Snodin. We still think 'In Snod We Trust' or 'A Snod's as Good as a Wink' would've been better. At least they're left open for Glyn Snodin to snap up. You can have those, Glyn.

is *Always Managing: My Autobiography*, and then he went off-piste with *A Man Walks On To a Pitch* and *It Shouldn't Happen to a Manager*. The latter two consist mainly of dubious anecdotes and best XIs and are thin gruel if we're honest. If the trend continues, Harry will end up with a book called 'Two Nuns in a Bath' containing nothing but shopping lists and Kevin Bond's petrol receipts.

However, at least Redknapp hasn't got a hashtag in his book title. Unlike Rio Ferdinand with his *#2Sides*. Hashtags is it now? We give it less than five years before we have a footballer titling his book with just emojis. Our money's on Jack Wilshere.

So how can they get it right? It can't be that hard. There's plenty of sensible middle ground in which to operate between 'My Story' and *Fuckin' Hell! It's Paul Cannell* (genuine title), right? You don't need to be all Brian Eno about it and call it *Stillness and Speed* like Dennis Bergkamp, but we do ask that you spend more than the 30 seconds it took Kelly Smith to come up with *Footballer*. Come on, Kelly.

Of course, a play on words around a name or nickname is a solid start. *Drinks All Round* (Kevin Drinkell), *Hell Razor* (Neil Ruddock) and *The School of Hard Knox* (Archie Knox), all deserve a pat on the back, while Phil Thompson (*Stand Up Pinocchio*), Paul Sturrock (*Luggy*) and Andy Morrison (*The Good, the Mad and the Ugly*) probably want more of an arm round the shoulder as they mine their physical failings for titles. It's okay, guys – did Christina Aguilera's 'Beautiful' teach us nothing?

There are one or two travesties out there too. Neville Southall, who in recent years has emerged as a potential leader of a glorious revolution on Twitter,[2] called his book *The Binman Chronicles*. Nev is doing himself a disservice there, as the greatest keeper in the history of Wales was only ever on the dust for three weeks, but it followed him in the press his whole career.

Leroy Rosenior's excellent *It's Only Banter* is a disturbing first-hand account of horrific racial abuse suffered as a footballer in the 80s – not a compendium of shoes being cut up or nailed to the floor. Rumours that Jimmy Bullard bought it and was sadly disappointed are unconfirmed.

Meanwhile, there's John Wark. Shut your eyes for a moment and picture John Wark. Noble moustache for sure; flowing locks

---

2 Of that 1985/86 Everton squad, the early signs were that it would be Gary Lineker that led us out of the darkness.

occasionally; dynamic running in his pomp; a whiff of my Uncle Stan about him in his playing dotage, perhaps – but for eight out of ten of you he's wearing an Ipswich shirt, right?

Whether it's got Fisons on it or not is probably down to your age, but it's Ipswich right enough. Of course it is. He played more than 500 games for Ipswich in three spells, won the UEFA Cup, was part of that lovely Arnold Muhren/Frans Thijssen[3] team under Bobby Robson, and was even the face of the club in that cringeworthy 'Alive & Kicking' Sky Premier League advert. We'd go so far as to say he's the first player we think of when we think of Ipswich (with apologies to Romeo Zondervan).

So what does he call his entertaining book? *Wark On*. He's playing on 'You'll Never Walk Alone', and the copy we read featured him in a Liverpool shirt on the cover. A real kick in the plums for the Tractor Lads, that.

There are those titles that ask more questions than they answer, too. Ashley Cole's is called *My Defence* with good reason, as he was taking stick from all sides when it was published. Dominic Matteo's is called *In My Defence*, but nobody's sure what it is he needs to be so defensive about. The cover gives us few clues, unless he's nicked that expensive watch he's flashing.

Mike/Mick Duxbury calls his book *It's Mick Not Mike*, so it has obviously bothered him for many years that people call him Mike not Mick … or Mick not Mike, we forget which now. And yet he doesn't address this issue once within his book. Not once. So now we're none the wiser. To be honest, he should think himself lucky people don't call him John Gidman and move on with his stories. Sorry, Mick/Mike.[4]

Duncan McKenzie calls his book *The Last Fancy Dan* but does very little within the pages to justify this. Rodney Marsh, however, uses the phrase 'loose cannon' upwards of 40 times in his autobiography to prove that he wasn't joking when he called it *I Was Born a Loose Cannon*. He's

---

3   One of your authors had a Frans Thijssen Unpuncturable Football as a boy. Not sure where that gets us, but it's true. The author's brother had one too. Why it was felt two footballs that could never be punctured were needed, we don't know.

4   Didn't Mick/Mike Channon have this same issue? We never heard him moaning about it and he named his book after one of his horses (*Man on the Run*). Incidentally, places we found Mick Duxbury referred to as Mike include: Wikipedia, Man Utd's official web page, the *Manchester Evening News* and on thefa.com's England player profiles. Poor bloke.

a Loose Cannon you see, and, like a Loftus Road Lady Gaga, he was 'Born This Way'.[5]

While we're on the subject of those 70s mavericks with skill to burn and questionable work rates, we can't ignore Frank Worthington's title, *One Hump or Two*. Terrific stuff. Rather than focus on his footballing prowess, Frank prefers to bring his sexy times to the fore. That title might not sound like a pun, but Frank is pictured drinking a brew on the cover (presumably with one or two sugars in), which doesn't clear things up that much to be honest, unless Frank was famous for advertising, or drinking, Typhoo back in the day. Hitting the pun mark much more cleanly and bringing just as much sexy to the table is Frank McAvennie. Both men are Frank by name and Frank by nature. McAvennie's *Scoring: An Expert's Guide* is so called because as well as being a goalscorer, he liked scoring with lasses an' that. Macca was also the subject of a Channel 4 documentary around the time of the book's release called *How to Score*, in case you were in any doubt that he liked doing it with girls. If we were being cynical, we might even suggest that it may also refer to scoring 'a wee bit of Charlie' now and again. In which case, hats off to Frank for a rare Triple Entendre title.

OTHER TITLES OF NOTE

- Johan Cruyff – *My Turn* (just lovely).
- Steve Nicol – *Five League Titles and a Packet of Crisps*.
- John Aldridge – *Alright Aldo, Sound as a Pound* (you can't go wrong quoting *The Anfield Rap*).
- Paul Parker – *Tackles Like a Ferret*.
- Duncan Shearer – *Shearer Wonderland: The Autobiography* (just for the sheer cheek of *Duncan* Shearer putting this out).

CHAPTER TITLES

As both Frank Worthington and Frank McAvennie will tell you, between the covers anything goes. That is to say, once you're hooked by the book title, we can all have fun calling our chapters whatever we want. This Liberty Hall approach led to some crackers such as 'Do

---

5 Half the authors of this book think Rodney should have called his book *Hot Rod* or *A Marsh a Day*, the other half can't get worked up about it.

Not Shit on David Seaman's Balcony' in which Paul Merson details shitting on David Seaman's balcony; 'If Only I Had Mark Hughes's Thighs', which goes a long way to explaining Robbie Savage devoting his media career to the promotion of Sparky's cause; and 'Blade Runner in Maryhill' in which Chic Charnley tells of that time he was chased around the Partick Thistle car park with a sword. We've all been there.

Some are more gifted at this sort of thing than they ever were at football. Paul Cannell alone gives us 'Grab a Granny Night', 'If It Moves Kick It, If It Doesn't Move, Kick It 'Til It Does' and 'One up the Bum, No Harm Done!', some of which come with stories you'll find within this book. He also gives us the cruel but funny chapter 'Meggy Thoo', which tells of Frank Clark's testimonial do. Frank got up to croon a certain Buddy Holly number, and with his 'slight speech impediment', Cannell describes him singing 'his very own rendition of "Meggy Thoo, Meggy Thoo, mitty, mitty, mitty, mitty, Meggy Thoo!"'

The manager who got the best tune out of Frank Clark was Brian Clough. Genius though he was, and perhaps deserving of his book title *Walking on Water*, we're not sure we can forgive him for calling a chapter 'Gazzamatazz and Hoddledygook'. And if he's pushing his goodwill to the limit with that one, then Lee McCulloch, having already had the temerity to call his book *Simp-Lee the Best*, severely tests our patience with the chapter 'Leeding out My Team'.

Lee shows us how easy it is to get a pun wrong, something we'll no doubt join him in as we go along, but when people get them right, only the most stone-cold-hearted would deny that they can be a thing of beauty. Therefore, let's take a moment to bow at the feet of Roy McDonough. The lower-league journeyman, who tells his life story in the extraordinary *Red Card Roy*, surely only joined non-league Heybridge Swifts and failed there so that he could call a chapter 'Heybridge Too Far': bravo.

Some people use their chapters to either show off their best friends, such as Mark Halsey's fawning 'Me and Jose',[6] or to grind an axe, as in Lawrie McMenemy's 'A Paine in the Grass', in which he tells us what an arsehole Terry Paine was to him at Southampton, or Stan Ternent with 'I Dreamed of Killing Him' – Ian Porterfield, since you ask. Thankfully he didn't go through with it.

---

6   Mourinho, not Feliciano or Maria Olazabal, disappointingly.

Let's finish up here with Joey Barton's excellent *No Nonsense* (warning: may contain traces of nonsense), in which the thinking man's thinking man asserts his indie credentials by having a chapter which takes its name from the Smiths song 'Sweet and Tender Hooligan'. Admirable though that is as a break from the Rod Stewart worship that's rife among the football fraternity, we can't help feeling it's a little too on the nose. Barton might have paid better homage by coming up with his own chapter titles that might also work as Morrissey solo tracks. That's what so many of his colleagues do.

Oh yes, they do. Look.

THE LAST FANCY DAN

(A fantasy Morrissey album. We even found the perfect cover featuring Duncan McKenzie and his carpet sweeper, which you can see among our pictures.)

1. This England   (Carlton Palmer)
2. I Should Have Tried to Understand (Brian Clough)
3. The Leaves That Never Fade (Bobby Charlton)
4. Life Is a Play Thing for You Foolish Clown (John McGovern)
5. Not Bitter But Angry (Graham Poll)
6. Is This All There Is? (Lee Sharpe)
7. The Kindness of Women (Carlton Palmer)
8. England for the English (Terry Venables)
9. The Biggest Mistake of My Life (Brian Clough)
10. Lovelorn in Rotterdam (Lee Sharpe)
11. Young Man, Are You Good Enough to Play for Me? (Brian Laws)

Told you.

2

The Legend of Andy McDaft

Petulant Cake

During a break from the research for this book, we were watching a 1982 episode of *The Big Match* because … okay, there's a fine line between research for this book and our typical leisure activities.

A very fine line.

In the show, South Coast Godfather and *How* legend Fred Dinenage was presenting highlights of a Graham Taylor-era Watford side (Barnes, Blissett, Rostron and all) soundly beating Arsenal at … well, wherever they played before the Emirates Stadium was built. Dinenage noted the criticism Watford had been receiving for their long-ball style, before claiming that, as a result, the Hornets were now known as the 'Wholesalers'.

Yes, the Wholesalers.

You know: 'Because they don't need any middle men'.

Now, as far as we're aware, this never caught on. For starters, it's a little convoluted, and what we've learned about footballers from reading all their books is that, in general, they prefer a nickname to be simple and effective – rather like Graham Taylor's Watford, in fact.

Now, some footballer nicknames do stand out like Peter Crouch at a Xherdan Shaqiri lookalike contest – there's the justifiably celebrated 'One Size' Fitz Hall, the bizarre 'Andy McDaft' for Kevin Keegan, and the baffling 'Vitch' for Ronnie Whelan. But on the whole, the football fraternity doesn't stray too far from the tried and tested rules of the nickname game.

For the most part, our reading has confirmed that still the most popular way of developing a nickname is to simply take the first syllable of a player's surname and then add a 'y' (or an 'ie' in special cases). Examples of this are legion, and, while some people might pine for a definitive list of footballers from the last 150 years whose nicknames conform to this simple convention, while this might be the time, it's not the place. Or this might be the place, but we haven't got the time. One of those.

However, there are plenty of obvious examples: Ryan 'Giggsy' Giggs; Ian 'Wrighty' Wright; David 'Platty' Platt; and, using a slight variation on the rule by utilising the second syllable of the surname rather than the first, Ally 'Coisty' McCoist.

In rare cases, the y-suffix name is almost inexplicably extended to a third syllable to take in the entire surname. This is strange, because surely the whole point of a nickname is to make it shorter or easier to say, particularly on the football field. In Ian Snodin's book (himself an interesting case – he tells his readers that he was known as 'Snods' everywhere until he joined Everton, where he became 'Snowy', presumably because the Everton players thought his name was pronounced 'Snow-din' (an issue commentators of the time certainly wrestled with[7])), we discovered that the Everton defender and later coach Mick Lyons was known as 'Lyonsy.'

'Lyonsy' seems to us an unnecessary mouthful, especially when there are clearly perfectly viable alternatives, like 'Micky' or 'Ly'. Or, thinking laterally, 'Tiger' or 'Puma'. Who wouldn't want to be known as Puma? Or even 'Liono', had *ThunderCats* not come along too late for him. An opportunity missed.

Then there's Rangers and Scotland legend Ian Durrant, or 'Durranty', as Lee McCulloch (among others) refers to him. Never in history, surely, has the y-suffix rule been so awfully abused. It's like nicknaming Gary Lineker 'Linekery'. It's more description than name: 'What kind of player is he?' 'Midfielder. Bit Durranty, I suppose.'

As Durranty and Gordon Durie are about the same age, we wondered if he was named 'Durranty' because calling him 'Durie' would have

---

7 It's cases like this that make structuring hard and fast rules for the awarding of nicknames extremely complex and a bit frustrating. Why didn't Snods point out that they were saying his name wrongly?

caused confusion. But while they both did play for Rangers, Durranty was there from 1984 and Durie didn't join until 1994, so the theory died there. Plus, as any fool knows, Durie's nickname was 'Jukebox' (one of the all-time great nicknames, that. Some might say it's a little obvious, but 'Broadway' would be the obvious nickname for Danny Rose (after 'Rosie', obviously) and there's no evidence Harry Kane or Dele Alli have ever called him that) so Durranty could have been Durie without duplication, even in the Scotland squad. Unfathomable.

And then there's Jimmy Greaves, who calls his book *Greavsie*. For a start, Greaves didn't need to be known as Greavsie. His nickname was already 'Jimmy', a classic, if not *the* classic footballer's name: easy to shout, easy to shorten if necessary, easy to work into a chant on the terraces. But that's beside the point.

What exactly is he trying to hide? What's his game? How did he go from 'Greaves' to 'Greavsie'? What happened to the second 'e'? Why is it 'Greavsie' and not 'Greavesy'? Just what is he trying to pull? Why have we all just accepted it for so long? And then, just to complicate things further, Ian St John would often call him 'James' on *Saint and Greavsie,* thereby turning his actual given name into a kind of nickname, and sucking us nickname scholars into a kind of Greavsie nickname vortex.

St John is a good example of a player who doesn't have a y-suffix nickname. For him, and many others, the formula simply doesn't work and an alternative needs to be found, usually by substituting the 'y' for an 'o', an 's' or an 'ers' (although in his case, he had the handy 'Saint' in between Ian and John). There are four distinct occasions when a deviation from the 'y' becomes necessary:

1. **Using the 'y' suffix will result in the player having a girl's name for a nickname.**

This obviously cannot happen. Certain players have had female nicknames, of course, but generally they're given by fans or the media. For example, Glenn Hoddle is often known as 'Glenda' to fans, but we found no mention of that name in any of the books we read, despite Hoddle popping up many times (and not usually in a complimentary manner). Then there's Robbie 'Lily' Savage, but again, this seems very much like a terraces nickname, rather than anything his peers gave him. Sav says that Leicester club legend Alan Birchenall did call him 'Lil' but adds (slightly unconvincingly): 'Luckily he was on his own with that one.'

But back to the point. We did not come across a y-suffix nickname that resulted in the player having a girl's name. David Beckham is not Becky (although 'Becks' is admittedly borderline), Jamie Carragher is not Carrie and Steve Vickers is not Vicky. There may be exceptions, but broadly, this is the rule.

2. **The player's surname already ends in 'y' or 'ie', thus rendering the nickname the same as the surname and, therefore, not a nickname.**

Examples: Wayne Rooney, Gareth Barry, Gary Kelly, Dele Alli.

But what happens in this situation? Well, we learned from Kerry Dixon that David Speedie's nickname was 'Speedo', making it the most redundant nickname in football history, as the only natural conclusion we can draw is that if his name had been David Speedo, he would have been nicknamed 'Speedie'. Why bother changing it?

Players stuck with a 'y' surname are often given an obvious alternative. Jason McAteer refers to Gary Kelly as 'Kells', for instance. But this isn't always the case – Dele Alli is apparently known as 'Delstroyer', which is at least imaginative, if a little long-winded.

Meanwhile, in Kevin Keegan's 1978 autobiography, he constantly refers to Don Revie, who had recently resigned as England manager, as 'The Revs'. Never just 'Revs', always '*The* Revs'. Keegan is the only player we've found who calls him this – it's like his own personal nickname for Revie, and it makes us hope beyond hope that The Revs, in turn, affectionately called him 'The Kevs'. However, by the time The Kevs wrote his second life story in 1997, it seems he'd totally forgotten this genial name, and instead only refers to him as 'Don'.

3. **It just doesn't sound right.**

For some reason, some surnames just don't work when shortened to the y-suffix. No one has ever called either of the Neville brothers 'Nevvy', and Kyle Walker is not known as 'Walky' – we're not even sure what he is known as, to be honest, but we'd bet on 'Walks'.

Whether or not the y-suffix works is something intangible – you can't always quite put your finger on why certain names just don't sound right. It means that sometimes footballers have to resort to using the 'ers' suffix (e.g., Terry 'Venners' Venables), which is traditionally more the preserve of the cricket fraternity: Michael 'Athers' Atherton, Henry 'Blowers' Blofeld, Phil 'Tuffers' Tufnell and so on. Tuffers is an interesting one, actually. Had he been a footballer, would he have been nicknamed 'Tuffy'? Feels like he might have been. Or 'Tufty', like the 1970s road-crossing safety squirrel. Choice of sport can have a huge impact on how people refer to you.

There are also rules for specific names. Anyone called Dean will be 'Deano', regardless of the suitability of their surname for the y-suffix. Dean Windass even called his book *Deano*, leaving the likes of Holdsworth, Ashton, Austin, Marney and Brian Deane with a pretty tricky task should they ever pen their much-anticipated memoirs.[8]

Similarly, Robbie Keane was known throughout his career as 'Keano', not 'Keaney' – and this would be the case for any other footballing Keane you can think of. Well, that's what we assumed. And then we read Lee Sharpe's autobiography, where, as well as delivering the unexpected revelation that he and Roy Keane were best mates at United, Lee refers to Roy, throughout, as 'Keaney'. We had always imagined if anyone called him 'Keaney' they'd receive his death stare at best, if not a full-on Haaland special. So what did Keaney call Lee? We're hoping for 'Sharpo', if only because of the enormous ructions it would send through nickname academia.

4. It would turn their name into another name or word.

No one with the surname Robinson or Robson has ever been nicknamed 'Robbie'; it's always 'Robbo'. The only person this may not have applied to was Sir Bobby Robson. He was, surely, always and only 'Bob' or 'Bobby'. Or, hopefully, in his younger days and as a mark of affection, 'Bobby Robbie'. Modern tabloids might even have referred to him as

---

8   Although, in fact, Windass himself was beaten to the punch for his catchy title by rugby star Dean Richards.

'BoRo', a bit like how Boris Johnson is known as 'BoJo'. They could have even gone on tour together: 'The BoRo–BoJo Roadshow' – although you suspect Sir Bobby would have had very little time for Johnson, so it probably wouldn't have lasted very long.

Similarly, David James could never be 'Jamie' so had to be 'Jamo', while calling Paul Merson 'Mersey' would've sounded like you were pronouncing the name of a river wrongly, so he became 'Merse'. Peter Beardsley would have been either Beery (inaccurate, as he was teetotal) or Beardie (inaccurate as he didn't wear a beard), so was known in some circles rather cutely as 'Pedro'. Having said that, Ian Snodin lets us know that Pedro had another nickname while at Everton. The lads there enjoyed a regular pub quiz at the Fisherman's Rest and Beardsley became known as 'Ceefax' because 'he knew everything about everything'. Not a bad nickname, but it seems old-fashioned now. These days, he'd be known as 'Wiki' or 'Google' … or possibly something quite different if you passed through the Newcastle youth system in the last few years.

POPULAR NICKNAMES

Beardsley's 'Ceefax' nickname is proof that footballers can and do go beyond the surname route when refusing to ever use the name their team-mate was given at birth. Outside the classics like 'Deano' and 'Smiffy', one of the most popular seems to be 'Trigger'. *Only Fools and Horses* is a real touchstone for footballers, particularly those who played in the 90s, and back then many teams named the dimmest bulb in the squad after the dimmest character in the much-loved sitcom.

Jason McAteer writes that he was the recipient of the Trigger nickname when he was part of the Ireland squad, but when he signed for Liverpool, there was already a Trigger in the shape of full-back Rob Jones. Rather than fall back to the classic 'Macca', though, the lads all called Jase 'Dave' – because, you may recall, Trigger used to call Rodney 'Dave' for some reason. All of which must've made things really confusing for poor Phil Babb, who would have had to remember to switch McAteer nicknames depending on whether he was playing for club or country.

According to Matt Le Tissier, Richard Dryden was the Trigger at Southampton: '(He) was so thick that he actually revelled in the nickname … when he was in digs he wasn't allowed to use the phone so he had to go to the call box down the street. One night he walked back and found the car was missing from the drive so he rang the police and reported it stolen – and then realized he had driven it to the phone box because it had been raining. It was still parked there.'

Tiss also tells us that Claus Lundekvam was 'Dave' at the Saints, not because he was thick and Dryden was already Trigger, but because he looked like Nicholas Lyndhurst, who played Rodney. Well, maybe if you squint. Arsenal players felt that Tony Adams looked like Lyndhurst too, but he wasn't 'Dave', he was 'Rodders'. Robbie Savage reveals that at Blackburn, their Trigger was David Bentley – fortunately, Bentley was there a few years after Jason McAteer, so there was no recurrence of the whole Trigger/Dave turmoil McAteer went through at Liverpool.

We also found two instances of pairs of players being known as 'The Krays'. Peter Storey wrote that Frank McLintock and George Graham were known by that name among some players at Arsenal in the 70s, 'on account of how close they were – like brothers'. While John McGovern says that after Brian Clough paired up Kenny Burns and Larry Lloyd as centre-backs at Forest, 'the players quickly and affectionately christened them "The Kray Twins"'.

But can you really 'affectionately' nickname people after murderous criminals? No one ever says: 'Here's my mate Steve, but we affectionately know him as Harold Shipman, because of his beard and that.' And surely at Arsenal there might have been a friendlier pair of brothers the players could have named George and Frank after? Mike and Bernie Winters were huge back then for a start.

Nicknames that have a mildly cruel, if sometimes affectionate edge, are not uncommon. In his book, Andrea Pirlo sadly tells the reader that when Roy Hodgson managed him at Inter, he would refer to him as 'Pirla', which means 'dickhead' in Italian. We suspect that was probably a mistake rather than an actual nickname, mind. Uncle Roy will be mortified if he ever finds out. No one tell him.

In his book, Sam Allardyce laments the loss of not-cool regional generalities like Mick, Jock and Taff, saying that the 'PC Brigade' would be all over the sort of nicknames that were once commonplace, but are now shied away from in football circles in case anyone feels offended: 'I've played with Gonk Head, Tefal Head, Dopey, Trigger, Plug, Squirt, you name them. Shall I go suing everyone who calls me "Big Fat Sam"? Do me a favour. I get even angrier away from football when we're told we shouldn't refer to it as "Christmas" any more, it should be "The Festive Season". What is this country coming to?'

Of course he's played with a 'Trigger'. Who hasn't? And perhaps it is a shame that the nickname 'Tefal Head'[9] has gone right out of fashion. Even so, it's a leap from there to complaining about how he's been told to refer to Christmas, but by that point he's in full rant mode, like a drunk nan at, well, Christmas. Or certainly during the festive season.

He's right about one thing, though: most nicknames are pretty harmless and they're usually taken in the spirit of joshing friendship in which they're meant. (Although Matt Le Tissier also mentions that Agustin Delgado's nickname was '"Tin Man" probably because he had no heart'. Not a lot of friendly joshing there.) Some players take this acceptance too far, however. Take, for example, Sheffield Wednesday cult hero Teddy Curran.

Yeah, old Teddy Curran. Winger. Sometime striker. Showboater. Self-acknowledged ladies' man. Teddy Curran.

Or 'Terry Curran' as he's known in the annals of football history and in any Rothmans you'd care to flick through from the era. But his real name is Edward, and for years everyone knew him as Teddy. That was until just after his professional debut, when Doncaster's assistant manager, Johnny Quigley, told the press his name was, in fact, Terry.

In Curran's book, which in the parlance of 80s tabloids is a genuine 'bonkbuster' (see 'Top Shelf' chapter for some of his more eye-watering passages), Teddy/Terry says that 'there was nothing I could do about it. I remember talking to Joe Slater, one of the local Doncaster journalists, and telling him straight that Terry wasn't my name. "Well, it sounds a lot better than Teddy!" he replied. Who was I to argue?'

And that's it. A journalist tells him 'Terry' is a better name than 'Teddy' (itself a highly contentious statement) and Terry/Teddy backs down and, for the rest of his life, simply accepts that his name has been irrevocably altered. Edward was his name, Teddy was his nickname, Terry then became his name. 'Who was I to argue?' It's your name, Ted! Surely, the single best and most qualified person to argue about the accuracy of a name is *the person who owns the name*.

---

9   For those who didn't live through the thrilling years of 1980s TV advertising, a 'Tefal Head' is a person looking like a boffin from a Tefal ad who had a massive 'spam' (meaning: forehead not covered by hair). To be clear, you would never call Steven Gerrard 'Tefal Head'.

NICKNAME NIRVANA: BOB, BERT, BORDER AND BUSY BOLLOCKS

In his book, Neil Ruddock, owner of one of the most famous nicknames in the game, reels off an astonishing list of nicknames from his Sunday pub team The Fox from when he was a young lad. They include:

'Phantom, Albert Hall, Dobber, Double Dobber (Dobber's big brother!), Padge, The Real Padgy, Mad Mutley, Poker, Strutter, Legger, Fagin, Spanner, Tonto, Shed, Yogi, Charlie the Limp, Bullseye, Satellite's German Boyfriend, Tradesman's, Signal Box, Bunger, Bambi and Turkey Tel'.

Absolutely phenomenal work. Thanks to the proliferation of surname-plus-y-or-ie nicknames in the professional game, it'd be easy to read that lot and assume that nickname creativity is the preserve of the vibrant amateur game, where people still play for the fun of ball-kicking, rather than the fun of earning millions for ball-kicking. But that's not quite true. Our reading has led us to plenty of nicknames that rival Razor's excellent list, either for the name itself, or for the reason behind it. Here are our favourites.

Name: Tony Galvin.
Nickname: 'The Russian'.
Reason: Says Ossie Ardiles: 'Because he studied Russian. He had finished secondary school and had taken on Russian at university. Why? I'm sure even he doesn't know why. Which is typical of Tony as a person. Being in tertiary education, he was absolutely an exception to the norm.'
Notes: This is a nice nickname, but feels a little on the nose. 'Lenin' or 'Tolstoy' would've been better. Or, if a football flavour was required, 'Lev' after legendary Russian keeper Lev Yashin would have been lovely. Also, we are confident that this is the only use of the phrase 'tertiary education' in footballer autobiography history, making it a new sort of Googlewhack.

Name: Dave Bassett.
Nickname: 'Harry'.
Reason: Obviously, everyone knows this nickname. But the reason for it is unexpected. After claiming the question of why he's known as Harry has 'plagued him all his life' (all right, mate, calm down), Bassett sets

the record straight: 'When I was a kid, just about everyone else that I knew was called either John or David. To avoid confusion among family friends I was first known as 'Harry's boy' and later as 'Young Harry'. Whether I liked it or not that name has stuck with me.'

Notes: Yes, they were simpler times in the 1940s and 50s in north-west London. No one even dreamed of calling their lads Jordan, Jordon, Kai, Jaxon or Arlo back then. You got John or David or your dad's name followed by 'boy', which isn't a name at all. This isn't hyperbole either – John and David were the top two boys' names in the UK in 1944 and were still the top two in 1954. Solid, dependable, less confusing times.

Name: Peter Withe.
Nicknames: 'The Mad Header'; 'The Wizard of Nod'.
Reason: Because he was good at heading. Former West Ham striker Clyde Best reports that Withe had these two puntastic nicknames while they were both playing for Portland Timbers in the USA.
Notes: We can just about buy 'The Mad Header', but 'The Wizard of Nod' just doesn't work. 'The Nodfather' wouldn't have been much better, but at least it's a proper pun.

Name: John Burridge.
Nickname: 'Budgie'.
Reason: Well, Burridge doesn't know for sure. He says he first got it from the other players as a 15-year-old while an apprentice at Workington, possibly because 'I was flying up and down doing jobs for them.'
Notes: Is it just us, or is 'Budgie' obviously just simple shorthand for 'Burridge'? The start and end of his name have been smashed together, with the classic 'ie' added on the end. Why hasn't John ever considered this? Does he think his nickname's similarity to his actual name is just a coincidence?

Name: Kenny Dalglish.
Nickname: 'Dogs'.
Reason: This was Graeme Souness's nickname for Kenny, because he was the 'Dog's bollocks'.
Notes: Fair enough.

Name: David Johnson.

Nickname: 'The Doc'.

Reason: Johnson received this nickname while playing for Liverpool in the 1970s. Kenny Dalglish writes: 'He used to carry one of those old airline bags to training. If somebody had a sore head or a cold, The Doc had a tablet ready. He had a remedy for everything.'

Notes: Good, accurate nickname. Particularly enjoyed the detail about the old airline bag. Plus, there's a bonus subtle echo in there of the great Dr Johnson himself, although there's no suggestion David ever attempted any serious literary criticism or great work of lexicography.

Name: Gary Neville.

Nickname: 'Busy Bollocks'.

Reason: Neville himself only goes so far as to claim his nickname was 'Busy', because after training in his early years he would spend hours kicking a ball up against a wall, first right foot, then left foot. Keith Gillespie, however, after noting how dedicated Neville was to football to the exclusion of all else, says they all called him 'Busy Bollocks – and with justification'.

Notes: Was Neville hoping he'd left this nickname behind once he retired and so refused to mention it in his book? Or did he only find out the full horror of his 'Busy' nickname once he read Gillespie's memoirs?

Name: Gary Neville.

Nickname: 'Simon Brown'.

Reason: The story behind this comes from Neville's enjoyable autobiography, *Red*. It happened at the 1995 Man United Christmas party. He admits he was a bit of a lightweight drinker, then aged 20, and after five or six ciders he ended up falling asleep on the pavement outside a Chinese restaurant, the Golden Rice Bowl (4.5 stars on TripAdvisor, if you're interested). He began throwing up so badly that a couple of team-mates put him in a cab and he asked to be taken to hospital: 'I was so terrified of being recognised that I checked in under the first name I could think of – Simon Brown. The lads got years of fun out of that. "Pass the ball, Simon."'

Notes: It's brilliant that even in his incredibly inebriated state, he was still so terrified of Alex Ferguson that he was able to muster up a way, flimsy as it may have been, to cover his puke tracks. Also, why Simon Brown? Was that a mate of his? We would have given him a lot more kudos had he checked in as 'Phil Neville'.

Name: Ron Saunders.
Nickname: 'Mr 110 per cent'.
Reason: Andy Gray, in his largely bant-free book *Gray Matters*, shows little love for his manager at Aston Villa. He reckons that Saunders invented the phrase '110 per cent' and that the press gave him the nickname because he used it so much.
Notes: It's rare that you get to discover where a really hoary old football cliché originated. So it's nice we can pin this one down. Gray notes, with contempt dripping from his fountain pen, 'He was proud of that nickname.'

Name: Julian Alsop.
Nickname: 'Bert the Brickie'.
Reason: Ian Holloway signed Alsop for Bristol Rovers in 1997 from Halesowen. Ollie says: 'The fans nicknamed him Bert the Brickie because he had a typical non-leaguer's attitude and was mad as a March hare, but a fantastic lad.'
Notes: This explanation makes absolutely no sense. We should also mention, as we've brought him up, that Alsop was once sacked by Oxford United for apparently attempting to ram a banana up the anus of a 16-year-old apprentice as a bit of banter that went too far. He also burned his boots on the pitch with a blowtorch after playing his last game before retirement for non-league side Bishop's Cleeve. Both incidents are classic brickie behaviour. Apparently.

Name: Graeme Le Saux.
Nickname: 'Rag'.
Reason: We were always under the impression that Le Saux's nickname was 'Socksy'. But in his book he says that the first time he joined Chelsea he was nicknamed 'Berge' after Bergerac, the 1980s detective based in Jersey, Le Saux's home island. Then, when he went to Blackburn, Kenny Dalglish started calling him 'Rag'. Le Saux reckons this was because he had a soft-top car, known as a ragtop in America, and that 'RAG' was part of the licence plate.

Notes: Berge may think this. But we suspect he was called Rag because he was always losing it (his rag), but no one told him. In case he lost it (his rag).

Name: Kevin Keegan.
Nickname: 'Andy McDaft'.
Reason: Keegan explains: 'Because I was always messing around and it has to be said that I didn't always get things right. My trousers, for example. I wore flares so wide that I couldn't see my shoes.'
Notes: Don't be ashamed of your flares, Kev. Those lads didn't know what they were talking about. While this doesn't explain much (why 'Andy' for a start?), the 'McDaft' bit was wonderfully ahead of its time, coming a good three decades before the hilarious *Boaty McBoatface* phenomenon of 2016.
True fact: 'Kevin' itself is a bit of a nickname. His real name is 'Joe'.

Name: Lee McCulloch.
Nickname: 'Jig'.
Reason: When he was a young man, Lee played for Cumbernauld United and he scored a few goals. In *Simp-Lee the Best*, he says that the local paper would write headlines like: 'Gigantic school kid scores again', which led to his nickname. Sort of: 'Now, because the first team used to always mention my "package" then it all started from there, saying it's "jiganourmous" then that was shortened to "Jig".'
Notes: Penises and banter about penises are a recurring theme in footballer autobiographies. But McCulloch is one of very few to apparently have a nickname based on the size of his knob. None of that explains where the word 'jiganourmous' comes from, though.

Name: John McGovern.
Nickname: 'Border'.
Reason: This nickname for the much-decorated former Derby and Forest midfielder originated after he was late back from curfew once, but avoided the waiting Brian Clough by using the back stairs of the hotel. The next morning, Clough berated the players he had caught, but McGovern got away with it by claiming he was in before midnight. Once Clough was gone, keeper Les Green was not happy. McGovern says

that Green shouted: "'You lying bugger! … I'm going to call you Border Mask from now on, a man with two faces." I eventually found out that Border Mask had been a losing racehorse in one of Les's accumulators. Obscure it may have been, but the name stuck, although the mask part disappeared, leaving me known simply as "Border".'

Notes: While this explanation of where it started makes sense, the reason why Green named him after a shit racehorse doesn't. Why is a horse a 'man with two faces'? More questions than answers here.

Name: Stewart Houston.
Nickname: 'Whitney'.
Reason: Garry Nelson, in his groundbreaking autobiography, revealed that this was the nickname for the Plymouth assistant manager during his time there. Because he shared a surname with the singer. Just to spell it out.
Notes: Brilliant.

Name: Mick Quinn.
Nickname: 'Bob Carolgees'.
Reason: Quinn had a whole feast of nicknames according to his jaw-droppingly indiscreet autobiography, *Who Ate All the Pies?* He must've been known as 'Quinny', as that's the law, but there was also 'Sumo', given to him by Coventry fans because of his waistline. 'Noah', because he was on such good form at one stage that he was scoring goals two by two (bravo). 'Fletch', after Ronnie Barker's character in *Porridge*, because Quinn spent some time in prison (see 'Call the Cops' chapter). And 'Bob Carolgees', because, with his famous Scouse 'tache, Mick resembled *Tiswas* legend and operator of the Spit the Dog puppet, Bob Carolgees.
Notes: Quinn adds that a West Ham fan once shouted at him: "'Oi, Bob, where's Spit?" I grabbed my bollocks and shouted, "Ask your missus!"' Yes, it is a bit of a perplexing anecdote. Does Quinn mean Spit the Dog … er, pleasured the fan's wife? Or that Mick made sweet love to the fan's wife while wearing Spit? You can almost see Mick running off laughing to tell his mates while the fans in the area look at each other, unsure about what just happened.

Name: Luis Suarez.
Nickname: 'Grunon'.
Reason: Suarez admits in his autobiography that this was his nickname back in Uruguay. It means 'Grumpy', after the dwarf of Snow White fame.
Notes: This nickname would have Sam Allardyce already bristling about an impending attack from the PC Brigade.

Name: Alan Waddle.
Nickname: 'Big Willy'.
Reason: Unclear. In his book, Phil Thompson remembers a goal Waddle scored against Everton for Liverpool in 1973 (of course he does – Thommo can remember every goal Everton have conceded in the last 60 years), and refers to him as 'Big Willy'. He adds, in brackets, 'work it out for yourself'.
Notes: Do you mean he had a big cock, Phil? Neil Ruddock is similarly coy in his autobiography – which is weird, because he's not coy about anything else – when he says that Mitchell Thomas's nickname was 'Length' – 'for reasons I won't go into'. You've taken us this far, Neil, you might as well just say it now.

Name: Arsene Wenger.
Nickname: 'Windows'.
Reason: Tony Adams says they called him 'Windows' when he first arrived because he wore glasses.
Notes: Bit childish, Rodders? Why not go full 70s-insult mode and call him 'Four Eyes'? Vinnie Jones and Dennis Wise did something similar with Andy Townsend, nicknaming him 'The Beak'. Vin adds: 'because of his massive conk'. That's how it's done, Razor. Good use of 'conk', too.

Name: Ronnie Whelan.
Nickname: 'Vitch'.
Reason: Another one as reported by Phil Thompson: 'Irishman Ronnie had this habit of saying "dust" instead of "just". Because of that he became "Dust" and then "Dusty". We changed it depending on the foreign opposition. When we were playing in Romania or Bulgaria he would become "Dustovitch" or "Dustovan" if we were in Holland ...

Dustovitch stuck and then he became "The Vitch" although it would change to "Dusto" if we were in Spain.'

Notes: Superb piece of etymology by Thommo.

Name: Marcon Wasilewski.
Nickname: 'Was'.
Reason: Short for Wasilewski. As revealed by Jamie Vardy.
Notes: Of course. Who's got the time?

Name: Stan Lazaridis.
Nickname: 'Skippy'.
Reason: Robbie Savage lists quite a few nicknames in his memoirs, many of them drawn from popular TV shows of the last century: Tugay was 'Wurzel Gummidge', Mark Crossley was 'Norm' and Steve Claridge was 'Cleggy'. Aussie Stan got Skippy because, famously, he has a marsupial pouch.
Notes: Not tons of thought went into this one. It was always going to be 'Skippy', 'Flipper', or, possibly, 'Toadfish', wasn't it? It could have been 'Robbo', because *Neighbours* legend Paul Robinson owned Lassiter's hotel, and Lassiter's sounds a bit like 'Lazaridis'. But they went with Skippy. Fair do's.

Name: Glyn Hodges.
Nickname: 'The Cake'.
Reason: In Dave Bassett and Wally Downes's book about the Crazy Gang at Wimbledon, Hodges is given space to explain that Bassett 'would always call me a "fat petulant cunt", only this time he got the words mixed up and just called me a "petulant cake". So for about six months my nickname was "The Cake".'
Notes: Sounds like a rude, cryptic clue from an old episode of *3–2–1*.

Name: Mick Smith and Steve Hatter.
Nickname: 'Ralph' and 'Potsie'.
Reason: In the same book, Downes sorts out the admin on this pair: 'Smithy, incidentally, became Ralph, along with Steve Hatter as Potsie, from *Happy Days*, an ironic naming for the pair bearing in mind their ferocity compared to the TV characters.'
Notes: Okay. Why call them that, then? Strange.

Name: Roy McDonough.
Nickname: 'German Porn Star'.
Reason: Because of his long hair and moustache.
Notes: Roy says he did his best to represent this name to the full, which will become vividly apparent after you've read the 'Top Shelf' chapter.

Name: Mickey Thomas.
Nickname: 'Pebbles'.
Reason: Paul Merson explains that this was because, like Fred and Wilma's baby daughter in *The Flintstones*: 'you could never understand what he was saying, he always mumbled'.
Notes: Strong, this.

Name: Frans Thijssen.
Nickname: 'Sam'.
Reason: This one comes courtesy of John Wark, who claims that Thijssen looked like Sam McCloud from the American police series *McCloud*.
Notes: Would it not make more sense to call him 'McCloud'? That would be more fun, right? Surely, if a player in the 80s looked like Magnum (which, to be fair, a lot of them did), they would get called 'Magnum', rather than 'Thomas'?

Name: Rob Styles.
Nickname: 'Thrush'.
Reason: Former ref Jeff Winter wrote of Styles: 'I have never come across a referee so roundly criticised by players, managers and supporters. And among referees he found few friends. He had a ruthless streak that surpassed anything I, and many others, had ever seen. Plus he seemed joined at the hip to (ref chief) Philip Don. I wasn't the only one to notice, for Rob earned the nickname of "Thrush". No explanation needed, I hope.'
Notes: Do you mean Don fed Styles regurgitated food, like a thrush does for its young? Or that he had a speckled belly? Oh. You mean he was an irritating … yes.

Name: Alan Shearer.
Nickname: 'Shocksy'.
Reason: Razor Ruddock comes up with this one, noting: 'I became great mates with Shearer, who didn't acquire the nickname "Shocksy" for nothing.'
Notes: We had no idea what he meant for a while, which was quite fun. So much mystery. We wondered if he kept giving off static. Then Razor later explains that it was because he was always shocking people by doing things like scoring a hat-trick on his debut. After that, the mystery faded and it doesn't feel quite so great.

Name: Vinny Samways.
Nickname: 'Vinegar Sandwich'.
Reason: Because his name sounds like 'vinegar sandwich'.
Notes: Lovely. This is another from Razor Ruddock, who bloody loves a nickname.

Name: Alan Kennedy.
Nickname: 'Belly'.
Reason: We turn to Phil Thompson once more for this one: 'We called him "Bungalow" at first "because he had nothing upstairs". Then it became "Moony" because the moon is a balloon. Then someone noticed a columnist in the *Daily Mirror* called Belle Mooney and so Al became Bell. Then it was extended to "Belly".'
Notes: They liked a convoluted nickname at Liverpool, didn't they? It's an enjoyable story, but we're still in the dark about the moon/balloon bit. How does that fit in?

We end this chapter by bowing deeply at the feet of the man with perhaps the most nicknames in the game.

Honourable mentions to Mick Quinn and Steve Nicol ('Chips' (liked chips), 'Henderson' (pretended to be old Rangers winger Willie Henderson when playing wide) and 'Chico' (no idea)), but standing atop the top of the shop is the absolute King of Nicknames, Sir Trevor Brooking. Naturally, like many Trevors, he was named 'Tricky'. So far so standard. But then you have:

- **'Lord Ted'**: Billy Bonds explains in his autobiography: 'As a keen golfer, like England cricketer Ted Dexter, Trev was at one time similarly known as Lord Ted among us.' What? He liked golf so you named him after a cricketer?

- **'Hadleigh'** or **'Hadders'**: Both Billy Bonds and Trevor Francis wrote that this was because the lads thought he was just like the upmarket main character from the TV series *Hadleigh* and had the hair to match. He does, too. Google it.

- **'Boog'**: This is properly obscure. Bonzo says it dates back to a tour of the US when West Ham were based in Baltimore. The name is a reference to a cult baseball player called Boog Powell, who played for the Baltimore Orioles: '(He was) a hefty, over-weight fellow whose running was definitely not his strong point. To do any good, Boog used to have to hit home runs. Otherwise he invariably ended up sliding his considerable bulk along the ground over ten or fifteen yards, arriving at base in a great cloud of dust. In his early days, Trev seemed to spend a lot of time on his backside … so we happily seized on Boog as his nickname, and it stuck forever after.'

- **'Cyril'**: Amazingly, this wasn't the only nickname Trev received due to his propensity to spend time on his backside. Brooking recalls that his manager Ron Greenwood once said, 'You're like the carpet man, you're always on the floor.' He was then named Cyril by team-mates because there was a TV ad at the time proclaiming 1960s carpet supremo Cyril Lord as 'The Carpet King'.

Trevor Brooking. One man, many nicknames. He's like an international spy. He's like *The Saint*. Which, come to think of it, wouldn't be a bad nickname for him either.

3

Be Our Guest
Hit the chickens

Fawlty Towers. The Shining. The Eagles. If history has taught us anything, it's that some pretty rum business goes on in hotels. And it would seem that footballers are responsible for more than their fair share of it. Exhibit A – Sam Allardyce on the first time he met a young Teddy Sheringham, then both at Millwall:

'He was a kid helping the kit-man with first-team duties and when I invited him into my hotel room to collect my dirty kit I was standing there stark bollock naked, as I towelled myself down.'

It doesn't bear thinking about, does it? Given the choice we'd go for the lift gushing with blood and the creepy ghost twins at the Overlook every single time. No wonder Teddy Sheringham sometimes has that thousand-yard stare of a Vietnam veteran. He's seen things, man; he's seen too much.

The hotel is the footballer's life in microcosm. These cosseted individuals are hermetically sealed – isolated from the common man. Their every whim is catered for as they focus on ensuring their body is at its absolute peak condition, preserving their maximum potential, like a coiled spring ready to explode into action in the imminent gladiatorial encounter for which they've been torn asunder from their loved ones and pressed into service. There's also access to minibars and fire extinguishers.

Yet it's not all hi-jinks, nudie-bums and shithousery. Sometimes in the hotel life of a footballer, you just have to find the right partner to get you through it. The Riggs to your Murtaugh, the Michael to your Ridgeley, the Dom to your Dick – that's right: the room-mate.

There's a peculiar chemistry to finding the right away day room-mate, and it's a rare thing of beauty when it comes together just right. Kenny Dalglish & Graeme Souness and Trevor Brooking & Billy Bonds roomed together for years quite happily, as did Mike Channon & Kevin Keegan, with Keegan informing readers that they would take it in turns to have a lazy day while the other basically waited on them. Nice.

Wally Downes describes a similarly domesticated arrangement between himself and Vinnie Jones at Wimbledon, but feels the need to say: 'In fact we were like a couple of old poofs, making tea, watching a film and going to sleep with quiz questions.' You know, that tired old homosexual stereotype of drinking tea, watching films and having quizzes at bedtime. We've all heard it a million times, haven't we?

Tony Cascarino also reports on the relaxed nature of a good room-share, just without the homophobia. He says that rooming with Andy Townsend reminded him of married life, although he does complain that 'Andy controlled the TV remote for the best part of ten years!', conjuring a delightful image of Townsend disapprovingly flicking through channel after channel, muttering 'Not for me, Clive' as he did so.

Occasionally, sharing a tiny kettle and a trouser press with a colleague will lead to a deeper appreciation of their character – an admiration grows. Neville Southall describes Everton and Wales roomy Barry Horne as 'the sort of person who was so clever that he could watch TV, read the paper and listen to the radio at the same time'. High praise indeed, because that's how we all measure intelligence, isn't it? Isn't it? Given this context, Barry Horne's post-football career as a chemistry teacher seems inevitable.

We all know that public school old boy Frank Lampard Jnr is one of the more academic players too, but it's one of his baser talents that got Rio #2Sides Ferdinand through the long, dark nights: 'We roomed together when we travelled away and Frank was funny! He used to get up in the middle of the night – religiously – and have the longest wee I've ever heard in my life! I'm sure it was just to make me laugh.' The mark of a good player is being able to turn it on at will, after all.

Perhaps most touching of all is the tale of Ian Wright and Dennis Bergkamp. When the non-flying Dutchman arrived at Highbury, he had a profound effect on those around him and none more so than

Wright, in terms of his all-round game, his diet – and his jim-jams. 'I remember the first time we roomed together, he went into the bathroom and came out wearing those immaculate pyjamas. I was staggered! All these years I'd been playing and staying in hotels with teams, I'd never seen another footballer wearing pyjamas – I'd just get into bed in the vest I'd been wearing all day. But straight away I thought "If pyjamas are good enough for Dennis Bergkamp, they're good enough for me." When I got home I went out and bought my first pair of pyjamas.'

What a heart-warming story: a sophisticated continental gentleman drastically alters the lifestyle of an English team-mate open to new ideas. Hollywood blockbusters have been built on less. For his part, Bergkamp is a bit coy about it in his own *Stillness and Speed*, saying, 'I don't usually wear pyjamas, so I'm wondering why I did. It's probably from my time in Italy.' Curious, no? Bergkamp then goes further in describing their nights together: 'I remember, in the hotel, I was reading a book, and he was falling asleep, like normal. Suddenly he gets out of bed and goes "Hello." Is he making fun of me? "Hello?" He walks to the door, and listens at the door and goes "Urgh!" "Urgh!" and makes other weird noises, and then returns to his bed, looks around and goes to sleep. And his eyes were open the whole time. It was really strange.'

The Arsenal pair obviously came to an understanding about Wrighty's sleepwalking because they got on famously, but it's a story that hints at the problems that can occur. As we said before, it's crucial that the chemistry is right. Mr Horne will tell you that once he's finished with Year 12.

Andy Gray, of Aston Villa, Everton and sexism fame, brings us a cautionary tale of just how wrong the room-share can go if the delicate blend of personalities is awry. While at Wolves, he saw 'troubled' midfielder Billy Kellock (who probably should write his own autobiography based on this) nearly murder winger Tony Towner. Well, it probably would have been regarded as manslaughter, but either way, it's less than ideal for team bonding. This happened while on tour in Sweden, and Gray was in the next room, when 'in steps Billy, white as a sheet. "It's Tony," he said, "I think I might have killed him." We rushed next door to the room Billy was sharing with Tony and sure enough there was his victim lying spark out on the bed with blood pouring from a gash over his eye. He turned out to be more shocked than anything else, but for a moment it was possible to believe that Billy had murdered him.'

Inevitably drink was involved, as Billy explained that in the dark of the room, and possibly of his soul, 'he'd got it into his head to chuck a chair through the window. Unfortunately for Tony, at this point he'd woken up and popped his head out from under the covers. The chair had caught him right across the forehead. I'm not sure if Tony ever recovered.'

It's a story that makes you wonder if there's more to it – 'I accidentally chucked a chair at his head when aiming for the window' seems an odd defence. Had Lieutenant Columbo been on the case, he might have asked if the curtains were open, as that might help to determine pre-meditation. But we're not detectives, and we're not grasses either, so we'll leave it there.

There are some social transgressions, thankfully short of Actual Bodily Harm, for which footballers will develop a tolerance, if only for the harmony of the room and the relationship. As we take a tour through some of them, feel free to find where you would draw the line.

There's the late-night eating for starters (and main course and pudding by the sound of it). If we were to give you, say, ten guesses as to which footballer was guilty of this crime, we think most of you would come up with John Hartson eventually. Luckily, he found a sympathetic 'roomie' in Robbie Savage:

'He was out one night, and I heard him come back around 3 a.m. I pretended to be asleep, because if he thought you were awake he'd do something like dive on you or switch on the telly or something. So I kept my eyes closed while he ordered a tray of sandwiches. Not a plate but a whole bloody tray. There was a knock on the door. Room service. Sandwiches, cans of pop and crisps. It was like being in a room with the Cookie Monster!'

One benefit of lying low and letting Hartson eat himself daft in the wee small hours is that he and Savage remained very different body shapes – we say benefit because being the same height, weight and build as the guy you're sharing with can bring its own problems, as Tim Cahill found out with Mikel Arteta:

'At Everton, whenever we had an away game, we'd share a room. Mikel and I are exactly the same size – same height, same weight – and before I knew it he'd have my suitcase open and be putting on all my clothes. I used to bring two sets of clothes to any away game, because I knew Mickey would snatch my best shirt, my new jacket, my favourite jeans.'

Everton do seem to have a thing about playing similar-looking midfielders together. Before Arteta and Cahill were strutting around the Goodison turf like twins, you had Thomas Gravesen and his little brother Lee Carsley. Despite the perils of Arteta stealing his clothes like a teenage sibling, Cahill seems to have enjoyed sharing with his Spanish chum. Less tolerant of his Iberian colleague is Jamie Carragher, who says of Josemi that he 'stayed up late, returning to the room about midnight and then ringing his mates in Spain. He was talking in Spanish on the phone until about one a.m.'

Annoying for sure, but does it make it worse if it's in Spanish? What about if he talked in some kind of dog language instead? You see, before he found his perfect partner in Andy Townsend, Tony Cascarino had to put up with Middlesbrough legend Bernie Slaven on Ireland duty, who, he says, '... used to call his dog every night. I'd be sitting in the bed alongside and Bernie would be howling like Lassie into the phone "Woof, woof, aru, aru, woof!" He'd be kissing the receiver and lavishing affection ...'.

Not right, is it? But at least Bernie was only on the dog and bone to his dog and bone. John Wark recalls Ipswich's David Linighan going one further and sneaking his dog on to an away trip and into their hotel room for the night: '... but when I wanted to answer a call of nature in the middle of the night I forgot about the dog's presence until it bared its teeth and let out a frightening growl. I tried to waken Lini but he was snoring away, so because the dog was between me and the toilet I decided not to bother and lay awake in some discomfort. What made it even worse was that the dog frequently broke wind and the smell in the room was close to unbearable. It wasn't until Lini stirred in the morning that he saw to the dog and cleared the way for me to relieve myself.'

What on earth would Frank Lampard Jnr have done in that situation? Imagine how long his piss would have been by the morning, and how much Rio would have enjoyed listening to it, had there been an animal guarding the loo all night. Wark also adds the fact that

Linighan's dog looked like Bullseye, Bill Sykes's dog in the movie *Oliver!*, because, as a Hollywood veteran of *Escape to Victory*, he knows how to paint a picture.

Without a shadow of a doubt, the unluckiest man with room-mates, according to his own accounts at least, is Stan Collymore, who brings us three tales that would make us think twice about signing the professional forms were we ever gifted enough to have had them laid in front of us. First, he shared with John Salako, and says that if he ever left to take a nice stroll around the hotel grounds, he'd return to find the born-again Christian having a right old time of it: 'almost invariably, he'd be lying on his bed, banging one out. Having a wank with Penthouse in front of him. I'd say, "I thought you were supposed to be fucking born again." And he'd be all sheepish and say, "I am, but we all succumb to our desires now and again."'

Did Stan never knock? Evidently not. Perhaps he felt he shouldn't have to, and he might be right, but surely they could have developed a system – a cautionary rap on the door from Stan, or Salako could have hung the 'Do Not Disturb' sign up – it wouldn't have taken much. Maybe we're prudish, but that 'invariably' really sticks with you doesn't it? Seeing that just once would be plenty, thanks.

After that experience at Palace, you would think Stan would be only too pleased with Jason Lee's different sort of eccentric behaviour at Forest. Collymore says that Lee had a 'fetish' for cleaning and would pack a proper scrubbing kit full of under-the-sink favourites to help disinfect the entire room when they arrived – and if someone like John Salako had the room key before them, who's to say he was wrong? 'Even though the hotel bathroom was always spotlessly clean when we checked in, he would make straight for it and clean the fucker out again. "I ain't going in no fucking bath that no fucking dirty bastard's been in," he would say.' Sounds to us like Jason should have washed his potty mouth out while he had the marigolds on, too.

Jason's Jif and John's Jism pale into insignificance, however, next to Collymore's worst room-mate – England keeper David James. The two shared a lovely country hotel room in Ireland together on a pre-season tour with Liverpool. To relieve the boredom, the pair asked for a selection of videos (this was the 90s) to pass the time. Except Jamo decided to pass the time with the innocent VHS tapes in his own inimitable style, as he sat on the bed throwing them against the wall and smashing them one by one, entirely without explanation.

Maybe it's something to do with goalkeepers. We were always told they had to be crazy. David James would have grown up in an era of John Burridge sitting on the crossbar and Bruce Grobbelaar walking on his hands and doing his wobbly-legs thing – perhaps the pressure was on to be kooky. The image of the crazy goalkeeper sadly seems to be a thing of the past now, with strict preparation and professionalism being the watchwords for the men between the sticks; the odd foray up for a last-minute corner is about as exotic as it gets these days, so it's important to preserve the tales of Crazy Keepers gone by. Les Green at Derby certainly adds to the legend, according to John McGovern's slightly terrifying account in *From Bo'ness to the Bernabeu*. He tells of the time Derby slept in a dormitory on an away trip, with Les running the full gamut of annoying behaviour – from refusing to switch the light off to grabbing people around the neck:

'Just as you were beginning to drift off for a good night's sleep, you would be woken with the sound of Les playfully strangling one of his victims, as they struggled to escape his vice-like grip. His other favourite was to imitate a German air raid, complete with flashing room lights and a running commentary from the German bomber commander.'

Unnerving, for sure, but it turns out Green wasn't the only strangler. Robbie Savage tells us that while at Birmingham he roomed with Paul Devlin and that the two of them would regularly have wrestling matches 'until someone submitted'. Sav takes up the tale: 'Before one Liverpool game, we were in our hotel room trying to bring each other down, and he got me in a death choke. That was his special move. The banter was fantastic.'

You see what we mean about the banter? Almost anything and everything is fair game under the umbrella of banter, including a man attempting to asphyxiate you before a big game.

The reason often given for these knockabout japes coming to the fore is boredom: players simply have nothing better to do than throw videos at a wall, choke each other out or play with their Salakos. Nowhere is this more acute than in international circles.

It's always struck us that if we were blessed with the chance to represent our country at a World Cup or two, we probably could suffer a few quiet weeks on the social front; but then we've never played the game, so we can't possibly understand the delicate sensibilities of the footballer that see him succumb to the silent killer that is boredom, despite having access to computer consoles, pool tables, great food, endless TV and, you know, books.

Boredom on international duty is a problem that managers have to address, and their approaches can differ. For example, according to Jack Charlton, Sir Alf Ramsey was very regimented about limiting sunbathing by players at the 1970 World Cup in Mexico:

'Trainer Harold Shepherdson would blow the whistle to indicate that we could start sunbathing, after 15 minutes he'd blow his whistle again to tell us to turn over, and after another 15 minutes he'd blow again to tell us it was time to go inside.'

Had no one heard of umbrellas, hats or sun cream back in 1970? And who's monitoring the effect of this one-size-fits-all policy on players? Half an hour in direct sunlight for, say, Peter Osgood, is fine but the same slot might have felt like a lifetime for a strawberry blond like Alan Ball. Let's not forget that at the 1994 World Cup, Steve Staunton of Ireland was even sent out for the anthems in a sun hat, only removing it at the last possible moment before kick-off, so as to protect his delicate alabaster skin. Just saying.

Glenn Hoddle felt the England lads could stand a little longer on the loungers in 1998, but with certain conditions attached: 'Players must have time to relax in their own ways and personally, I think that lying in the sun for up to 45 minutes a day can revitalise the energies. No reading, listening to music or chatting – just concentration on the sun. It's a form of meditation that provides thinking time without distraction.'

So, they must relax in their own ways, but without books, music or chatting. Not the most controversial views Hoddle expressed during his England tenure, but it seems a little unfair. The 1970 lads got 15 minutes less but were no doubt busting out the Harold Robbins paperbacks and the Mungo Jerry all over the place. No such luck around the pool for the '98 squad, but Glenn did make provisions inside: 'We planned to allocate rooms for reading (for the likes of Tony Adams and Graeme Le Saux), rooms for television and videos, and even a "mini arcade" with pool tables, table tennis, darts and video games.'

This sounds like the best youth club ever, but it couldn't keep Paul Merson happy. He tells us he spent most of that World Cup being beaten by Michael Owen at pool, driving games and, well, pretty much everything else that was available. He also laments that he'd lost his drinking buddy Tony Adams to the reading room as the newly reformed Tone had 'gone all intellectual and was talking quietly in *Countdown* conundrum words. I couldn't understand him any more.'

Terry Curran says that Alan Ball likened being kept in hotels to being in prison, and 'He got the idea from visiting a prison at Preston during his Everton days as part of the club's community work.' Presumably, if Little Alan Ball hadn't been to visit a prison, he would never have understood the concept, apparently not having seen *Jailhouse Rock*, an episode of *Porridge* or the *News at Ten*.

Even in a more modern age, with distractions like mobile phones, tablets and Tamagotchis, boredom remains a problem. Rio Ferdinand (*#2Sides* – #NeverForget) writes that in his day there were times when the lads like JT, Ash and Shaun Wright-Phillips-y would arrange for loads of sneaky takeaway food to be smuggled into the camp. Not for the grub you understand, just for the buzz of it.

'It was quite an operation: the food would be delivered through the dark of the hotel by one of the lads' drivers. In the normal run of things you'd never think of doing that; it would only ever be once in a blue moon. We're not stupid. We know what to eat. But we were stir-crazy: we'd been locked away for like a week and no one had any food they really enjoyed. At times like that that kind of stuff tastes fantastic. It's a reaction to being bossed about.'

Maybe it's a male thing. Perhaps only the men get bored. Kelly Smith fondly recalls trips away with the England women's team, with talk of travelling with their own table tennis table, and she sounds grateful for the Wii and the board games. She even says they got creative: 'One night Alex and I organised a team game involving all the England players plus some of the coaching staff … It concerns team bonding and it's based on a game show we had seen in America. The game is called *In It to Win It*.'

Continue, Kelly, you intrigue us strangely.

'It was good fun to do. The two of us researched different topics on the internet so that we could make up our own games. A good example is wrapping a pedometer to the front of a team-mate's head with medical tape and getting them to move their heads back and forth as quickly as possible'.

Good, wholesome fun there then. All perfectly reasonable. Can you imagine the lads coming up with such stuff? Nah. The guys are much more about this sort of thing, from John Barnes: 'Our room was twenty floors up and Gazza was hanging out of the window trying to hit the chickens with bars of soap.'

You heard.

Even when Bobby Robson caught them at it and asked what they were doing, his first thought wasn't to discipline Gazza for animal cruelty or misuse of soap, or even to simply find him something less destructive to do. Rather, he asked:

'"Can you really hit them from here?"

'"Yeah, of course."

'"Go on then," said Bobby, "show me." Gazza took aim with the soap and scored a direct hit on a chicken. Bobby just walked out of the room, laughing and shaking his head.'

It all comes under the banner of 'Banter', of course. Even the word makes us shudder – but it looms so large in the life of a footballer that it runs through this book like the letters on a stick of rock. And even though the whole concept has its own chapter elsewhere, let's take a moment to focus on some specialist hotel-based b-word starting with that time Alan Shearer almost had his career ended by a pissed-up Neil Ruddock.

Matt Le Tissier explains in his book that it all happened on a Southampton away trip in Shearer's early days. The scene is set with Alan enjoying a nice, warm bath – for all we know, he might have been relaxing beneath the bubbles with some candles on the go and a bit of Enya on the stereo. But his tranquillity is destroyed by Ruddock and his fellow booze hounds, who've come to raid his minibar, suspecting Al wouldn't have touched it. They burst in on him, tip vodka over him and steal his fridge, leaving a trail of smashed glass along the corridor behind them.

Big, wet, slippery Al naturally gave chase with 'nothing on his feet', or, presumably, anywhere else; 'and as he ran through the shards of broken glass he practically severed three of his toes. They were cut to the bone and almost hanging off. Everyone sobered up pretty quick when they saw that. It is no exaggeration to say his career was hanging as precariously as his toes.' As in every footballer medical emergency, the only sober guy left standing drives, and they rushed the fledgling England striker to A&E, where a doctor 'managed to sew the toes back on', and in so doing paved the way for an unlikely league title for Blackburn, years of blissful memories for Newcastle fans and that Lucozade advert in his back yard. It's fair to say this bit of larking about got out of hand.

Paul Sturrock tells us that between meetings with Rod Stewart, the 1986 Scotland World Cup squad got up to some much milder, student-level mischief at their Santa Fe camp: 'One night when all of the backroom staff had gone out, the master key to the hotel bedrooms was appropriated. When they came back they found cellophane had been placed over the toilets; various pot plants from the hotel grounds now adorned their rooms, and physio Hugh Allan could hardly get into his room.'

The aforementioned Wally Downes and Vinnie Jones, perhaps inevitably, were fans of the stronger stuff as, according to Dave Bassett, 'The pair ran riot. They would strip rooms, hang hotel beds out of windows.' We get tired just thinking about the effort involved in this – it must have been exhausting. When we arrive at a hotel we like to kick our shoes off, bounce gently on the bed, look at the view, see what TV channels we have and maybe make sure the Gideons have been – the thought of instantly setting about ways to destroy everyone else's room and hang their furniture outside is too much to contemplate.

Had Paul Merson been less good at football, he might have fitted in well with the Crazy Gang vibe, as he was the scourge of his team-mates from check-in to check-out, with poor old Perry Groves regularly on the receiving end: 'Grovesy was used to stick. My party piece was to shit in his pillowcase just to really wind him up. I used to love seeing the look on his face as he realised I'd left him a little bedtime pressie. When he caught me the first time, squatting above his bed, letting one go, he couldn't believe his eyes.'

Presumably he couldn't believe his eyes because he's a reasonable human for whom shitting in a colleague's pillowcase is not the norm. Given that Merson also threw Groves into the sea, and Roy McDonough admits to treating him badly in his early days at Colchester, we're beginning to think that Perry might be short for Perennial Victim.

For a different nasty surprise left in a bed, we must look to Paolo Di Canio. When at Celtic, Paolo shared a room with Peter Grant, 'one of the kindest and nicest people I've ever met'. Presumably then, as he was such a nice guy, Paolo gave silent thanks for an easy time at the hotel and relaxed. Or, he drew the following conclusion: 'In some ways he was too nice. To liven things up, I decided to mess around with him. By sheer chance I discovered that he had a phobia about fish.' So, Paolo did what any self-respecting hotel-dwelling footballer would do – he sourced a salmon head from the hotel kitchen: 'It was still fresh and rather creepy. The salmon had one of those eyes that seemed to follow you around the room. Even I was a little freaked out by it, and I love fish. I placed the salmon head in a clear plastic bag and went back up to our room. Peter was lying on the bed.

'"For you!" I said cheerfully, tossing the fish head on his bed. Peter must have jumped three feet into the air. I've never seen him move so fast. He ran to the other side of the room and started yelling. I couldn't quite make out what he was saying but it was clearly to do with the fish.'

Oh, do you think it was something to do with the fish, Paolo? You're probably right. Amazing powers of deduction. Quite the Inspector Montalbano.

It's always the staff we feel sorry for, having to clean up afterwards, put rooms back together and get rid of all the stains and smells. You might expect it from Led Zeppelin, but not from Middlesbrough. Jack Charlton tells a tale in which property damage crosses over with the other great hotel pastime among footballers – a bit of how's your father. After getting a bill for a broken skylight after his team stayed in a hotel for a Grimsby away game, it transpires that it came about because one of the players (who he doesn't name, possibly to preserve a delicately hanging marriage) 'said that he had succeeded in enticing a young lady back to his room, and once the word was out, his team-mates, in the manner of these things, had climbed out on the roof to look through the skylight.

'Unfortunately one of them got so excited that he fell through the bloody thing ... I turned to the baby of the team, Stan Cummings, a lad of 17, and said, "Hey, I hope you weren't up there on that roof."

'"No, boss," he says, "I were in the cupboard."'

Jack blithely accepting, there, the idea that of course if there's sex going on, then every other player is going to want to watch. It's such an odd culture – they're not quite all at it, but there are several instances of it (see our 'Top Shelf' chapter for more gory details). However, even the most prudish among us can enjoy the 'Carry on Confessions of a Footballer' comedy stylings of a player being so excited that he fell through the roof.

In his Republic of Ireland days, Jack Charlton was known to occasionally keep a keg of Guinness on tap in his hotel room. That may or may not have contributed to the sight that beheld Ronnie Whelan as he stepped from the lift in the hotel after Ireland beat England at Euro '88: 'This figure was running down the corridor with a black blanket round his shoulders and trailing behind him like a cape. It was Tony Galvin. And he was there on his own. And he was running up and down singing, "I'm a bat! I'm a bat! I'm a bat!" And I was looking at him, totally puzzled at first, before I cracked up. And he went by me again. "I'm a bat! I'm a bat!" And then he disappeared round the corner. It was hilarious. It was mad. But on the night, it all seemed to make sense.'

The wistful ending to this anecdote is enjoyable. It gives it a whiff of *The Wonder Years* – ideally, it would be accompanied by Joe Cocker's version of 'With a Little Help from My Friends'.

Of course, aside from the banter, the damage to hotel property and charging around like a creature of the night, it's sex with a stranger that some footballers like to pass the time with.

Dave Bassett tells us of the time one of his teams became involved with a wedding party, of all things, during one hotel stay. 'Harry' charitably describes the bride as 'not a bad looker' and tells us that 'she and her bridesmaid seemed "game for a laugh" as they say, and spent a short while with the boys before the bride retired to her room and her groom'. Bassett declares them to be 'soccer groupies and a good time was had by all' before sharing his concerns that a marriage built on such a shaky start might not have lasted the course. He might be right; still, at least the lads didn't get bored.

Terry Curran says that such things are inevitable: 'Girls almost throw themselves at footballers and when a gorgeous-looking woman offers you sex when you're in a hotel room feeling lost, it takes a strong bloke to say no – and I didn't.' Great honesty from Terry there; though he does appear to completely absolve himself from blame, as if the woman just appeared like some kind of sexy Fairy Godmother, and as if he was contractually obliged to do the deed; but if he's only too happy to admit to his indiscretions, then not everyone is.

Graham Roberts says that he had to deny to his wife that he'd been involved in a threesome after his Rangers room-mate, Davie Cooper, had been caught out at a hotel with Miss Scotland. As he's at great pains to tell us, Graham was nowhere near it, 'as I didn't much fancy playing gooseberry, I would bunk down with Ian Durrant or one of the other lads'. Best out of it, Graham.

For all of Frank Worthington's kissing and telling in the scandalous *One Hump or Two,* he rigorously denies the suggestion that Lawrie McMenemy caught him in flagrante at the team hotel while at Southampton. Gallant Frank insists that they were only having a cup of tea together because they were fans and 'They were hardly Miss Worlds.' McMenemy sent him home regardless.

The ultimate denial, and on the grandest scale, however, belongs to Johan Cruyff. We've all heard the infamous story, broken by German tabloids at the time, of Dutch players cavorting with naked German models in the hotel pool the night before the 1974 World Cup Final, but, naturally, Cruyff denies it: 'I was supposed to have been there and Danny (Cruyff's wife) got to hear about it. They later also managed to get quotes from a few of our second-choice players who had told them that, before the final, I'd had my furious wife on the phone for hours.'

Is it us, or is Cruyff denying the wrong part of the scandal here? The phone bit isn't the problem.

'As for the story itself, well, Danny was in our second home in the mountains near Andorra, in a place that didn't yet have a phone connection, so we couldn't even have contacted each other on the telephone, let alone argued.'

So there. He couldn't have done anything with those girls and had a row with his wife over the phone because she didn't even have a phone. That's all right, then. That clears it up. Fancy not having a phone when your footballer husband is staying away in a hotel, though. How's he supposed to chat to the dog?

4

Food & Drink & Drink

212 steak and kidney pies

As young lads, we used to love reading those little questionnaires footballers would be asked to fill in for weekly mags and comics like *Match*, *Shoot!* or *Roy of the Rovers* (and later, with a bit more of an edge to them, in the brilliant *90 Minutes*). These Q&As would furnish us with the tiny details about the lives of our heroes that were never revealed during *Match of the Day* commentaries or on Oracle – pretty much our only other sources of football information at that time (we were never allowed to ring ClubCall).

No matter which player gamely filled these in, these would, in the main, be the answers given:

Favourite Car: Ford Capri

Favourite TV Shows: *A Question of Sport* and *Minder*

Favourite Music: Diana Ross and Phil Collins

Favourite Food: Steak and chips

Favourite Drink: Tea

It was for kids. They all said tea, but even then we didn't believe them. Some of the autobiographies we read felt like a throwback to those days as we collected a whole heap of deliciously inconsequential footballer facts. In terms of food, we discovered that:

- Pat Van Den Hauwe likes his steak almost raw ('two flips, that's it') …

- … while Ian Snodin prefers his very well done ('like a block of coal')

- Jack Charlton kept pigeons, but also liked to eat them ('... any pigeons we wanted rid of, we just wrung their necks and had them for dinner the next day') (Different times. Can't imagine John Stones doing that)
- Paolo Di Canio likes tiramisu so much that he put a recipe for it in his book
- and Robbie Fowler celebrated his five goals v Fulham in the cup with special fried rice, barbecue sauce and a tin of Irn Bru from his local chip shop.[10]

In terms of drinks, it's perhaps surprisingly not all about alcohol. Terry/Teddy Curran, never much of a drinker, admits to preferring Coke, and claims in his book that sometimes he would knock back up to 35 bottles of the stuff in one evening. 35! Even if that's the tiny 200ml bottles you get in pubs, that's still *seven litres* of Coke in one night – more than *12 pints*. Obviously, we have to take into account changes in recipes, but based on recent scientific evidence, that's roughly 210 teaspoons of sugar he imbibed in just a few brief hours. He must've been pissing brown by midnight. More importantly, how annoying was it to go to the bar 35 times in an evening? Or did he line them up, six or seven at a time, to save his legs?

Curran's not the only one with a Coke addiction, though – Paolo Di Canio says that as a child he adored it: 'That fizzy sweetness hitting my throat was like a drug. I would drink two or three litre-bottles a day, furiously guzzling it down whenever I could get my hands on it.' Coca-Cola, then, seems to be the beverage of choice for the Sheffield Wednesday maverick. Gerald Sibon is probably a Coke ambassador back in Holland, while Chris Waddle likely uses it as a sort of crutch to get through 5 Live commentaries with grumpy old Alan Green.

And then there's John Aldridge. At the end of each chapter in his book, he presents a few Top 8 lists. Top 8s, because he wore the number eight (of course). These lists, oddly, are not ranked, and that, along with rigidly sticking to exactly eight things, can diminish their effectiveness. For example, at one stage he lists 'Eight Big Money Liverpool Players'. But that's literally all it is – eight players who cost Liverpool a lot of

---

10 When Fowler scored what was then the fastest Premier League hat-trick in 1994, he added ribs to that order. It's like he allowed himself specific rewards for specific achievements – four goals in a cup final, for example, might have meant special fried rice and barbecue sauce, ribs, Irn Bru *and* some prawn balls. No goals at all meant he went to bed hungry.

money. It's not the eight most expensive Liverpool signings at that time of writing. He doesn't even say if they're good or bad signings. It's just eight names vaguely tied together by their large transfer fees.

He does the same thing with eight Spanish Liverpool players. It's not his eight *favourite* Spanish Liverpool players. It's not the eight *best* Spanish Liverpool players in his opinion. Or the eight worst. Or the eight most expensive. And it's not a list of all the Spanish players to have played for Liverpool. It is simply the first eight players Aldo could think of that are Spanish … and … wait for it … have also played for Liverpool. Invaluable info for any reader.

So, it quickly becomes clear that he's painted himself into a corner with the gimmick – and his Top 8 favourite drinks list is a good example:

1. Red wine.
2. Tetley's Smooth Flow.
3. Cristal Pilsner.
4. San Miguel.
5. Tea.
6. Coffee.
7. Guinness.
8. Water.

'That's seven, Aldo – any more drinks you really like? … Water? … Okay … No, that'll do. It's fine. Not like we're ranking them, is it?'

You'd think that if he lists his Top 8 drinks, he'd also list his Top 8 foods, but he doesn't, so we'll forever be wondering about that one. (We say that, but his favourite will be steak. It's always steak.) However, because a lot of the book references his work for radio covering Liverpool games, he does give us some valuable insight into the grub served to the press boys and girls at various grounds, including this nugget about Arsenal: 'It's like a five star restaurant there, with fish and chips at half-time and Ben and Jerry's Ice Cream if you want it too.'

Indeed, nothing says 'five star' like Ben & Jerry's ice cream. None of that Wall's muck at Arsenal. Just the good stuff. But, in the words of any great infomercial, that's not all. Aldo also provides an exhaustive Top 8 list of Press Room Grub 'in case you've ever wondered what the press get to eat at the match'. Now, between your two authors, we've been going to football for a combined total of nearly 80 years. We checked, and in all that time never has it occurred to us to wonder, even for a brief second, what Oliver Holt and his mates eat before (or even during) a game.[11]

And yet, perhaps we're wrong to be cynical, because Aldo absolutely lifts the lid on this subject. Top of the list is an absolute pearler:

1. Portsmouth – nice people but I didn't enjoy the food at times.

Straight off the bat. He tells us he'll be revealing the best food at football grounds, then starts the list with a club where he thinks the food is a bit shit. Brilliant. Liverpool (obviously) make the list for their roast dinners, although Everton do too, for their breakfasts. Hull City get a mention for a great curry he had there once. And the Arse get a second namecheck for their 'five star food and desserts'. Yeah, Chunky Monkey on tap.

Still, this is only Aldo's opinion. It's important to get corroboration for his love of the Arsenal nosh, and we found it from Alex Ferguson. It comes in his most recent autobiography, when he's writing about the Battle of the Buffet, when Man United and Arsenal engaged in a childish (and brilliant) food fight at Old Trafford in 2004. We join it well into the anecdote:

'Anyway, the next thing I knew I had pizza all over me. We put food in the away dressing room after every game. Pizza, chicken. Most clubs do it. Arsenal's food was the best.'

There we go. Confirmation. And what detail from Fergie. Here he is, finally giving his definitive version of what happened in the tunnel that fateful day, and still he finds a moment to give Arsenal props for their catering. Superb.

If you're a fan of food and drink being used in violent ways inside dressing rooms, though (yes, sounds a bit niche, but whatever gets you through the night), the place to go is West Ham. In *Always Managing*, Harry Redknapp tells a phenomenal story about a frenzied Paolo Di Canio lifting a giant barrel of Gatorade over his head (were they at the Super Bowl?), lobbing it across the dressing room and ruining poor Shaka Hislop's smart white linen suit.

---

11 OK, there was this one time one of us wangled our way into a press room and beat Bobby Gould to the last free biscuit. But that's it.

Redknapp also tells a story in one of his other books about the time he (Harry, not Paolo) threw a platter of sandwiches at Don Hutchison for being a smartarse, saying that Hutch ended up with 'egg, cheese and tomato right across the nut'. It's a nice story, but as it's Redknapp you have to wonder if he's remembered it right, because Neil Ruddock tells a similar but different tale:

'Harry went ballistic in the dressing room and John Moncur in particular, received the mother of all tongue-lashings. "Monc" himself went mad and, in his rage, kicked a tray full of sandwiches … They flew everywhere; one hit Harry in the face and another skewered a clothes peg perfectly and that's where it stayed. We were all dying with laughter.'

So did Harry throw sandwiches at Hutch or did Monc boot sandwiches at Harry? Or, did very similar things happen in the same dressing room at around the same time? One thing we are certain of is that Razor took a comical bite out of that sarnie while it hung limply off that clothes peg. No doubt about it.

SUPERSTITION AND ROUTINE

Footballers love a superstition, whether it's putting their left sock on first, being the last player out of the tunnel or kissing someone's baldy head for luck – but quite a few of their routines involve food or drink.

Jamie Vardy's revelations about his drinking habits during Leicester's title-winning season are a great example. You probably already know them, but they're worth repeating: a glass of Tawny port on the eve of a game and his habit of dissolving Skittles in a three-litre bottle of vodka until he had fermented some kind of Taste the Rainbow™ liqueur.

For the record, he didn't dissolve all the colours of Skittles, just the red and purple ones, 'because when I eat them I don't fancy the orange, green and yellow ones'. Bit fussy, Jamie? They all taste basically the same. But this is confusing. Jamie says he put about 20 batches of red and purple sweets (the ones he did like) in the vodka. So does that mean every time he busted open a bag of Skittles he put the reds and purples in the vodka then chucked the rest? Or was he constantly choking the green, yellow and orange ones down? Did he sacrifice his love for the reds and purples for the sake of some sickly sweet Skittle vodka syrup further down the line? Playing the long game, if you like? Or did he allow himself three or four from each pack before putting the rest in the vodka? How did this system work, for Christ's sake? Sadly, he withheld the crucial details, possibly because he plans to mass-produce and market Vardy's Skittle Vodka after retirement. What he does tell us is that after a while 'you can drink the vodka neat and it tastes just like Skittles, so you don't get that minging taste'. Why bother buying vodka if you hate it that much? Just get an alcopop, mate. Or, you know, just eat the Skittles. That said, we're definitely going to try it.

Here are a few of our other favourite pre-match routines and superstitions involving food or drink:

Name	Routine/Superstition
Carlton Palmer	Carlton had all sorts in his routine – wearing the same boxer shorts until they lost; sitting on the right of the coach; always last on to the pitch. But he also enjoyed a small sharpener before the game: 'I would wander into the lounge area in the main stand at Hillsborough, past the surprised sponsors and besuited executives, jog to the bar where the bar staff had lined up my drink, swig it down, and run straight onto the pitch.'
Gary Neville	As you might expect, Nev had his routine down pat: 'The day before a game, it was always the same – 8 a.m.: breakfast of cereal and orange juice. Noon: fish, potatoes and vegetables 3.30 p.m.: cereal and a piece of toast. 7 p.m.: pasta with soup. 9.15 p.m.: lights out. I'd even take cereal and my own bowl and spoon on the train if we were going down to London. I'd sit there at 3.30 precisely munching my Weetabix as the train rolled through the countryside and the other lads pissed their sides.'
	Wonderful work. He also liked a Ribena at lunch on matchdays.
Filippo Inzaghi	Having a big purge before games crops up quite often in autobiographies – Tony Gale loved a good vomit according to Leroy Rosenior, while Jackie Charlton admits he always had a proper pre-match poo. It's no different in Italy, reassuringly. Andrea Pirlo's description of Inzaghi's ritual is sublime: 'Simply put, he crapped. Crapped a hell of a lot. That isn't a bad thing in itself, but the fact he'd do it at the ground, in our dressing room, just before the game, got on our nerves somewhat. Especially if the dressing room was small ... Often he'd go three or four times in the space of 10 minutes. "It brings me luck, boys," he'd say.'
	Three or four times in ten minutes? Christ. A frightening ratio – although still less than his ratio for offsides per 90 minutes.
Tommy Smith	The most intriguing of all doesn't involve consumption, but simply getting the belly right before a game. Jimmy Case writes that while at Liverpool he was fascinated by Smith's peculiar ritual: 'Ronnie Moran rubbed Tommy's chest and out would come a great loud belch ... Tommy said it was to prevent him getting a stitch in his side at the start of the game.'
	First of all, we were under the impression no one talked about getting a 'stitch' past the age of about 14. Secondly, how did it come about initially? What was the first time like? Did Smith do this during his youth career? Who did it before Moran? Like with Vardy and the Skittles, this offers more questions than answers.

CULINARY CHRONICLES

If you take just one nugget of information away from this book, then let it be this: Leroy Rosenior's sister invented the machine that makes Maltesers: 'she basically adapted a cement mixer', he says, trying to make it not sound like a huge deal. In terms of family kudos, Leroy was a very good, top-level footballer … but his sister whipped up a contraption to make Maltesers out of some bog-standard construction equipment. We're afraid there's only one winner there.

Andy Gray chucks out a lovely tale too. He joined up with the Scotland squad on one occasion and at dinner he blithely ordered a prawn cocktail as a starter. Scotland manager Jock Stein was unimpressed: 'You're from Drumchapel in Glasgow laddie. What do you know about prawn cocktails? You'll have soup like the rest of us.' Yeah, poncey old Andy Gray – goes south of the border to play his football and what happens? He comes back up, thinking he's Margo out of *The Good Life*, demanding to eat prawn cocktails, cheese and pineapple hedgehogs and Black Forest gateau.

There were never any problems with the ponciness of prawn cocktails with the England squad. They were happily eating it at least as far back as the 1966 World Cup. Bobby Charlton writes that it was on the menu at the post-match do following the disappointing 0–0 draw with Uruguay in their opening game. But not all of it was consumed: 'A few of the players, having become bored by the ceremonials, and partaken eagerly of the wine that accompanied the buffet, sent some of the local dignitaries home with prawn cocktail and potato salad that had been slipped into their suit pockets. Such laddish behaviour, had it found its way on to the news pages, might not have hugely enhanced our image as we prepared for the next match against Mexico.'

'Laddish behaviour'. That lot were the original Crazy Gang. Not Sir Bob, of course – he only heard about all this japery through Nobby Stiles.

Stein wasn't the only manager we read about who could get wound up by food. Ian Snodin relates one story where Everton manager Colin Harvey went berserk at the coach driver because he brought him seeded rather than seedless grapes for the long coach ride home from an away game. You can see Harvey's point, to be fair. Where was he going to spit all the pips? It's a right bloody faff eating pip-filled soft fruit on a coach. A coach driver, of all people, should know that, surely?

Like Jock Stein, Don Revie took a keen interest in the diet of his players, and, while a youngster at Leeds, Norman Hunter found himself prescribed a weird health snack by The Revs after he'd complained of feeling lethargic: 'a special potion consisting of a glass of sherry with raw egg mixed in it. I had to swallow this concoction every day before I left home for training. It was dreadful … Revie made sure it was the best – Harvey's Bristol Cream and I suppose the eggs were free range and fresh! But … that potion tasted absolutely vile and there was the odd occasion early on when it made me throw up.' Norm should have tried dissolving some Tooty Frooties in it (no Skittles back then, of course) – to get rid of the minging taste.

At least Hunter did what he was told by his elders as he made his way in the game. Not so Archie Gemmill, who turned his nose up at the first meal offered up by the landlady of his digs as a youngster at Preston: 'A meat and potato pie floating in the middle of a bowl of tomato soup might cut it for some people, but I'd never encountered anything like it before. I'm ashamed to say, I went straight back upstairs, grabbed my belongings and fled.'

It's weird, though – ever since we read that, a meat and potato pie floating in Heinz tomato soup is all we fancy. It seems magical, somehow. Was the pie abnormally buoyant due to a particularly light and flaky pastry? Or was the soup just supremely viscous, like a gel? Tantalising.

Still, at least Archie apologised as he bolted out the door. One West Ham squad had no such manners. They were on tour in Bermuda (it's an absolute nightmare being a footballer sometimes, isn't it?), and after one game Clyde Best took the whole squad and all the backroom staff to meet his family. There was a reception of about 100 people to welcome them. It sounds wonderful. But then Clyde writes:

'You might have imagined that the guys would have been keen to sample some local culinary delights. Far from it. What they wanted was Roast Beef and Yorkshire Puddings – the very same dish I had grown accustomed to in the UK. I can't remember how my mum felt about that – she probably wanted to make something typically local – but, being the accommodating person she was, and a great cook, she somehow managed to pull it off.'

We read some pretty rum stuff in these books – mostly to do with footballers getting mixed up with booze, women, violence and petty thievery. But this may just be the worst thing we came across. A bunch of lairy players, welcomed to a team-mate's mum's home, looking around, raising their eyebrows and demanding a roast dinner. Next time someone says 'West Ham won the World Cup,' tell them about the time a very similar West Ham were arseholes to Clyde Best's lovely mum.

Robbie Savage loves a bit of food-based banter, and isn't afraid to show it in his life story. He proudly recounts a prank he played on Leicester legend and club ambassador Alan Birchenall. Birch, it seems, used to take a meal home from the canteen to eat in the evenings (which seems a bit bleak, but good luck to him). So once, and you'll like this, this is an absolute classic, Sav crept into his office, removed the foil from his covered dinner, then threw the food in the bin – before re-covering the bowl! Genius, really. Poor Birch took the empty bowl home, settled down for a quiet dinner, ripped the foil off and found his dinner had gone. He was probably forced to eat cold cheese and crackers to keep him going until morning. If only there had been someone there to see his face!

Of course, there wasn't. Birch lived alone. So Sav was laughing at something he could only imagine. But he wasn't laughing the next day when Birchenall playfully shoved his face into his hot lunch: 'I found myself up to my nostrils in boiling-hot jacket potato. My nose was seriously scalded. I even had to see the club doctor.'

Oh, well. Guess you learned your lesson, though, Robbie? You definitely didn't go on to comically loosen the top of a salt shaker so that goalie Simon Royce ended up with a ruined meal, did you? Because that kind of thing, as you know from experience, can have consequences. What's that? Oh, you did. 'He couldn't take a joke … The lads were killing themselves, but Roycey didn't see the funny side. He tipped his dinner all over my suit. We nearly came to blows over it.'

Three things to note here. First, this trick is a bit clichéd, isn't it? Who does he think he is, Dennis the Menace? Second, were people, genuinely, 'killing themselves' with laughter? Really? And third, it's a bit rich for Sav to accuse Roycey of not being able to take a joke when he almost started a fight after Roycey's response.

Plus, Sav's own reactions to a bit of bantz aren't always exactly graceful. For instance, one Christmas the Leicester lads were enjoying a festive night out when Dennis Wise took to the stage saying he'd bought a gift for Robbie. He then pulled out a vibrator in a wig and a Leicester kit with 'Sav 8' on it, and said: 'To the only prick in a Leicester shirt.' Savage, who tells us Wise was particularly close with then boss Dave Bassett, produced a remarkable response: 'I looked round and spotted dessert: chocolate fudge cake. I spread the chocolate all over my face as though it was poo. "That's what you look like when you come out of the manager's office," I said.'

It was only a joke, Sav – that seems a bit much. How does smothering your face in chocolate help you win the argument? It seems doubtful the rest of the squad were stood around thinking, 'Touché, Robbie. Touché,' or 'Your move, Wisey. Top that, mate.' More like: 'I think you just proved Wisey's point, Sav.'

Away from pranks, Jimmy Case tells one story of the day a supporter at Liverpool offered him a pie during a break in play: 'I took a big bite out of his pie, much to the amazement of the rest of the crowd, who loved it. That's Scouse humour for you. Of course, they wouldn't allow it now.' As we all know, Scousers are natural comedians – no other region in the country produces the comic mind necessary to decide to take a bite out of a pie during a football match.

But what worries us about this anecdote is the end: 'Of course, they wouldn't allow it now.' Who are these 'they'? The officials? The stewards? Health & Safety? The FA? Remember, the Sutton United keeper who ate a pie on the bench during the 2017 FA Cup tie with Arsenal was fined for breaching betting regulations, not for taking on extra calories. We'll go out on a limb here and say that if Tom Davies (it needs to be a Scouser, no one else would think of it) were to take a bite from a crowd pie this weekend he probably wouldn't be fined or banned or sentenced to 40 hours of community service. In fact, he might even be lauded for his courage in risking eating any kind of stadium food.

The weirdest eating story we found came from Glenn Hoddle in his 1998 World Cup diary. The backstory is that one night Glenn was being interviewed by the super-smooth Ray Stubbs. However, he'd been talking so much that he lost his voice, so Stubbsy kindly gave him some Fisherman's Friends.

The next day, Glenn was giving a press conference and was relieved to have a few FFs at his disposal, so he signalled to Stubbs, who was standing at the back of the room: 'Ray couldn't work out why I kept putting my thumbs up and pointing to my throat, but in the end he realised. Those Fisherman's Friends really had come up trumps.'

It's sweet in a way – for Ray, the gesture was so small he'd evidently all but forgotten about it. For Glenn, it meant so much he needed to thank Ray publicly via the medium of charades. It's kindness such as this, and the good karma it generates, that's going to see Stubbsy come back as Dougie Donnelly in the next life.

Despite his Partridge-esque final line, Glenn is sadly yet to be hired as the face of a Fisherman's Friend ad campaign. Imagine the series of adverts they could produce: in each one, Glenn finds himself in a situation where he needs to say something important (in a press conference; coaching a team of youngsters; warning someone that they'll pay for their sins in future lives etc.) but he's lost his voice! Quickly, he takes out and sucks on a Fisherman's Friend, which allows him to make the vital communication. After that, he turns to the camera and says: 'Those Fisherman's Friends really came up trumps,' before giving the thumbs up (possibly to a confused Ray Stubbs).

NUTRITIONAL BOLLOCKS

As we all know, Arsene Wenger introduced pasta to the British Isles in 1996, and since then nutrition has become a bit of a hot topic in footballer autobiographies. Usually, it's to complain about how horrible it is to not be able to eat junk food all the time, but very soon, this will probably die out. The players of the 70s, 80s, 90s and noughties seem to have spent their early careers feasting on whatever filled them up, and so resented the changes forced on them by bastard nutrition experts, whereas these days, the Rashfords, Kanes and Pickfords of this world have probably been eating raw veg and quinoa since their early teens.

For the generations before this lot, things were different. Accepted wisdom seemed to be that as long as you trained properly, the quality of what you shoved down your throat didn't matter too much. And neither did the quantity – which brings us to the incredible phenomenon of eating contests.

The king of these monumental events appears to be former Arsenal defender Steve 'Bouldy' Bould, with both Paul Merson and Ray Parlour expressing their awe at his incredible ability to tuck away mountains of food.

Parlour remembers one contest that took place on the way back from a game at Newcastle: 'We were like, "What should we do today? Let's have an eating contest." No reason really, it was just something to do.' How many possibilities did they go through before alighting on that idea? Apparently, Bouldy ate nine dinners, but they had to stop the competition when other players were chucking up outside the coach.

Parlour gives the impression it was a one-time thing, but in *How Not to be a Professional Footballer*, Merse makes out like it was pretty standard for away days: 'We'd have eating competitions to kill time on the journey and he (Bould) would win every time. Prawn cocktails, soup, salmon, roast chicken, lasagnes, apple pies, cheese and biscuits – he'd eat the whole menu and then some. Everything was washed down with can after can of lager.' What menu? How did this apparently mobile restaurant that serviced the coach work, exactly? We like to think they had to pull alongside and keep up with the coach, like the police in *Speed*.

Bould had little competition at Arsenal, but a sort of Eating Contest FA Cup might have been interesting, with clubs each putting forward a champion for a barf-inducing showdown. For Manchester United, step forward another centre-half, Graeme Hogg. Mick (not Mike) Duxbury remembers the time Lou Macari offered Hoggy £100 to eat ten burgers while on tour in Magaluf. The first two went down fine, but the lads wanted the dice loaded in their favour, so: 'While he's drinking, we're putting promotional flyers that we had been handed into the burgers. All sorts of things. He gets to about seven or eight and simply cannot take anymore. Because of the things we'd given him extra, he was more than worth that £100, so he got it.'

Seems a bit odd that Hoggy wouldn't simply remove the indigestible bits of shiny paper from his burgers, but fair enough. Based on that evidence, we'd still be backing Bouldy to walk away with the inaugural Eating Contest FA Cup sponsored by Harvester. Jason McAteer and Gary Kelly probably wouldn't give him much of a test either. McAteer recalls an Ireland game where he and Kells were on the bench, so the day before the pair of them decided to take on 'Harry's Challenge' at a local restaurant: 'Basically you get this massive piece of battered cod, about eight foot in length, 3 million chips and a huge portion of mushy peas, all washed down with tea, bread and butter. If you complete the challenge the meal is free.'

Leaving aside the hyperbole (any keen angler knows an eight-foot cod is frankly ludicrous, particularly with the head cut off, and you surely can't wash anything down with bread and butter – come on, Jase), it does sound like some task. Neither of them manages it, and Trigger/Dave later chucks his guts up on the side of the Lansdowne Road pitch.

The one man we reckon could challenge Bould is Billy Kellock. As we've already seen, he appears to have been fairly unstable, but Andy Gray also reports that Kellock beat another team-mate, Alan Dodd, in a hamburger-eating contest, which involved about a dozen burgers each: 'It was an absolutely extraordinary exhibition of scoffing,' he writes.

Some might see these contests as a classic symbol of excess among the young and wealthy in a modern capitalist society. But we prefer to imagine that these lads are just so competitive that there's nothing in their lives they can't turn into some kind of contest, even something as mundane as eating food on a coach trip.

Eating contests are at the far end of the spectrum. More common among the players of late 20th century Britain was the simple wish to eat unhealthy foodstuffs, but on a (slightly) more moderate scale. Jimmy Bullard reckons that Neil Ruddock once kept a food diary for a while at Liverpool and the club worked out he ate '212 steak and kidney pies per year'. That's roughly a pie every 41 hours. An incredible rate.

Ruddock himself claims that while he was at Liverpool and struggling a little with his weight, a dietician recommended he stick to 'things like Sugar Puffs, beans on toast and pasta'. Now, we'd never normally dream of questioning the wisdom of dieticians, but we'll make an exception here. Sugar Puffs? Even in 2015, after a recipe change and a name change that absolutely no one told us about (they're now 'Honey Monster Puffs'), *The Telegraph* reckoned there was a super-sweet 8.7g of sugar per 30g serving (and if Razor was going to eat Sugar Puffs we'd guess his servings would weigh somewhat more than 30g). So if that was an improvement for Razor, what on earth was he eating for breakfast before? Some kind of special breakfast sandwich? Possibly a Yorkie encased by two hot buttered Pop-Tarts? Now we've said it out loud, we'd like to eat this for breakfast ourselves, holding it in one hand while flicking a V-sign at Jamie Oliver with the other.

Matt Le Tissier fell foul of the old diet diary too: 'I was too honest for my own good and wrote down everything, the burgers, the chips and the fry-ups. Her [the club dietician] jaw hit the ground when I showed her the list. She questioned how I was still alive let alone playing at the top level. I did try the poached eggs on toast for a fortnight but it didn't make a bit of difference, so I went back to what I liked.'

Now, we're not Southampton fans, but, like many of you, we love Le Tiss, and for many reasons. There's *that* goal of course, and *that* goal and *that* goal (it doesn't matter which goals you think we're referring to, they're all bloody brilliant). There's the fact that even when his career had pretty much gone, he still came on as sub in the last game at the Dell to volley a beauty into the net, in the last minute, to snatch a win against Arsenal. There's that clip where he's not bothering to stifle a yawn moments before kick-off. There's the still-weird fact that he went out with Marilyn from *Home and Away*. And, perhaps most of all, we love him because he didn't sign for Chelsea that time.

But.

Come on, Matt. You can't make an attempt at eating well then sack it off after two weeks because you didn't think it was helping. Two weeks of poached eggs can't reverse 25 years of daily McFlurries. We'd have some sympathy for his position (whatever works, works, kind of thing – we're all different and that), but in the same book he also admits: 'I was once carried off in training after a fainting fit caused by eating too many sausage and egg McMuffins before we even started.' So, as long as he didn't *actually pass out* during training while on the revolutionary poached egg diet, surely it *was* helping?

He's far from the only one complaining about dieticians ruining fun time, either. Keith Gillespie appears to avoid anything green unless it's his Northern Ireland shirt: 'Nutritionists tried to change that, prescribing a list of foods and giving me a chart to fill out my daily intake. After a couple of days, I ripped it up, and went back on the cheese and ham toasties. I couldn't be arsed with all that hassle.' You really start feeling for the poor nutritionists when someone thinks making some food that isn't cheese and ham toasties is a 'hassle'.

In some cases, though, the players are arguably not completely responsible for their junk food obsession. Lee McCulloch writes that McDonald's once sponsored the league in Scotland and the players all received gold cards so they could eat for free: 'It was brilliant. We were there four or five times a week.' Amazing. Not only did McDonald's slap their name all over the Scottish football product, they let players eat free in their outlets, so fans would see them in there, so that would improve their image and people would eat there even more. Genius, really. A kind of genius, anyway.

Paul Cannell reports that Bill McGarry decided to ban sweets and crisps at Newcastle in the late 70s, but Alan Kennedy was so addicted to crisps he couldn't give them up, and used to suck on them at the back of the bus so McGarry wouldn't hear the crunch. Which is properly desperate, because what's the point in eating crisps if you can't crunch them? The clue's in the name. Maybe he was eating Skips. Melt in the mouth, they do.

If you're sucking on crisps all the live-long day, your throat is bound to get a bit parched, and that brings us to tales of thirsty footballers. Almost every autobiography we read included tales of extreme drunkenness and/or players fairly regularly abusing their bodies with unhealthy food intake. It's often justified with assurances that they always put 100 per cent into training. 'Play hard, train hard' was the prevailing belief for decades: the established route to team spirit came via the bottle – the successful Everton side of the 80s seems to have been particularly big on this (Stuart Pearce recounts one game – admittedly played after Everton had already won the league – where he could smell alcohol on their breath), as was the Arsenal side of the early 90s. As were, in all probability, most teams: we've seen the phrase 'Win or lose, on the booze' attributed to Neil Ruddock, Bobby Moore and Tony Adams, while Peter Storey says it was practically the motto of the Arsenal team in his era.

The Republic of Ireland certainly seem to have been enjoying themselves during their golden period of the late 80s and early 90s, and John Aldridge is quick to credit Jack Charlton's liberal attitude to a few beers: 'He'd let us drink before games and wouldn't run us too hard in training. He wanted us to keep all our energy for the match. As far as I was concerned that was good psychology because when the game came along you wanted to run the beer off.'

You can't argue with that kind of logic, can you? Drink more booze, don't train too hard, because then you'll really want to shift the calories when you play an actual game. We believe this was exactly the regimen the great Dame Jessica Ennis-Hill stuck rigidly to during her preparations in France before taking heptathlon gold at London 2012. She absolutely hammered the old Kronenbourg 1664 for months while many experts assumed she was concentrating on conditioning – but just look how it paid off once she got to the 110m hurdles! Absolutely blew the field away as she worked to run off those calories.

The main thing we learned when it came to alcohol was that the attitude of British footballers towards booze was very different to the attitude common on mainland Europe. If that sounds a little stereotypical, here's what we mean:

The Full English: Ray Parlour (Eng)

Ray and a few Arsenal team-mates were on tour and went down to a local pub: 'There were only five of us, and I will never forget, one of the boys went to the bar and said, "Thirty-five pints, please."' Thirty-five pints. Why? Could they literally drink faster than the tap could pour?

The Continental: Gilles Grimandi (Fr)

Parlour adds that they turned round to their French team-mate, who must have been looking round expecting the rest of the squad and the backroom staff to walk in at any moment to take their drinks, and asked him what he wanted. 'A small glass of wine please,' was his incredibly brave answer in the face of such severe peer pressure.[12]

Still, the 35-pint order was tame compared with Ian Snodin's revelation that Norman Whiteside once told him that he, Paul McGrath and Bryan Robson once sank 27 pints of Guinness *each* in one session. Robbo, of course, trained the next day as if nothing had happened, because he was Robbo.

* * *

The Full English: Mick Quinn (Eng)

Read Quinn's description of his typical intake while still playing, bearing in mind he describes himself, in relation to this, as 'a heavy social drinker': 'Four or five pints followed by a few vodkas with alcopop mixers and perhaps a few brandies as a nightcap.' Isn't a 'nightcap' supposed to be

---

12 Incidentally, it's unclear if Parlour meant there were five of them plus Grimandi, or including Grimandi. If it included Grimandi, 35 pints is an odd order as 35 is not divisible by four, is it? That's just standard maths.

singular? You know, like a cap? You're topping off something large with something small, not with several something smalls – otherwise they're just part of the 'large' part, surely? Anyway, the impressive thing there is that he drank vodka *with* alcopops. What innovation. Like cheese on toast, but substituting the bread with some cheese.

The Continental: Andrea Pirlo (Ita)

While Quinn drinks cocktails of Smirnoff and Hooch, Pirlo, not much of a drinker, has a cocktail named after him: 'The "Pirlo" is the most famous Brescia aperitivo going. The ingredients are simple: sparkling white wine, Campari and tonic water.' Sure, Andy, but wouldn't it taste better mixed with a bottle of blue WKD? Just to give it a kick?

* * *

The Full English: Carlton Palmer (Eng)

Carlton Palmer admits he once played for Sheffield Wednesday against QPR while drunk after Chrisses Woods and Waddle took him out for an all-nighter the day before the game knowing, but not telling him, that they wouldn't be playing.[13] Once on the pitch, he was still so drunk that Sir Les Ferdinand, playing against him but ever the gent, kindly had to point him in the right direction when the brightness of the floodlights left him confused and disorientated.

The Continental: The Sampdoria Squad (Ita)

Graeme Souness writes that soon after he joined Sampdoria, he found the players giddy with excitement about an away game at Avellino. When he asked what they were so excited about, they answered: 'Wait till you taste the coffee down there … They ate their dinner so quickly that night and were all racing to get to the bar for a coffee.'

It's a different world, isn't it? The Sheffield lads came to London and were bang on the booze. In Italy, once in the provinces, they're delighted to sip a quality espresso. The equivalent, we think, would be The Waddler, Woodsy, Carlton and the rest getting all hyped up about a trip to Plymouth so they can indulge in a proper cream tea.

* * *

---

13 See 'Celebrity' chapter for more details on this night out.

The Full English: Roy McDonough (Eng)

During pre-season training with Southend, Roy had naturally been drinking before a training run, and possibly copped a bad pint. Unfortunately this led to him getting caught short, panicking and having to take a dump on the beach (like the Chris Rea song), 'squatting between two sun loungers to release a chocolate Mr Whippy into the sand.' Beautiful image, isn't it? When he says he was between two sun loungers, was he squatting unaided, or was each arse-cheek supported by the edge of each lounger, thus creating a makeshift pit below? And, cat-like, did he bury his mess afterwards? We don't know.

Anyway, there was, naturally, no available loo roll, so he ran back to the hotel to get clean: 'I went to the bar to straighten out with four beers, before dealing with that dirty arse.'

Wow. There were so many options available to Roy here. He could have ordered a beer and sorted 'that dirty arse' while it was being poured. He could, if he was that keen, have ordered and taken a few almighty gulps before sorting his bum out. At worst, surely, he could have sank one then had a clean up. But four? Four pints while the rancid stench of alcohol-fuelled shite wafted about his person? Remarkable commitment to the booze, there.

The Continental: The Atletico Madrid Squad (Sp)

While managing Atletico Madrid in 1988, Ron Atkinson had a player called Sergio Marrero, who was caught drinking whisky in a bar during the week. The next day at training, Ron 'could sense a stigma around him', and the club secretary had to explain that the squad 'had cut him dead'. They saw drinking as abuse of the body, and if you hurt your body, you hurt the team.

* * *

In contrast, Southend boss Dave Webb actually congratulated McDonough on his return to the hotel, so impressed was he that he had managed to complete the run despite the booze inside him.

Fortunately, not all Brits come across as lairy lager louts. Bobby Charlton, when reminiscing about the celebrations after the World Cup win, sounds more like a sort of old-fashioned Victorian gent: 'The Playboy Club was maybe not my natural habitat, but I enjoyed it well enough even while following my habit, formed after excessive celebrations as one of Manchester United's youngest first-teamers, of merely sipping an exotic World Cup cocktail. I suppose I didn't want to blur the edges of my contentment.' It's a little-known fact that Sir Bob's book was ghostwritten by Charlotte Bronte.

And then there's dear old Kevin Keegan, who manages to sound more like a hard-bitten detective in the mould of Philip Marlowe. Try reading this in your best inner Humphrey Bogart voice: 'During my early days at Liverpool I would occasionally go to night-clubs, which I found to be lonely places filled with people who were trying to create a false world for themselves. The lighting would be subdued and people would drink and talk out of character, as an escape from the normality of their everyday lives. It was almost as if they were actors and actresses, wearing masks and changing their personalities to suit the surroundings.'

Kev's absolutely nailed what it's like to be sober at a nightclub, hasn't he? It's enough to drive anyone to drink. He adds: 'And then I saw her, slinking to the bar like a panther after a hard day sleeping – she looked cute enough to pet, but you'd risk losing an arm if you ever tried it. I drank my whisky and watched her order. Several men thought about approaching her and then decided against it. When she wanted company, she'd take it, and not before – and you wouldn't necessarily have a choice. Who was this dame? What was she doing in this godforsaken dive in downtown Liverpool? And why was she drinking Vardy's Skittle Vodka?'

Well, possibly not.

5

Celebrity

Brian Tilsley

Many of you will remember that, strange as it may seem, Tony Adams once dated the model Caprice after meeting her on the star-studded occasion of an episode of Ian Wright's much-missed chat show. But, until we read Adams's book *Sober*, we weren't aware that another guest, Ulrika Jonsson, also 'slipped her number on a piece of paper into my pocket'. Now, you don't have to have been a subscriber to *Loaded* and *FHM* to see that that is, by all reasonable standards, an enviable 90s evening's work from Rodders.

And so our dip into the endless crossovers between the worlds of football and celebrity begins. Very few of them are of a romantic nature, but they are all, hopefully, interesting, surprising and entertaining. Jamie Vardy being friends with *X Factor* winner Sam Bailey isn't going to cut it here, nor is Kelly Smith geeking out when she met Take That. Very much more the sort of thing we're looking for are the facts that Leroy Rosenior used to hang out with Massive Attack when he was at Bristol City; John McGovern being BFFs with AC/DC's Brian Johnson; and the fact that a young Stan Ternent helped to build mountaineer Chris Bonnington's house. Oh yes, that's very much more the sort of thing.

Some of these chance encounters are one-time deals, as our stars pass like ships in the night. But sometimes the same old names crop up. The repeat offenders, the usual suspects. And none of these refer to Kevin Spacey.

Let's begin, then, by handing out a Gold, a Silver and a Bronze medal to the stars who are the most frequent flyers across the night sky of our football heroes, starting with the undisputed Guv'nor.

GOLD - ROD STEWART

We haven't read Rod Stewart's autobiography, but we can only assume it is mainly about meeting footballers. There can't be much room for anything else. Every anecdote must involve a footballer appearing from somewhere. From what we can tell, his life is literally just tight trousers, singing, blonde women and a constant stream of footballers passing through and telling the tale in their own memoirs. If Rod were to repay the favour and namecheck every footballer he'd met in his life, his book would be longer than *War and* sodding *Peace*.

Whether you like Rod Stewart or not (for the record, there are some absolute bangers like 'The Killing of Georgie', but we can take or leave a lot of it), you categorically do not like him as much as the average footballer does. We've read stories from players that have lifted every trophy you can imagine, and risen to the very top of the world's greatest game, but it seems that, almost to a man, they can go weak at the knees at the sight of Rod the Mod. For example, Alan Brazil and the Scotland squad had a night out with Rod and his first wife, Alana, in Spain in 1982 and Brazil remembers it wistfully: 'I looked at Rod's face and wiry body and honestly wondered if he was made of the same sort of bones and blood that we were.'

It does sound like a good night, though: 'My most vivid memory of that night is that at one stage Rod, Alan Hansen and I were all dancing on the bar.' And Alan Brazil is not a man easily fazed by fame; after all, he went to school with Jim Kerr out of Simple Minds.

John Wark was also there that night in the middle of the World Cup, along with the rest of the Scotland squad and a fair number of the Tartan Army, and he takes up the story: 'Rod was in his element and it wasn't long before he leaned over to Alana and said: "Why don't you go back to the hotel. I'm staying on here with the lads." She did exactly that and after an extraordinary sing-along – I remember 'Sailing' was a particular favourite – we said our farewells to grab taxis for the journey to the team hotel.'

Elsewhere, Vinnie Jones claims Rod as a friend, and Frank McAvennie says he met him in his own first flush of his fame, along with the likes of Elton John and George Michael, but that 'I was particularly impressed with Telly Savalas'. Bit rude, Frank. After all, did Telly invite the whole 1986 Scotland World Cup squad to his LA house for dinner? No, he didn't. Did Rod Stewart? Of course he bloody did.

Rod also invited Archie Gemmill, along with his wife and guests, backstage at an NEC Birmingham gig. While Rod was playing the convivial host, he was unfortunately told it was time for him to go. Archie regales us in similar moony-eyed terms as Alan Brazil: 'At that, a young girl, who couldn't have been more than nineteen, stepped forward and Rod held his arms out by his sides as he was stripped right down to his underpants. Well, Betty and Christine watched this performance wide-eyed, giving each other a little look that said, "If I come back in another world, I want that job!"'

Stan Ternent also got freebies to see Rod in concert, albeit from the wings in a full body cast and wheelchair after an injury. Rod had a gig in Newcastle you see, so naturally spent the week before limbering up for it by training with Sunderland and making friends with striker Billy Hughes. Stan says, 'His mate from The Faces, Ronnie Wood, tried to keep up but he was knackered and in the bath drawing on a fag after two minutes.'

The magnetic charm of Rod has cast a spell over more than just Maggie May, Britt Ekland and every Scottish footballer ever; it's also responsible for Carlton Palmer getting caught playing while pissed – sort of. As we mentioned earlier, Carlton was tricked into a night out on the pop with two injured Chrisses – Woods and Waddle – before a Sheffield Wednesday away game in the Smoke against QPR. The midfielder would have got away with it if it hadn't been for those pesky photographers, who were outside Tramps nightclub as they left, waiting for the singing royalty to emerge. Worse the wear for drink, and still in his tracksuit, Carlton and his drinking buddies made to leave:

'I hauled myself atop England's current goalkeeper and we wobbled precariously out into Jermyn Street and the bright early morning sun. To my mind, even though my mind was in fact barely functioning, it still seemed a bit early for there to be so much light. Then, by degrees, I understand that the dazzling light was the result of flashbulbs going off, the paparazzi being out in force to snap Rod Stewart who was, apparently, also inside Tramps. This was what had lured Waddler and Woods to the club in the first place, they were always going to end up there.'

It's not all songs of joy and tears of laughter with Rod, though. Two of our favourite mentions revolve around the tragic circumstances of

Jock Stein's untimely death while managing Scotland as they drew with Wales at Ninian Park in 1985 in a vital World Cup qualifier. First of all, Lawrie McMenemy doesn't let the sad day of Stein's funeral deter him from a spectacular name-drop: 'At the service I stood next to Graeme Souness and Rod Stewart, so packed was the service.' Lawrie has a name-drop for any occasion, don't you worry about that.

Top of the shop though has to be Mickey Thomas, speaking about that night in Cardiff, when Welsh World Cup hopes were dashed before the football world realised it had lost one of its greatest managers: 'What had preceded this was now completely irrelevant. A great man of football was dead. Nothing else mattered.

'The only small consolation for me was that I managed to get Rod Stewart's autograph and later met him with my big mate from The Alarm, Mike Peters.'

Brilliant. Nothing else matters after such a tragedy – except a celebrity autograph. But then this is Rod Stewart we're talking about – king of all the celebrities.

SILVER - ELTON JOHN

As with all good medal ceremonies, there's an element of doubt about the validity of the results, and if there is anyone here who is performance-enhanced, it's Elton John. He is, after all, involved in football as a long-term chairman of Watford. Still, Tommy Trinder and Eric Morecambe were club chairmen too, and they don't feature in footballer autobiographies anything like as much as Elton Hercules John.

Let's start at the very beginning, before the man who would be Elton even had that name. As a fan of the music scene in the 60s, a young Terry Venables, being the hip, swinging guy he was, would hang around the Tin Pan Alley offices of Mills Music. 'At the time there were two youngsters working there as general dogsbodies in the basement of the offices, Reg and Eric.' Nothing of note so far, but El Tel goes on: 'Reg was a little fat fellow, who had a superb gift as a mimic, and could do a brilliant impression of *Carry On* star Kenneth Williams, while Eric was an extremely extroverted character.'

It turns out that Eric was Eric 'Monster' Hall, and Reg was Reg 'Tiny Dancer' Dwight, before he burst out of his basement cocoon and emerged as Elton John.

Frank McAvennie's reminiscence of Mr John comes from his full-on 80s daft hat phase, when the two met in Stringfellows and then carried on partying back at Elton's. 'Elton was a generous host with drinks of any kind available on demand and lines of the best coke I had ever had.' Before you get on your high horse, Frank was injured at the time. And if a man on the injury list can't pass the time by doing a 'wee bit of Charlie' off of Elton John's cistern, then we don't know what the world's come to.

Tony Adams tells us he met Elton much later at an awards bash in more sober times, and the two did charity work together. But not everyone is so enamoured with the singer – Brian Laws says that Brian Clough was having none of it: 'Elton was a big admirer of Cloughie and would even be invited into our dressing room before games. Once he came in and told Cloughie he had some tickets for a concert he was doing at the NEC in Birmingham. Cloughie said he wasn't interested – but we would be.' Lovely stuff from Cloughie.

Any discussion of Elton John and football shouldn't shy away from the lovely image of Graham Taylor as best man at one of his weddings, but it's another former Watford manager we turn to here for his stories. Step forward Dave 'Harry' Bassett.

After he'd greeted Elton with his standard opener of 'Hello son', the two got on famously for Bassett's brief stay at Watford. He remembers with fondness a visit to Elton's house with his wife, Christine, when the singer showed them a wardrobe full of furs: 'He selected a magnificent full-length coat and insisted that Christine try it on for size. Mouth agape, she slid into it – and it fitted her perfectly and might have been made for her. "It's yours," he said simply. I've never known Christine to be speechless for quite so long. In fairness to Elton, I know that he is now a keen conservationist and no longer buys real furs.' The 'in fairness' here is lovely, but there's no news on whether Christine had a similar attack of morals and lobbed the coat out for the bin men to take.

Although Dave struggled to live up to Taylor's achievements during his brief reign at Vicarage Road, Elton was certainly keen to get him there in the first place. He imparted on Dave a particular pearl of wisdom during tense negotiations with Bassett's employer at Wimbledon, Sam Hammam: 'Sam was asking Elton for money. He eventually agreed to it. I remember Elton saying afterwards, "When you've got a clinker up your arse you need to remove it."'

With a turn of phrase like that, it's no wonder Bernie Taupin wrote the lyrics, is it?

BRONZE – FREDDIE STARR

Dipping for the line and taking Bronze while dressed as Hitler and wearing wellies … it's Freddie Starr. Starr doesn't crop up nearly so many times as Elton John, and certainly not as many as Rod Stewart, but the quality of his appearances gets him on the podium. First of all, there are the standard glitzy nights out in choice company with Frank Worthington: 'We'd go out for meals to Bailey's cabaret club where we met stars like Lulu, Guys and Dolls, Gary Glitter, Freddie Starr and the Grumbleweeds.'

Frank is no stranger to a celebrity (his foreword is written by Bill Maynard for goodness' sake), but I bet he wouldn't boast about every one of those celebrity big guns these days. Guys and Dolls were shit for a start.

Freddie Starr goes beyond such chance encounters in nightclubs, though – he's always gone the extra mile to involve himself with footballers. Alan Ball tells the story of when Freddie threatened to get involved at Exeter and take the club over.

'I never imagined that we would see him but, sure enough, he appeared on the Friday and came to the training. The players hardly believed it as he joined them. He was chipping, juggling and executing all manner of tricks with the ball. He was telling jokes, moving around with his funny walks and then when he knocked the ball into the net he went down like Elvis Presley, calling "Yo" as he lay there. The lads were in creases of laughter and he got up to tell them if anybody scored in the following day's league match the manager and players all had to go down giving it the Elvis "Yo".'

We like this story firstly because we have no idea what he means by the 'Elvis Yo', and secondly because he didn't buy Exeter at all. It would seem he just came down to dick around a bit. This becomes a theme with Freddie, particularly on cup final days.

John Barnes says of the morning of the 1984 FA Cup Final: 'The relaxed approach continued on the day. Michael Barrymore was with us. Freddie Starr was on the coach to the stadium.' Now, this is slightly puzzling because we're old enough to remember the coverage of this final. And while Michael Barrymore was representing Watford with his comedy stylings (which included a horrifically racist skit on *Grandstand* made up as John Barnes himself), Freddie Starr was with the Everton squad, so how he ended up on the Watford coach we don't know.

Having said that, Freddie Starr seems to have been on most coaches to Wembley in the 1970s and 80s. He just found his way on there, as a sceptical Lawrie McMenemy witnessed when Southampton made it to the League Cup Final against Forest in 1978. Despite not knowing Starr personally, and without him having any apparent affiliation to the club, Lawrie took a call from the comedian asking to come and visit. He had done so once before, prior to their 1976 FA Cup Final appearance, and not arrived. This time, however, Starr was as good as his word, turning up at the hotel and relaxing the players with his impression of Alan Ball, which to be fair, we could all probably have a go at. But if Lawrie thought the hotel visit was an end to it, he was very much mistaken. 'When I stepped on the coach I noticed Freddie Starr sitting at the back, uninvited, talking to the players. It was 1.15, rather late, and I decided to let him stay.'

Given that they were late leaving the hotel, mainly due to Freddie Starr dicking around doing Alan Ball impressions, the Saints were inevitably a bit late arriving at the stadium too. 'In view of the time, we walked straight up the tunnel out on the pitch to test it. Starr came with us and marched in front of the band waving his arms about. I was surprised no one went to him and asked who he was. He'd struck me as being a complex character, funny but zany.'

Really enjoying Lawrie's stab at trying to understand the man behind the mask here. You would think it would end there, and Lawrie clearly did, but no. As the manager took his seat on the bench (for a cup final, remember!), 'I spotted Freddie Starr sitting behind us! He'd gate crashed right to the best seats in the stadium.'

This is the level of commitment that has got Starr one of our medals. It's bizarre. Lawrie's never met him before, but he gets on the coach, the pitch and the Southampton bench. He really did, you can see him on YouTube and everything. This book isn't big on statistics, but it seems to us that Freddie Starr is on 57 per cent of all cup final coaches, maybe.

* * *

Other celebrities who crop up more than once include Nick Faldo, Michael Parkinson, Mick Hucknall and Norman Wisdom.

Nick Faldo gets two mentions, with wildly differing outcomes. On the one hand, former Palace chairman Simon Jordan is a very unsatisfied customer, having successfully bid 'an extortionate amount' and won a golf day with Sir Nick for his brother. 'When my secretary contacted Faldo's secretary to arrange the lesson, he was extremely non-committal on dates.'

Oh dear. Jordan, who is not averse to a celebrity spat (see Pete Doherty later), eventually lost patience when he got no answers and wrote Faldo a letter saying 'as far as I was concerned fuck his one-hour golf lesson. Mind you, given his rapidly declining form he probably needed it more himself.'

On the other, more positive, hand, however, is the fact that the three-time Masters champion saved Paul Merson's life – well, sort of – and without even trying. Paul Merson, you see, was terrified of flying and recalls the time he got over it: 'My shirt was soaked through with sweat and I was thinking of doing a runner, but as I was sitting there, Sir Nick Faldo got on to the plane. "Oh my God," I thought. "We're going to be OK. Nick Faldo isn't dying in a plane crash." I was fine for the rest of the flight.'

This is impeccable logic, right? Nick Faldo is more famous than me, so there's no way he's going to crash in a plane. By that reasoning, all you have to do to avoid a plane crash is to make sure you have someone more famous with you on the flight – though The Big Bopper may have taken issue with that, were he still with us.

For his part, Michael Parkinson pops up a couple of times, mostly to upset people. Kenny Dalglish takes him to task for criticising him at Blackburn, and Ian Wright was hurt when Parky 'slaughtered' his chat show – especially as the criticism wasn't because the show seemingly made Tony Adams irresistible to women.

Now, we're surprised that the professional Yorkshireman had time between Muhammad Ali anecdotes to criticise a fellow chat show host, but his words clearly stung poor Ian: 'I was shocked more than anything else by how horrible he was being about me. Michael Parkinson is The Man when it comes to chat shows, the one everybody aspires to be because of what he's done and who he's sat down with. Him going out of his way to belittle me would be like Pele having a go at me for trying to play football.'

Fortunately, Ian managed to put all criticism of *Friday Night's All Wright* behind him, to go on and make *The Wright Ticket* and *Wright Around the World* before TV executives ran out of Wright puns and he had to go back to football punditry. Light entertainment's loss is *Match of the Day*'s gain.

Mick (not Mike) Duxbury tells of a dressing-room visit by Simply Red's Mick (not Mike) Hucknall, which clearly still troubles him. 'If I'd have been in my right mind, in any other situation, I would have loved nothing more than to go and shake his hand and probably do something stupid like bow down in front of him. But I was doing my pre-match thing of zoning out and completely allowed the moment to pass me by. I've regretted that ever since.' Ever since? Maybe Mick (not Mike) could have asked Mick (not Mike) if anyone had ever mistakenly called him 'Mike' and they could have bonded over that.

Norman Wisdom comes up a couple of times for his Freddie Starr-like ability to attach himself to footballers, and not just because Gordon Hill, Peter Taylor and Kenny Sansom are constantly getting mentions for their impressions of him (see 'Banter, Tomfoolery and Hi-Jinks' chapter). The pick of his stories, though, is clearly this one from Peter Shilton when he picked up an injury at Leicester:

'I turned up at the treatment room only to be told that it was occupied. Having hung about outside for some time, I decided to go in and see who needed such lengthy treatment. And, much to my surprise, there on the table was comedian Norman Wisdom. Norman was appearing in a show at a local theatre and had injured himself while performing one of his comic falls. The club were only too happy to offer him treatment.'

Priorities were clearly in order at Leicester back in the day where any showbiz legend passing through town could hop on the massage table for a rub-down before the players got a look in.

DROP IT LIKE IT'S HOT

The flip side of the recurring celebrity is the recurring name-dropper among our footballers. Who loves to breeze through their chapters, liberally scattering famous names here and there? Well, quite a few of them actually.

Paul Cannell has his musical boasts of seeing both a young pre-Police Gordon 'Sting' Sumner perform with his first band in Newcastle, and of chatting with Jerry Lee Lewis in a Memphis bar.

Stan Collymore's name-drops are mainly regarding his sexual conquests, but let's focus on Stan's encounter with OJ Simpson, who he bumped into at a restaurant: 'He called me over. He said he knew who I was. I thought he was okay.' So that's all right, then. We thought this would be the ultimate example of 'speak as you find' until John Burridge said that Uday Hussein, who once offered him a coaching job, 'came across as a nice guy. He didn't seem cruel at all.' That's Uday Hussein, of murder, imprisonment, torture, rape, kidnapping and son of Saddam fame. Following this logic, Fred West might have been okay because he let someone out of a side turning once.

Frank Worthington's celebrity shenanigans err more towards showbiz and romantic entanglements than brutal killers, thankfully. He speaks of hanging around in Philadelphia with AC/DC, Bad Company and Humble Pie, and he tells us of his friendship with Rick Wakeman, though only to set up a mention of his fling with the first Page 3 superstar, Jilly Johnson, who was friends with Rick's wife. He also tells a seedy Mills & Boon pastiche story of the day he copped off with Dick (no relation to Unai) Emery's make-up artist. 'Oo, you are awful.' Yes. Yes, he is.

John 'Aldo' Aldridge can't quite keep up with Frank's level of celebrity acquaintance, but he does, typically, boil it down to a Top 8 (always a Top 8 with this guy). This time it's simply: '8 People I've Played Golf With'. We'll give him Stan Boardman and John Bishop, though as Scouse celebs they may be contractually obliged to play golf with any half-decent ex-Liverpool marksman. Down a rung are jockeys Kieren Fallon and Franny Norton. Then the list is stretched wafer-thin with four football folks. I'm sure that Alan Kennedy (and his crisps), Don Hutchison, Mike Dean (!) and Nigel Spackman are lovely company, but it's hardly Tarby, Lynchy and Brucie, is it?

Rio Ferdinand can count Olly Murs and Tinie Tempah as his celebrity friends, as both are enthusiastic wearers of his clothing line, #5 – there's that hashtag again. Harry Redknapp talks about hanging out with Bobby Moore and the access it got him and his mates to *Top of the Pops*, where they would 'mix with the girls from Pan's People, but it was never really my scene'. Harry says he preferred spending time 'at my local pub the Blind Beggar, in Whitechapel, where Ronnie Kray shot George Cornell. They were great days at West Ham.' Well that's a different sort of name-dropping; extolling the virtues of a murder scene for a night out, but whatever floats your boat, Harry.

If there were good times at West Ham, though, they were nothing compared with the giddy days at Bournemouth when Jim Davidson was on the board and 'we had the time of our lives. It was real laugh-a-minute stuff.' Apparently Jim had 'strippers in, the lot', and one day on the motorway when the Torquay coach came past them, 'Jim Davidson stood up and pulled a moonie at them.' He's lucky he didn't get nick-nicked.

Simon Jordan is a sod for a name-drop. As we've seen with Nick Faldo, he's no stranger to a bit of celebrity confrontation, but elsewhere he's happy to talk about people he's met at parties, like Chris Eubank, Ray Winstone and Victoria Beckham, and he doesn't mind you knowing that he dated Sophie Anderton and Alex Best. But his finest celebrity anecdote took place on a visit to Anfield as Palace chairman: 'I turned away handing my coat off to one of the boardroom attendants to hang up. Unfortunately it wasn't a boardroom attendant, it was Chris De Burgh the singer of "Lady in Red". How embarrassing. But in fairness, he did hang it up for me.'

Lovely stuff. We think and hope it was a case of mistaken identity rather than De Burgh actually working there, but we can't be certain; we've all got to pay the Ferryman eventually.

Mick Quinn gives the name-dropping title a good shot, peddling weak anecdotes about a Miss World he doesn't bother to tell us the name of and the time Simon Le Bon invited him to visit him and Yasmin in London – though regrettably he couldn't make it. His best effort, though, involves meeting Robin Williams in Malta, while on tour with Wigan – of course. Williams was filming *Popeye* on the island and performed a stand-up routine at the hotel they were all staying at. All seems like it went well until Mrs Williams mentioned how hard Robin had been working on the film, and Quinn and team-mate Colin Methven became needlessly aggressive with the poor lady: '"If he thinks fannying around having make-up put on is hard work, he should try shovelling coal down the pit for eight hours." "Yeah," I joined in. "Or be in a family of four in Liverpool living on sixty pounds a week.'" Is this what the youngsters call 'whataboutery'? Quinn says that Patch Adams took it in good spirit, had a chuckle and signed a pound note for him.

That note didn't stay in Mick's possession for long, though. At the next bar, he was a quid short for his round: 'I looked at it, thought "Fuck it", and handed it over. Easy come, easy go.'

But, as with Rod being the King of the Celebrities, there can only be one winner when it comes to name-dropping, and that is, as you might expect, Vinnie Jones, what with him being a Hollywood actor these days and all. During the course of his engaging memoirs, Vinnie talks of meetings with the likes of Charlton Heston, Dustin Hoffman (who he claims 'mentioned something about "the new Bruce Willis"'), Michael Caine, Bob Hoskins, Patrick Swayze, Quentin Tarantino, Ronnie Wood, Roger Daltrey, Eric Clapton, Bill Withers (whose house he moved into), Robert Duvall, Brad Pitt, Angelina Jolie and inevitably Rod Stewart. But his best celebrity anecdote involves a bit of self-deprecation, when he lived next door to Pete Sampras.

Vinnie knew that Sampras was getting married, and he had been fishing for an invitation:

'I came home one day, got the letter from the Sampras family, opened it up – boom! I'm thinking, I've got it! I ran up to the house and they were all there looking at me. So I said, "Here we are, then, Stath [Jason Statham, of course]. Have a look at this then!" I opened it up and read it out: "Dear Vinnie, we're getting married on Saturday. Can you please turn your sprinklers off at 6 p.m."'

VERY IMPORTANT PEOPLE

But it's not all singers, actors and sports stars. Occasionally, our heroes will cross paths with heads of state and heavyweight political figures. Eamon Dunphy, for example, fondly recalls the time Prime Minister Harold Wilson came into the Millwall dressing room before a match against his beloved Huddersfield – 'No one was interested.' Ah.

Rodney Marsh was equally unimpressed when his adventures in the USA meant he met former secretary of state Henry Kissinger at the 1979 Soccer Bowl Final (whatever that is):

'Yes, he wanted to talk football. However, despite being a person who spent his life as a peace envoy around the world, he turned out to be one of the most boring individuals I have ever met. After three minutes I made my excuses and left to talk to the tea lady instead.'

For a start, we think he's making the bit up about the tea lady. For seconds, we doubt US soccer teams even have a tea lady, do they? A coffee lady, maybe. Finally, it's a fair bet that this fictional tea lady might have had similar thoughts about Rodney, had she been thrust into an unwanted conversation with him about what a loose cannon he is. Where's her autobiography?

Another one of our brave boys who sallied forth and did so much to build the profile of soccer in the USA was Newcastle's Paul Cannell. In a jam-packed career across the Atlantic, he played indoors and outdoors for the likes of Washington Diplomats (where he captained Johan Cruyff), Memphis Rogues, Calgary Boomers and Detroit Express, but his best stories are all about his partying, like this one about a night out in Washington: 'I spotted this attractive girl who seemed to be the centre of attention. Full of alcoholic and chemical bravado,[14] I sauntered, well staggered over and asked her if she wanted to dance. To everyone's amazement she said yes!' His success was all the more remarkable because the woman was surrounded by security men at the time: she was Susan Ford, the daughter of President Gerald Ford.

One man who turns up with a frequency and a vivid wardrobe to almost rival Rod Stewart is Nelson Mandela. The great man must, naturally, have been an immense inspiration to all who met him. Except perhaps Paul Merson: 'When we played in South Africa a few years later, we were presented with a guest of honour before the match, a little black fella with grey hair. When he shook my hand, I nudged our full-back, Nigel Winterburn, who was standing next to me. "Who the fuck's that?" I said. Nige couldn't believe it.

'"BLOODY HELL, Merse, it's Nelson Mandela," he said. "One of the most famous people in the world."'

So you can be imprisoned for 27 years for your cause, be a figurehead in a powerful emancipation movement, and be elected as the first post-apartheid president of South America, but until you've won the Masters three times, Paul Merson will not regard you as famous enough to be his crash buffer on a commercial flight.

---

14 We're sure we saw Chemical Bravado playing at the Forum once.

Ray Parlour was on the same tour and at the same meeting – surely he must have felt a little more of a sense of occasion, right? 'I remember shaking his hand. We knew what kind of a life he had been through, what a hero, and it was a great privilege, but I can't say we had much of a conversation. I wanted to take him down the pub but I reckon he was too busy at the time.' This proves that there is literally no occasion that shouldn't end with Ray Parlour in the pub.

He does make a valid point about struggling to have a conversation with the South African leader, though – Robbie Fowler had the same trouble when he met him with Liverpool: 'He came across to have a word with me, and it was then I discovered that he is a bit mutton – he had these great big hearing aids in his ears, and they were whistling so loud they were playing a tune. It wasn't exactly a sparkling exchange either.'

Between Robbie's nasal mumbling (which he says was a source of amusement to his team-mates, who called him Lester Piggott), and Nelson's hearing aid feedback, the two struggled to make a connection. 'Mind you, I did joke with him that Robben Island was a picnic compared to chucking-out time in Toxteth.'

Back in dear old Blighty, royalty is still the top of the pile, right? And luckily they have their own built-in hierarchy. Let's pause briefly on our inevitable climb to the top of the ladder to take in Mickey Thomas's meeting with Prince Charles at the 1979 FA Cup Final. 'Martin Buchan told his Royal Highness I was from Wales and he enquired, "What part of Wales are you from?" I told him Colwyn Bay and he added, "Oh yes, I have been there." Quick as a flash I asked him, "You haven't been with my missus, have you?"'

Except you didn't really, did you, Mickey? His entire book, *Kickups, Hiccups, Lockups*, is littered with instances of his quick wit being brought to the fore in inappropriate places like royal line-ups and police cars. *L'esprit de l'escalier* is strong in this one.

The tip, the top, the cream of the crop, though, is of course the Queen herself, who some of our lucky heroes have met by virtue of receiving an honour from her and attending the ceremony. You would think they would have unreservedly had a lovely time, but not so. Stuart Pearce is full of admiration for the royal family (of course he is), and was in awe of a fireman he got chatting to, but it doesn't stop him moaning: 'My only complaint was that there was nothing to eat! It would have been nice if they had knocked up a few bacon sandwiches at that time of the morning but there was only bottled water.' Perhaps those guests that had to bring their own packed lunch along to Harry and Meghan's do shouldn't have been so surprised after all.

In his thoroughly enjoyable book, the late, great Cyrille Regis had no such complaints about the buffet when he received his MBE, but he does reveal that Her Maj has developed a neat trick over the years: 'After about 30 seconds, the Queen shook my hand and gave a slight little push towards me, which is a subtle and elegant way to let you know it's your time to move away and her turn to meet the next person. An onlooker couldn't tell, but it certainly reminds you that when you've had your moment with Her Majesty, it's time to move on.'

It seems that honest old Cyrille decided that there was contact but not enough to go down. Your modern lads would've been sprawling all over the red carpet and appealing to the Equerry for a penalty.

Finally, when Kelly Smith received her MBE, it seems she was left with more questions than answers: 'As soon as the Queen left the room, she disappeared. It was like she had never been there with us. I don't know where she went. The castle's so vast, there might have been a secret, special room she went through or something. Whatever she did, she just seemed to vanish.'

Peculiar behaviour from Her Majesty there. What's her game? Maybe she's magic. You would think after all these years she might have introduced an element of that into the ceremonies, wouldn't you? She could disappear in a flash and a puff of smoke, for instance.

And speaking of slipping out unnoticed …

ESCAPE TO VICTORY

(Spoiler warning – do not read this section if you've never seen *Escape to Victory*. In which case, what have you been doing with your life?)

We're all familiar with bank holiday staple *Escape to Victory*, aren't we? You know the one. Ipswich defender Russell Osman brings down the Third Reich by urging his team-mates to go out for the second half and fight back for a creditable 4–4 draw, then the whole team scarper before extra time.

The film is a baffling but rewarding combination of footballers and actors, best exemplified by Michael Caine being the star, and Kevin

Beattie (one of a number of Ipswich players involved) playing his body for the football bits.

It will surprise nobody that there is no correlation between the quality of the player and the quality of the book he or she writes, which is why Pelé is not the go-to guy for *ETV* tales. Pelé is, of course, one of the greatest players the world has ever seen, but is his book an exciting thrill ride? No. No it's not. He even manages to be dull about the disco and cocaine hedonism that surrounded New York Cosmos when he was there, so if you want the skinny on the inglorious days of the North American Soccer League in the seventies, you don't go to Pele, you go to Paul Cannell. And if it's *Escape to Victory* you want to hear about, you don't go to Pelé either, because you'll get far more out of John Wark.

Wark had a nice time on the film, despite having his few lines overdubbed by somebody else, and speaks highly of Michael Caine. However, he's less enamoured with the film's other headline star, Ol' Rocky Rambo himself, Sylvester Stallone. Pelé tells us that Sly didn't let anyone else sit in his chair on set, and Ossie Ardiles says that he needed 17 takes or more before he saved the penalty at the end of the film, but Wark goes into greater depth: 'Stallone was nowhere near as sociable. He and his entourage, which comprised several minders, were even booked into a different hotel.'

You can feel the disdain dripping off the phrase 'several minders' there, can't you? Because there's nothing more disdainful in the eyes of a footballer than a fella who can't look after himself. Warky also says that Stallone decided he could do without coaching from Ipswich keeper Paul Cooper, and wanted to finish the film with his goalkeeper character, Hatch, going past five players and scoring (which, to be honest, we'd have liked to have seen). He saves his greatest scorn, however, for the filming of a scene where all the players/prisoners share a shower. All the footballers immediately stripped off completely, probably even before they were asked, but 'we spotted that Stallone preferred to wear a pair of mini briefs and all these years later I still can't help wondering what "Rocky" wanted to keep hidden from us'.

Wark is clearly implying here that Sylvester has a small cock, so he's definitely got it in for him. It's interesting that 'all these years later' he still finds himself wondering about Stallone's junk – we're told if you watch the right films, John, it's there for all to see. Also, worth considering that he's a professional actor and didn't get naked for a scene that he didn't need to get naked for. All the football lads get naked at the D of an H whether they need to or not.

However, we will forgive Wark his bitchiness on this subject because he does also tell us that one of the German players in the film (who scores twice) is Ferenc Fulop, the father of future Sunderland goalkeeper Martin Fulop. So there.

BRIEF ENCOUNTERS

Some of our favourite brushes with celebrity as detailed by the great and good of the game.

Sam Allardyce & Tony Knowles

For those that don't know Tony Knowles, he was a high-ranking snooker player back in the heady days of the 80s when snooker was the new rock 'n' roll. Knowles had the looks of contemporary chart-topper Paul Young, was part of the cool gang with Jimmy White, Alex Higgins and Kirk Stevens, rather than that square Matchroom Mob lot, and was good enough at snooker to be on our tellies a lot. Because snooker was on our tellies a lot.

Knowles was quite a playboy and told tales of snooker groupies (nuts are we, thankyou), but there was one girl he missed out on: the future Mrs Allardyce. The three of them knew each other as teenagers in Bolton, with Sam convinced that Tony fancied Lynne but couldn't win her hand from him. An early victory against more glamorous opposition ground out by Sam there.

Pat Van Den Hauwe & Brian Tilsley off of Coronation Street

You'll find Pat Van Den Hauwe peppered throughout this book, whether it's other players telling us how hard he was or his own accounts of his off-the-field activities (which you'll mostly find in the 'Top Shelf' chapter), because his book is genuinely so very entertaining. One of his anecdotes pleased us more than the rest, though, and that was his celebrity spat with Chris Quinten, who played one of Gail's many husbands in *Corrie*.

The two of them didn't hit it off when they were introduced in a nightclub. 'As far as I was concerned he was Christopher Who? No fucker knew who he was until the name Brian Tyldesley [sic] was mentioned.'

Pat was with Mandy Smith (Bill Wyman's ex-teenage bride) at the time and very much on the social scene, so this must have been like two rutting stags under disco lights. He says Quinten was with 'a couple of slappers' and a small disagreement and scuffle ensued, with the two of them separated by Teddy Sheringham, who was, as you've probably already guessed, double-dating with Mandy's sister Nicola at the time.

It all seems to have been over very quickly, but later Van Den Hauwe says of another party, 'It was wall to wall with real celebrities and Chris Quentin [sic] was nowhere to be seen! I was introduced to an odd-looking gentleman who said he was "Right Said Fred".'

Firstly, Chris must have really got under Pat's skin to warrant this second mention, and secondly we think Right Said Fred is two people – or three if you count the lad who isn't bald. Although, for all we know, he may now be in another band with the one out of Bros who wasn't a bros and the one out of ZZ Top without the ZZ Top beard (yes, yes, we know he's called Frank Beard).

Leroy Rosenior & Gary Glitter

We've gone for the headline a bit here. West Ham favourite Leroy was actually best mates at school with Gary Glitter's *son*. That was until, in one of the worst acts committed by a member of that family, Glitter Jnr did a terrible racism and called him something unrepeatable. Understandably, after that, Leroy didn't want to be in his gang any more.

John Robertson & David Soul

After an away day at Plymouth, John 'Supertramp' Robertson spotted David Soul (Hutch off of *Starsky & Hutch*) in the hotel bar.

'My mother-in-law at the time was a big fan of his and I went up to him in the hotel, saying, "Excuse me, would you mind signing this for my mother-in-law?" His quote back to me was, "I've signed 500 of these today," and it was said in such a manner that suggested he could do without it. He signed it, gave it me back but I ripped it up and said,

"Thanks very much but I don't want it now." Later on, to his credit, he came over and apologised and sent over a drink for the boys.'

It's good that Soul saw the error of his ways and tried to make amends with the stocky winger. I like to think that this incident is what he's singing about on 'Don't Give Up on Us', but sadly we don't think the dates work.

Ray Parlour & Bobby Davro

Within the game, Ray Parlour is known as a hard-working midfielder who embraced the brave new world of Arsene Wenger and flourished in successful Arsenal teams. A reputation well earned. In legal circles, however, Ray Parlour is known as a landmark divorce case in which his ex-wife was awarded 'at least a third of my future earnings'. The ruling clearly gave Ray a certain notoriety among divorced celebrities, as he explains in an encounter with TV's Bobby Davro in the boxes at Royal Ascot: 'He came in to say hello and said, "What have you done to me? I am getting divorced and all I hear is Parlour v Parlour this and Parlour v Parlour that …" "Bobby, I lost as well. It's not great for me either." We were all laughing about it in the end.'

Terrific divorce banter. Of course, anyone who has seen that YouTube clip with Bobby Davro in the stocks with his trousers round his ankles will know that divorce might not be the worst thing that's happened to him. (Go on, you know you want to.)

John Lyall & Billie Whitelaw

These days there aren't many managers who survive relegation from the Premier League without losing their job, or even get to hang around once the writing is on the wall. The past was very different, with relegation often seen as an occupational hazard, but not the end of the world. Without the financial disparity of today, it could be no more than a bump in the road, and it was perfectly possible for a decent manager to keep his job in the hope of bouncing back.

West Ham's John Lyall was one such man, who, following relegation in 1978, consolidated and came again, but not before he took advice from that obvious source of wisdom on the subject – Billie Whitelaw. You know, Billie Whitelaw. You would recognise her, depending on your age, as the creepy nanny in *The Omen*, the Krays' mum in that

Spandau Ballet one or the hotel landlady in *Hot Fuzz* every other night on ITV2. Who else would you turn to as you faced life in Division Two? John wrote in *Just Like My Dreams* that just after the end of the season he took a call from Ms Whitelaw, whose son was a fan:

'She told me that she had reached a point where she realized she was no longer examining the qualities of her performances. She simply took them for granted. At that time she took a decision to look at her career more deeply and make herself work a little harder with people perhaps not quite so efficient or professional. So she went into provincial rep; she moved from the first division to the second. She made the decision consciously. We didn't, but she said we might find it had the same effect. She found working in smaller theatres a refreshing and stimulating experience, and it gave her the chance to look at her career and performance in a different light. I have always remembered the advice she gave me in that conversation. I thought to myself: "Well, maybe some good will come out of relegation." West Ham were about to perform on a smaller stage, just as she had done. I was determined to make the experience work for me, just as it had done for Billie Whitelaw.'

Imagine an equivalent now. Tony Pulis says it's okay that his team has gone down because Pauline Quirke said it might turn out fine.

Lawrie McMenemy & Jeremy Clarkson

'There is a danger that exposure on the box can change you.' As a man who was invited on telly to tear apart the first-ever episode of *The Young Ones* as a load of rubbish, while insisting he's no 'fuddy-duddy' in the face of Julie Walters's spirited defence of the landmark comedy show, we know Lawrie McMenemy speaks from a position of authority.[15]

The object of Lawrie's ire is the leader of Richard Hammond's gang, Jeremy Clarkson, who he had the misfortune to be seated next to at the BBC Sports Personality of the Year awards. Quite what Clarkson was doing there is not clear. Lawrie describes him as 'surprisingly rude'. Why Lawrie is surprised by this is not clear, either. 'I said: "Hello, good evening," and by way of conversation, "what car did you arrive in tonight?" Not the wittiest thing I have said but not the worst. He took one look at me, turned, and without a word, a blue one would have sufficed, found another seat two rows in front.'

---

15 *Did You See?* BBC, 26 November 1982.

Lawrie is suitably wounded by his Partridge-esque banter falling on stony ground and worries that 'maybe he saw me as "yesterday's man"'. This seems unnecessarily maudlin, but whatever his reasons, Clarkson is out of order. Unless, of course, he just didn't hear Lawrie and was in the wrong seat in the first place.

Before we leave Lawrie, though, here's some casual name-dropping amid one of the worst celebrity anecdotes we've ever heard, ripped from the pages of the enjoyable *A Lifetime's Obsession*: 'At Sir Bobby Robson's memorial in Durham Cathedral in 2009 I was talking to Steve Cram and Brendan Foster when we were joined by the two young television performers, Ant and Dec, whom I had never met before. I had read that Ant McPartlin had gone to St Cuthbert's and I asked him if he was any relation to the art teacher I had with the same name. Not so, he had never heard of him.'

Notwithstanding the sad circumstances, and the impressive gathering of Geordie royalty, this is poor. Surely even Lawrie would concede that this would have been a marginally better story if he *was* related. Not a great story, but certainly a better one.

Diego Maradona & The Pope

Diego's is a life lived, that's for sure. One of the very best players ever to lace up a boot, he would be well within his rights to bow to nobody on earth.

Which is, perhaps, why his meeting with the Pope rankles with him so much. Far from coming away with a feeling of being blessed by the Pontiff, Diego instead feels, well, mugged off by him.

'I met the Pope. It was disappointing. He gave a rosary to my mum, La Tota. He gave a rosary to Claudia. When it came to my turn he said to me, in Italian, "This one's special, just for you." I was very nervous. I said thank you. I couldn't get any other words out. As we walked around I asked my old girl to show me hers, and it was the same as mine. So I said to La Tota, "No, mine is special, the Pope told me it was special." I went back to him and asked him, "Excuse me, Your Holiness, what is the difference between mine and my mother's?" He didn't answer. He just looked at me, gave me a little pat on the back, smiled and carried on walking. Total lack of respect – he just patted me on the back and smiled, that's it!'

The Pope's clearly pulled the Bruce Forsyth trademark 'You're my favourite' move here, and Diego's having none of it. 'So yes, I fell out with the Pope.' The Hand of God snubbed there by God's right-hand man.

Simon Jordan & Pete Doherty

As mentioned earlier, Simon Jordan is not shy of dropping a celebrity name as he goes about his business, but one of his encounters deserves a closer look. It concerns the time he played in a celebrity five-a-side tournament against Pete Doherty of The Libertines, Babyshambles and Kate Moss fame.

The two clashed, as it appears they were both taking it a bit too seriously. 'After one particular scything challenge I enacted on him, he got up in my face full of testosterone and I suggested, "There was no need to get the needle," referring to his much publicised heroin addiction.' If you have to explain it, Simon, it's not funny. File this one under 'Needless to say, I had the last laugh.'

Jimmy Case & The Drummer out of Coldplay

We love a surprising friendship, and the revelation that one of the hardest men in football, Jimmy Case, is good mates with Coldplay drummer Will Champion came as a pleasant surprise. We particularly enjoyed the story from the start of their relationship, which leads to one of our favourite sentences.

'So one night we went out for a drink to a local wine bar, but they wouldn't let Will in because he was wearing trainers. Fortunately, the owner knew me so I told Will to swap shoes with me and it would be ok. And that's how the drummer of Coldplay ended up wearing my shoes.'

Maybe we should open this up as a competition. Send us your best 'And that's how the drummer ...' stories and we'll read them and really enjoy them. Or tweet them. Or something. But probably just read them.

Alan Ball & Whitesnake

Alan Ball was a World Cup winner and England captain, but after Don Revie left behind the bingo and carpet bowls of Leeds and took over as the national team boss, he was swiftly dumped due to a personality clash. One of the reasons Ball suggests for this is the fact that, when staying with the England squad in north London, he would occasionally go under the wire in a quiet moment and 'go along to my friend Bernie Winters's house'. The Revs couldn't have been too furious with this, though, as it's not as if strong drink was taken, with Ball insisting 'we drank tea and chatted', which sounds nice.

Tea seems reasonable. Even if it's a secret, off-camp, celebrity tea. But then looking after his body must have been what allowed Alan to play on so long. I bet he even dropped the biscuits on the floor for Schnorbitz when Bernie wasn't looking.

It's no surprise, then, that Alan opted out of his other good celebrity story, this time involving drink. Talking about his friend, the Portsmouth director Jim Sloan, Ball tells us of a chance encounter in a Midlands hotel on an away trip with 'Here I Go Again' merchants Whitesnake: 'They had just finished a gig. I told Jim that I was off to bed as the lads would be up fairly early in the morning for a light run. Jim said not to worry, he fancied having a bit of fun with these lads and their roadies.

'When I came down the next morning there were bodies lying all over the floor and chairs of the hotel foyer. Jim had wiped out Whitesnake and as I went in to breakfast he was sitting there, bright-eyed, saying: "Morning Mr Manager. Breakfast? Same again?"'

Whitesnake and their entourage scattered all over the lounge bar is a lovely image. Hair everywhere, we shouldn't wonder.

Wally Downes & Mickey Rourke

Let's not beat around the bush about this. Wally Downes has got a tattoo done by Mickey Rourke. Not a tattoo *of* Mickey Rourke, which would be odd, but not outrageous. A tattoo *done* by Mickey Rourke.

This came about through their mutual friendship with Vinnie Jones, who writes that one day they were round Rourke's house, and: 'The next thing Wally has got his shirt off and is getting a tattoo done by Mickey!'

There's no mention of what the tattoo is, but we think the story is all the better for it. We're woozy enough from the revelation that Wally Downes, Crazy Gang founder and portly sometime football coach, has a tattoo done by old Angel Heart himself, without knowing what it looks like or speculating about where it is.

We think we need to end here. It really doesn't get better than that.

6

Hard, Harder, Hardest

Dancing Queen

It is a question that has taxed the finest minds over the centuries – Descartes, Freud, Keys: What do we mean by 'Hard'? It is the contention of this book that a 'Hard Man' needs to have specific credentials:

a. He must be tough (natch).

b. He must be willing and able to dole out physical violence when necessary (and possibly when unnecessary).

c. He must happily take violence in return without blinking.

d. He must buy you a pint (not a half) afterwards and not bang on about what's gone on.

In this chapter, we'll seek to discover who really is the hardest in the sport. Who is the one true hard nut to rule them all? Who would be last man standing in a game played in an underground car park with no ref? We'll look at several contenders and weigh up their individual merits before coming to our conclusion. And we'll do this by calling on all the information we've gathered and allying it with our gut instinct as to who we would least like to see lining up on the opposite side of the tunnel before a match.

Being a hard man doesn't simply mean going in where it hurts. It also means being reliable in a crisis. It's a quality that both team-mates and managers appreciate, and it's something that Frank Worthington, somewhat tritely, calls 'Trench'. As in 'they are someone you would want in the trenches alongside you'.

The 'In the Trenches' trope occurs frequently in the books we read. It seems to us that if playing football is in any way like the Great War, you're probably doing it wrongly. Still, the ability to appear able to take your place alongside someone as you wait to go over the top towards certain death is apparently seen as a desirable trait within a football squad.

For example, Graham Roberts says that 'Paul Miller was the type of guy you'd want beside you in the trenches', and this exact quality obviously plays on his mind because he also says of Davie Cooper: 'If you were in the trenches you'd want Coop alongside because he would never let you down.'

Lee McCulloch talks in general terms about 'some guys that I would want in the trenches beside me', while Neil Ruddock has a similar broad sweep when calling into question the character of the overseas lads: 'Some of the continentals, however, are a bit soft for my liking. Technically gifted, sure, but you wouldn't want too many of them in the trenches with you.' And they don't like the golf and the booze and the gee-gees so much either, we shouldn't wonder.

Worthington himself not only describes former Brighton team-mate Jimmy Case as: 'the sort of solid down-to-earth character you would love to have alongside you in the trenches', he also goes so far as to compile an XI of those he would want there among the muck and bullets with him ('The Trench XI') and then names those he feels would be far better suited way back behind the lines, perhaps in a Parisian brothel sipping Crème de Menthe ('The Non-Trench XI').

Among those he turns his nose up at are:

- Lawrie McMenemy (who comes up a lot in people's bad books throughout their, well, bad books)
- Kevin Dillon (see 'Why Can't We All Just Get Along?' chapter)
- Alan Biley (he of the spectacular 1980s hair)
- David Armstrong (he of the no 1980s hair)
- Chris Hutchings (he of looking a bit like Kurt Russell and following Paul Jewell into disastrous jobs fame).

Some of their transgressions from the way of the Trench are documented in *One Hump or Two*, but many others are just left hanging, as if they know what they did and that's enough.

Interestingly, Frank can't find room in this Band of Chuckle Brothers that he wouldn't want near him in a combat situation for Leicester team-mate Keith Weller. This is despite his saying Weller was a selfish player who wasn't popular in the dressing room and who Frank accused in a slanging match of: 'behaving like a big f****** girl' – so now we're confused about the rules.

Those lucky enough to be at the Somme alongside Corporal Worthington include the aforementioned Case, Sam Allardyce (of whom more later), Huddersfield's Jimmy McGill (who we're sure is in *Better Call Saul*) and Mark Dennis.

So what has this last notorious hard man done, while with Frank Worthington at Southampton, to deserve his inclusion? Let's turn to the apparently Non-Trench Lawrie McMenemy to describe one episode involving 'rascal' Mark Dennis, a man he describes as 'not the most disciplined of men'. It's an intriguing story: 'The RSPCA phoned me to say that Mark's neighbour had contacted them in tears claiming his dog had eaten her cat. She was extremely upset and I do not blame her. He explained: "The cat was in our garden, the dog was not in theirs."'

We have so many questions about this incident. Firstly, do dogs even eat cats outside of cartoons? Secondly, does it really matter *where* it ate the cat, Mark? It seems to have eaten the cat, Mark. Finally, why is Lawrie McMenemy having to deal with this? It feels like more of a private or a police matter. This is the sort of incident that would these days be covered by one of those fabled player liaison officers – you know: get a player's gas switched over to a different provider, find somewhere for visiting relatives to stay, pay off a weeping next-door neighbour as the player's dog spits out a 'Tiddles' collar. They're dab hands at that sort of thing. Either way, this doesn't seem particularly Trench behaviour from Dennis – though admittedly with correctly channelled aggression the dog might be useful.

Luis Suarez prefers to do his own biting rather than hiding behind a dog, but that definitely doesn't make him Trench. Even apart from the cowardly nibbling, there's this: 'I cried when Ajax fans said goodbye to me. And I could never understand why Jamie Carragher didn't do the same when he waved goodbye to Anfield for the last time as a player. Come on, a tear – at least one.' No way. Not Carragher – Carragher's Trench, for sure. Or at least he was before all that spitting business. That must have lost him 'proper football man' points within the community.

Despite all Frank Worthington's efforts, though, we're still scratching our heads a bit as to quite what the seemingly undefinable quality of 'Trench' actually is. It's possible that, very much like the soldiers in the trenches, we're getting a bit bogged down in it. And let's face it; in a discussion of tough guys, you want us to get straight to people walloping each other, don't you?

So, where better to start, particularly as we've been on the subject of biting, than with Norman 'Bites Yer Legs' Hunter? Except – breaking news on this, and we think this might even be a *Booked!* exclusive – Norman Hunter doesn't actually bite yer, or even your, legs – and that's despite calling his book *Biting Talk* (small ripple of applause for that, by the way). In fact, the rehabilitation of Hunter has been one of the pleasant surprises of the research for this book.

Previously we had dismissed him as a dirty player in a dirty team, a cynical Revie foot soldier who strutted through his era sneering at the weak and looking like one of the baddies from *Straw Dogs*. However, having read his book, we like him a lot. It's an interesting read, and he's a sympathetic character who describes himself as 'actually quite friendly', while dismissing his own hard-man reputation on the basis that he could see danger coming and simply protected himself accordingly: 'The real hard men were those who went into challenges without even sensing danger or caring how they might end up. They were truly fearless.'

Hunter effectively rules himself out of the 'hardest player' running here by being so very reasonable and nice, and instead nominates George Kirby and Andy Lochhead as his toughest opponents.

Other forwards who felt his breath on their neck speak highly of Hunter too. Kenny Dalglish, who himself admits that 'I was such a competitive player that I have punched defenders in my desire to win', says that Hunter would kick you, but then shake your hand; while Kevin Keegan can't praise him highly enough, saying that he voted for him for PFA Player of the Year and that 'for me, he could have won that award every year. Norman could kick when he felt it was necessary – that was part of his makeup – but he did not get enough credit for his skill. He could flight the ball so accurately with his left foot.'

Much-loved Norman, then, is practically a teddy bear. He can't possibly be one of the contenders for our toughest of tough guys can he? And yet, like Keegan and his skirmish with Billy Bremner, Hunter was involved in one of the most treasured on-field scraps of the 1970s, and we can't skip over that.

His 'little punch-up' with Franny Lee remains a high-water mark of the genre, and on the off-chance you're not familiar with it, we urge you to take a break, make a cuppa and look it up online. It is joyous. It begins with Hunter becoming furious after he believes Lee dives for a penalty (which, to be fair, he definitely does). It continues when Hunter later takes his retribution and whacks Lee for it. And then sit back and revel in little Franny's arms going like a windmill at Hunter after the two have been sent off. It's the sort of fight Gene Hunt would approve of.

The Leeds man says it didn't even end once the pair had gone down the tunnel, the whistle had blown, and the crowds had dispersed back home for a Watneys Red Barrel in front of some brown curtains, no doubt. Hunter tells us: 'I'd had my testimonial and picked up £35,000 and he challenged me, on TV, to fight him in the street for it. He said he'd give me 3 to 1. Well I didn't fancy that one little bit.'

Footballers publicly fighting in the street, like in *Rocky V*! We'd be all for that in the modern game. In an age when testimonial money means less and less to players, a few proper scraps on the cobbles would soon see them start to earn their corn again. Exactly what Hunter had to gain from such a public brawl is unclear (unless Lee was offering shares in his bog roll business if he lost), but the fact remains that Hunter bottled it. By his own admission, he ran away from a square go with Franny 'Scrappy-Doo' Lee. Sorry, Leeds fans, he's not our guy. But, as we say, he comes across as a thoroughly decent chap and we're sure he'd take this news with quiet dignity – and not by chomping on our calf muscles.

Certain classic hard men – Kenny Burns, Larry Lloyd, Ron 'Chopper' Harris and Julian Dicks, for example – do get mentions in the books we read, but sadly for them, not much more than that. Meanwhile, notorious hard man Tommy Smith comes across more like a bully – Ronnie Whelan remembers him threatening: 'I'll break your back' (a favourite Smith catchphrase) after a ball had ricocheted off a teenage Ronnie into Smith's face. We're not having it.

Whelan himself was considered tough by some, including Neil Ruddock, who says: 'Ronnie, in particular, was a right dirty so and so who gave as good as he got and knew when and where to put the boot in.' We hadn't previously considered the elegant Liverpool midfielder as a tough nut – it's a nice surprise – and another surprise is finding out that Whelan himself rates Coventry's Lloyd McGrath as a hard man he always tried to get the better of.

Elsewhere, Alan Brazil describes Ipswich team-mate Paul Mariner as 'one of the hardest men I have ever met in the game. If I had been a defender I would have thrown a sickie rather than face Mariner.' Again, Mariner is not a name we necessarily expected to see in such a discussion, yet there he is. Perhaps more predictable names that are mentioned in dirty dispatches are Johnny Giles (by Sam Allardyce) and Dennis Wise, who Jimmy Case says used to pinch him under the arm during games, while John Wark gives the hard-man nod to Billy Whitehurst, Norman Whiteside and Joe Jordan.

Jordan has his own war stories about breaking John Wile's jaw and taking a sneaky punch from Brian Kidd at a corner, but he comes up in Wark's book because he headbutted him early in his career. Later, when the pair were Scotland team-mates and Wark felt on a surer footing, he gently reminded Jordan of the incident, expecting them to laugh about it like the old friends he clearly hoped they were. Instead, Joe 'just shrugged and replied "That's me, that's how it is" and the conversation was brought to an abrupt end.'

Before we get to the upper tier of our tough guy pyramid, let's just ditch a few names who might reasonably expect to be there or thereabouts. Paul Ince is ruled out on the basis of calling himself 'The Guv'nor'. Steve McMahon is out of the running because John Wark says so: '[he] thought he was hard, but I could tell he was scared of [Norman] Whiteside'. And, sorry, Forest fans, we're also losing Stuart Pearce at this stage of the game.

There's no doubt Psycho was (and is, actually – we wouldn't say any of the following to his face) a daunting figure. Just read Joey Barton's description of his pre-match routine, observed while hidden in a corner: 'It was some show … He wore nothing but his socks, shinpads and a pair of white pants. He would work himself into a frenzy, stretching, striding, jumping, grunting. He'd be sweating, scary. I'm thinking, "What the fuck is this? He's a lunatic."'

Intimidating as that sounds, it's not enough. Even the slightly odd words of Sir Bobby Robson can't help him here: 'Ask Stuart Pearce if he would prefer a fillet steak or a good tackle and he would go for the tackle every time. He loves a tackle that boy.' High praise indeed from Psycho's gaffer at Italia '90, but it's the mention of that tournament that does for him. After all, as much as we might like to think of Pearce, bloodied but unbowed after Basile Boli put the nut on him two years later, it's Pearcey in tears after missing his penalty in Turin that really sticks in the mind.

Now, we're modern gents who firmly believe that the odd tear doesn't make anyone any less of a man (indeed, your authors can't get through *Paddington 2* or *Toy Story 3* without weeping these days, and don't get us started on *Up*), but this is *Thunderdome* now. Only the toughest of the tough need apply, and, as Brian Moore said in his commentary that night[16]: 'And I thought he was a really hard man.' Admittedly Pearce did once play on a broken leg, but, as we say, the crying swings it. We don't make the rules. Oh, hang on a minute – we do.

As we move towards the top contenders, we reach John Fashanu, who's as high in our hard-man thinking as anybody who forged a television career by shouting 'Awooga!' can be. Carlton Palmer isn't someone who scares easily, but he makes his thoughts on this subject very clear: 'You didn't fuck with Fash.' Palmer says he always made a point of being nice to Fash (nicknamed The Bash, lest we forget), because he was intimidated by him: 'He was a martial arts expert and, I gather, could handle knives.' This seems fair enough, Carlton, but we think there comes a time when you have to trust that the officials, while they are checking studs and jewellery, won't allow players on the pitch armed with blades.[17]

Referee David Elleray is full of praise for Fashanu, claiming he was 'always the politest and most pleasant of people off the field. On the pitch it was a different matter – although he was always well spoken and correct, he was very, very tough.' Elleray then expresses sorrow that he was forced to wave Fashanu off into retirement with a red card as he was being stretchered off following a terrible foul on Ryan Giggs. John Wark also names Fashanu as a tough opponent, along with his Wimbledon team-mate Vinnie Jones, but says that both were covering up playing deficiencies.

Jones is a case of somebody who talks up his own hard-man reputation a bit too much for our liking, and therefore loses points in our

---

16 What do you mean, you were listening to Motson on BBC One? Philistines.

17 Unless, of course, it's former Derby, Norwich and Wolves defender Paul Blades.

complex hard-man algorithm. He does, however, tell an entertaining tale from his time at Leeds when he was out of favour with boss Howard Wilkinson and puzzled about what do: 'I wanted to have my say, but I had so much respect for the gaffer I bit my tongue and thought my hard work would do the talking.' A noble sentiment. And one that Vinnie did well to maintain ... right up until the moment he threatened his beloved boss with a shotgun.

That's right. Arriving to meet the coach for an away game feeling disgruntled, and with his shooting kit in the boot of his car, primed for a weekend away after the game, Jones found the set of circumstances irresistible. Taking the firearm from the boot, he boarded the coach and went up to Wilkinson, who at that point must have been regretting sitting at the front. 'I put the end of the twelve-bore right up his nostrils with my finger on the trigger and said, "Now, are you going to bloody play me at Luton tomorrow?"'

Understandably, Wilkinson was worried, but once he knew his midfielder was joking and wasn't actually going to blast his actual head off his actual shoulders, we're told that 'Howard appreciated it more than anybody'. In fact, Howard appreciated it so much, he sold Jones to Sheffield United at the earliest opportunity.

So, Vin doesn't come into the final reckoning, partly because of his boasting but mostly because he pulled out a shooter, and everyone knows that the truly hard don't need tools. For a very similar reason, we're ruling out spectacular flash in the pan Salvatore 'Toto' Schillaci, who Paolo Di Canio genuinely heard threatening someone's life – and not a vague 'I'll kill you' threat, either, but the very specific 'I will have you shot.' Connected, you see.

We feel that the genuinely tough leave it for others to say. They're hard by deed, rather than word. Too many players spend too much of their book telling us how tough they are – and grot-peddling Arsenal enforcer Peter Storey (see 'Call the Cops' chapter) is definitely one for this. His take on the modern game is that 'I am not really equipped to talk about hard men in the game today, because there aren't any'. Yep, things were definitely better in Peter's day, when dinosaurs ruled the earth and referees allowed the hatchet man one free whack at the opposition's Fancy Dan just to settle a game down. 'Tough guys and rugged tacklers have been victimised. If I were playing today, the chances are I'd be sent off inside five minutes for giving some foreign striker a stern look.'

Foreigners, you see, they've ruined it. Zola, Bergkamp, Silva, Hazard – coming over here with their skill and wanting to play football instead of going in studs up – what are they like? Actually, we take back our sarcastic tone: Hazard kicked a Swansea ballboy up the guts a few years ago, didn't he? Not even Storey did that. Peter does name Roy Keane as the last of a dying (presumably now dead) breed, though, and we will get to him soon enough.

Graham Roberts is another who talks about himself as a hard man, and goes so far as to call his book *Hard as Nails*. Despite the fact that he lost two front teeth in a cup final and played on, we're afraid that there just aren't enough tales from his opponents to put Roberts in the frame as one of the very toughest. However, he does subscribe to the true hard-man mantra that 'spitting is the lowest of the low in my book'. We've never quite understood this, yet so many footballers say it. Granted, spitting on someone is distinctly Non-Trench behaviour, but we think, in the unlikely event of being given the choice, we'd rather be spat at than have somebody, for example, kick us in the throat.

Roberts relates one story that involves him tackling Charlie Nicholas so hard in a north London derby that it left the striker on the wrong side of the advertising hoardings and Roberts down on his knees. With Champagne Charlie unfit to retaliate, the sneaky Arsenal physio ran on to treat both players and asked Graham if he was okay, 'before decking me with a right-hook. The cheeky bastard connected right on my nose and there was blood everywhere.' Both for attacking a player decidedly outside of the hard-man code, and for then getting done over by a medical professional in breach of his Hippocratic oath, Roberts finishes even out of the Europa League spots of our hard-man Premier League.

Jimmy Case is an interesting, er, case. He does have the anecdotal evidence to paint him as one of the very hardest men, but he also blows his own trumpet a little. He calls his book *Hard Case* when, as we say, we think that's for others to judge; and, like Storey, he decries the modern game and the modern footballer's toughness, or lack of it. He claims that the likes of Thierry Henry wouldn't last five minutes against him, and that 'if I'd come up against a player like Ronaldo, within the first ten minutes I would have taken a good yellow card, something just short of a red, to sort him out and then we'd see just how brave he really is. That's what makes me think that the likes of Messi and Ronaldo would have found it a lot harder if they'd been around then.'

Firstly, we admire how confident Case is that he can judge the exact line between a good yellow and a red, like an expert accountant keeping their client just the right side of legal. Secondly, we hate this argument. It's not as if Ronaldo and Messi haven't been kicked all through their careers by the likes of Busquets and Ramos. Diego Maradona flourished in an era when he was kicked to ribbons by players like Case, whose job it was to stop him.

But such 'in my day' thoughts can't detract from Case's own strong, er, case. We already know that Frank Worthington regards him as none-more Trench, and Ronnie Whelan adds to the legend: 'Jimbo was an iron man. And he was deadly. I played against him many a time when he moved to Brighton and then on to Southampton and he was the hardest player I ever came up against.' Persuasive words, yet the sheer weight of books we have read for this project tells us that there are at least six more players we would regard as harder. A dirty half dozen if you will. One of those would be 'Red Card Roy' McDonough, who lays claim to being the most sent-off man in English football.

Admittedly, much of McDonough's hard-man reputation comes from his own words, but you simply can't argue with the number of times he's been ordered from the field. Suffice to say that not many were for diving or two bookable handball offences. McDonough was an angry man on the pitch and had no end of running battles, but it seems that nobody got his dander up quite like Tony Pulis.

Long before he was a dour manager, prowling the touchline wearing everything it's possible to buy from a club shop while overseeing his own particular soporific brand of football, Pulis was a combative midfielder for the likes of Bournemouth and Bristol Rovers. And while he was at Newport he had the misfortune to run into Red Card Roy himself, who generously describes our Tone as 'pathetic, a little fucking squirt'.

McDonough goes on to say, with an air of *The Beano* about it, that he'd like to 'fill his big gob with a knuckle sandwich'. But after some heated words in the tunnel at a Southend v Newport cup tie, Roy's more Dennis Nilsen than Dennis the Menace in his description of an attempted tackle after Pulis miscontrolled a pass and allowed the ball to linger around chest height for a terrifying moment. Well, what's a card-carrying Hard Man to do? 'I launched myself through the air like Bruce Lee, striking the ball hard with a flying kick, but making sure I followed through into his chest.' Pulis went down, as you would, only to find McDonough was trying to 'finish the job by messing up his head with my studs'.

Pleasant.

We shudder just at the thought of that challenge, and may even have fainted if we'd been at Roots Hall that night to see it, but Roy falls short of the hard-man top table for two reasons. Firstly, he admits to spitting at poor old Perry Groves – decidedly Non-Trench behaviour, we're sure you'll agree. And secondly, he once tried to dispense medical help on the field. Surely, the true hard man uses an injury break to go and scratch his studs to a point on the goalpost or something, not hang around trying to help. On the occasion he describes, it was Southend team-mate Shane Westley who suffered a hand injury. Now then, of course McDonough called Westley a 'big soft c***' for moaning, and yes, he may indeed have ruptured the tendons in the defender's hand trying to fix some dislocated fingers, thus causing more than the original damage – but the point remains – help is help, and there's no room for it in the hard man top five. Sorry, Roy.

If Tony Pulis was the victim of one of our hardest guys, then his Brother-from-Another-Defensively-Minded-Keep-You-Up-But-Bore-You-Silly-Mother is certainly on the other side of the fence. Sam Allardyce, for it is he, with 'the biggest head I've ever seen, like one of those giant papier-mache things you'd see on *It's A Knockout*', comes in at number five on our list. The above quote comes from Roy McDonough again, who speaks highly of Big Sam and his Big Head, despite a tussle in which Allardyce splatted McDonough's nose across his face for him. Through the blood and the snot Roy expressed respect for Allardyce. There seems to be a code among these men, you see. Roy says he enjoyed it.

For his own part, Allardyce concedes that the only person he ever intentionally fouled was Mick Harford, because he 'thoroughly deserved it'. Harford, of whom more in a minute, is certainly one who honours the code – indeed, wears it as a badge of honour, alongside the scar he still has from where Sam elbowed him and split his lip so badly you could

106

see his teeth through it. All forgotten afterwards, of course. There are no grudges between these men. Just business. If you've ever seen the 1980s extended pop video that is *Highlander* – well, it's similar to that. These folk walk among us, and for the most part keep themselves to themselves, happily wandering about the place only engaging in battle with each other. But God help the mortals who get in their way.

Leroy Rosenior recounts a telling incident about Allardyce which has clearly traumatised him to this day. During a Huddersfield v Fulham game in the mid-80s, Jeff Hopkins of Fulham was sent off when he broke the leg of a Huddersfield player: 'Playing for the Terriers that day was Sam Allardyce and he wanted retribution. Fists clenched, he was screaming at Jeff, following him from the pitch, being held back by the coaching staff, telling Jeff exactly what he wanted to do with him.'

Leroy went off injured himself later, and was trying to console a distraught Hopkins in the dressing room when 'suddenly a fist came flying through the door. Through the door! It was as if the Incredible Hulk had arrived at Bloomfield Road. It wasn't, it was Sam Allardyce, though he was just as angry and just as scary.'[18]

What we love about this is that Leroy feels the need to clarify that it wasn't actually The Hulk coming though the door, just 'the mass of muscle and malice that is Sam Allardyce'. Your authors regularly hid behind the sofa when Bill Bixby turned into Lou Ferrigno back in the day (ask your mum or dad, Ruffalo fans), but we can't imagine that anything we were missing while we curled in a ball by the radiator was even remotely as scary as a rampaging Sam Allardyce hell-bent on revenge. And that's why we feel compelled to include him so close to the top. Since reading Rosenior's account, we've had countless sleepless nights trying to rid our minds of the image of a Green Even-Bigger Sam, dressed only in the tattered remains of his trousers and a gold chain, trying not to spill his pint of wine as he rampages through the countryside. It doesn't bear thinking about.

It's also worth noting that Allardyce himself doesn't even seem to remember the incident, or at least doesn't think of it as a big enough deal to include in his own memoirs. Maybe he was always busting through doors like Jack Nicholson in *The Shining*. 'Here's Sammy! Of course, if I was called Allardici, you'd let me straight in.'

---

18 We'll forgive him the Bloomfield Road mistake too, shall we? He was clearly terrified.

Then we come to Pat Van Den Hauwe. We honestly can't recommend his autobiography enough if what you want are tales of debauchery and scrapping. It's fair to say that the Wales full-back features most heavily in our 'Top Shelf' chapter for his sexy adventures; and here for his sheer hard-bastard nature.

We are talking, after all, about a man that committed a tackle so bad that a referee wanted to pack it in. Hats off, Pat. David Elleray it was, who says after sending Van Den Hauwe off for 'one of the worst fouls I have ever seen on a soccer pitch in England', he had 'sat in the dressing room and not wanted to go out for the second half'. High praise indeed.

Van Den Hauwe seems to have picked up different nicknames at his various clubs. Former Spurs team-mate Neil Ruddock tells us that his fellow defender was known as Reggie, as in Reggie Perrin, because 'he would go AWOL for days on end without any explanation; missing, presumed dead'. Ruddock explains that 'I think even the managers he played for were scared of him, or wary of him, and he got away with things other players wouldn't'. And with good reason, it would seem – Ruddock also mentions an incident when 'Reggie' forced his way through a metal gate by ripping it off its hinges.

Frank Worthington reveals that at Birmingham, Pat had the more traditional soubriquet 'Psycho' because of 'the way his eyes glazed over when he was riled, which I have to say was fairly often'. And not just when Brian Tilsley out of *Coronation Street* was around either.

The Birmingham team around that time had a fearsome reputation, as not only was Van Den Hauwe there, but also the likes of Martin Kuhl and Mark Dennis – later on, Julian Dicks passed through the nervous metal gates of St Andrews, too. Our old favourite Roy McDonough was also there for a time, and it's his recollection of a friendly with Sporting Gijon in Gibraltar that secures Van Den Hauwe's place in our top four.

It all started when a fight broke out because, according to impartial witness Red Card Roy, a 'dirty Spaniard' punched Don Givens, and another Gijon player gave him a kick to the head. Inevitably, the place soon resembled a Wild West saloon brawl with Van Den Hauwe in the thick of it, swinging wildly. As a side issue, it seems that one of the linesmen got knocked out with a chair by a couple of fans, but Van Den Hauwe remained front and centre stage as he 'chinned another couple of people as we punched a hole through the ruck to reach the other side of the ground, while glass rained above our heads'.

Given that McDonough admits to trying to stay out of trouble during this Royal Rumble, and that he relied a bit on Van Den Hauwe to get him out of it, it seems a shame that Roy then appears in the dock to give evidence against his old mucker that keeps him from top spot.

The two came up against one another in a Southend v Tottenham cup tie and, inevitably, they clashed, with the Spurs man throwing a punch at Roy and being admonished with a 'Behave yourself, pal.' When it happened again a few moments later, McDonough says he was able to flatten Van Den Hauwe, and manager Terry Venables took the prudent decision of moving his man away from McDonough to elsewhere on the pitch. Without wishing to go back to the tortured 'trench' analogy, being taken out of the firing line is never a good look for a hard man.

Into the top three, and we have to find room for Mick Harford. While he doesn't appear to have his own book (yet), he receives a vast number of mentions in the accounts of others for his toughness. Standout stories are rare, but there's just an appropriately heavy weight of passing anecdotal evidence that Harford was as tough as they come. Sam Allardyce says he 'took no crap'; Carlton Palmer puts him on the same pedestal as knife-wielding Fash, saying that they were 'the only two footballers I played against who demanded that you be nice to them'; and Graham Roberts names him as the hardest player he ever played against. A lot of people say the same, and the lack of a killer incident shouldn't stop Harford from taking his place on the podium.

And so to our top two. In an ideal world we'd love to see these two duke it out on a football pitch, in a boxing ring, in an octagon, in the Colosseum, or wherever they want, but until that happens we've had to make a decision. Not only are the two of them extremely tough, but, pleasingly, they couldn't half play. We've changed our minds several times on which way round this pair should go, and if you see them, please tell them that. We really, really, wouldn't want to get on the wrong side of either of them.

Number one is still to come, but for now we're putting in second place a man who was undoubtedly tough as both a player and manager, and particularly when he combined the two. That man is Graeme Souness.

Our Chief Assessor in all things hard, Roy McDonough, is here again with his appraisal of Souness, who he says would do whatever it took to win, 'whether that meant going over the top of a player, or punching or elbowing his opponent to force the upper hand. I had so much respect for Souness.'

So much respect. Never mind that he was an excellent player who went to three World Cups and won countless trophies in a glittering career, it's all about the hardness.

We've all seen the crazy tackle against Steaua Bucharest (which we think might have led directly somehow to the fall of communism in Romania), the red card against Hibs that announced his arrival in the Scottish game with Rangers, and the planting of a flag in the centre circle after a heated Turkish derby when he was Galatasaray manager. This all points to a man who gives not one solitary shit what you think about his actions, and surely there's not much harder than that. This trait was certainly put to good use when breaking down barriers and signing Rangers' first Catholic for around 75 years in Mo Johnston, and, memorably, the club's first black player in 1988 in Mark Walters. But he can also simply be admired in the context of giving several players a right good wallop from time to time.

Harry Redknapp tells a story of a time when he, Jim Smith, Trevor Francis and Souness had dinner together and reminisced about old times. Francis had the temerity to suggest that Italy's infamous hatchet man Claudio Gentile was a bit scary and had once waited for Souness down the tunnel: 'But Graeme didn't even let him finish the story. "No, he didn't," he snapped. "Not a fucking chance." He really had the hump about it.'

We like both that Souness was offended merely at the idea that somebody else was hard and the image of this meal descending into awkward silence as they pushed their food around the plate and tried not to upset Souey any further. Imagine the mood when it came to splitting the bill.

Graeme Souness is clearly as intimidating at a nice evening meal as he was as a player and as a manager. For his further adventures, please see both 'The Gaffer' and 'Fight! Fight! Fight!' chapters, where he shows a very cavalier attitude to wearing clothes over a series of showdowns. But we'll leave the final word on Souey to Ronnie Whelan, who we now know was part of the hard men's union, and who could only look on in awe at Souness when he shared a Liverpool dressing room with him:

'He wanted to be the top dog, he wanted to be the alpha male. He had a high opinion of himself and he liked being the centre of attention. He had the designer gear, the hairdryer in the dressing room and the fancy bottles of cologne. The 'tache was always nicely groomed too.' Well, of course the 'tache was nicely groomed. Putting the fear of God into opponents is no excuse not to look your very best now, is it?

Our champion, however, is somebody who gives the impression that he not only never uses a hairdryer, but that he'd rip the plug off of yours if you tried to fire it up in his presence. A man who, like Souness, managed to be as frightening as a player as he was excellent, before graduating to being a scary manager too. Moreover, while Souness shows a more mellow side in his TV analysis these days, this man even manages to be that rarest of things – a terrifying pundit.

Roy Keane, then – our gangster number one.

When we think of Keano and his hard-man reputation, thoughts immediately turn to his savage challenge on Alf-Inge Haaland.

Keane gives us an insight into the mindset of the hard man when he says of course he was thinking about nailing Haaland, just as he would think about Rob Lee, David Batty, Alan Shearer, Dennis Wise and Patrick Vieira: '"If I get a chance, I'm going to fuckin' hit you." Of course I am. That's the game. I played in central midfield. I wasn't a little right-back or left-back, who can coast through his career without tackling anybody.' A lovely bit of self-justification here from Keane. We're all at it, not like those namby-pamby big girl's blouse full-backs. This must come as a blow to Gary Neville, who receives a bit more of the same elsewhere from Roy.

Of the infamous tunnel incident at Highbury, Keane says The Neviller came in from the warm-up complaining that the Arsenal players had said stuff to him: 'The last thing I wanted was Gary in my earhole, going, "They've been shouting at me in the tunnel." My attitude was, "Fuckin' deal with it. You're not eleven."'

But how could he be expected to deal with it? He's just a full-back, not a dyed-in-the-wool, fully fledged midfield hard man. Presumably the logic here is that the full-back has the luxury of knowing where a tackle is going to come from, as the touchline has his back, whereas in midfield you need the peripheral vision of a barn owl, or perhaps a tawny owl, to see where the danger might be coming from.

On the 'bullying' of Gary Neville, 'one of the weaker' United players, Keane interestingly says it would have been okay if they'd done it to Nicky Butt, Wes Brown or, of course, himself, because they could take it. It gives us yet more insight into the code: 'I never went looking for a full-back who'd never done anything to me. I'd look for people who were in my position or were physically important for their team. I'd always thought, "They can give it back to me."' There he is again with his full-back loathing; from what we can gather, it seems mostly based on Gary Neville, to be fair.

To finish on Haaland, Keane says, 'There are things I regret in my life and he's not one of them.' Tellingly, he also says that he's disappointed in the response of the other Man City players that day: 'They didn't jump in to defend their team-mate. I know that if someone had done it to a United player, I'd have been right in there. They probably thought he was a prick, too.' Fair point. Besides the fact that he really doesn't like old Alf-Inge (he devotes *pages* to it), we love the fact that Roy is disappointed that people didn't swarm at him wanting a fight, like he's Begbie or something.

This air of quiet menace carried over into his brief time as a manager. Anybody who's seen those press conference clips can feel the shudders in the room full of seasoned journos. More than any amount of Nigel Pearson suggesting you might be an ostrich, just a look from Roy Keane if your phone goes off when he's talking might be enough to make us soil ourselves.

Lest we forget, since he has slipped down the pecking order in recent years to playing second fiddle to Martin O'Neill and Paul Lambert, Roy Keane's managerial career started well. Having rescued a plummeting Sunderland after Niall Quinn thought anybody probably could have a good go at it, Keane got the self-styled Black Cats promoted and for a while they looked happy enough in the Premier League. The reasons things started to go wrong are likely myriad and complex, but one reason we can be sure of is that someone started playing ABBA in the dressing room before games.

The unnamed staffer responsible, we're assured by Roy, soon moved on, but the damage was clearly done. What alarmed Roy, you see, was not the ABBA per se (in fact he concedes, 'Fuckin' "Dancing Queen". I wouldn't have minded if it had been one of Abba's faster ones.'), but rather that his players were allowing a member of his staff to take charge of the stereo pre-match, rather than find their own motivational music. He was concerned that it pointed to a lack of leadership in the dressing room, worrying that 'none of the players – nobody – said, "Get that shit off."'

Now we can stand here all day and debate the merits or otherwise of Sweden's greatest export outside of flat-pack furniture, but clearly the damage was done. They lost that day and the rot had set in. We only wish we knew who the ABBA fan on the Stadium of Light staff was. If he's prepared to slip on a bit of *Arrival* in a Roy Keane changing room, maybe he should be on our list too.

Clearly, Keane would only want the right sort playing for him – as he tried to sort the willing from the weak, the transfer market must've been a bit of a minefield. Matt Taylor seemingly had the option of signing for Sunderland at one stage, but perhaps felt that Roy was a bit too scary to play for. Keane picks up the story at the end of their meeting: 'I walked him to his car, told him to take his time with the decision. I was walking to my own car when I got a text – from Matt Taylor. I could still see him, still in the car park, driving out. I've decided to sign for somebody else.' Quite right too. Discretion is the better part of valour and all that. I bet he even kept the windows wound up and the doors locked.

The other great Roy Keane at Sunderland transfer story is the one involving Robbie Savage, and while it doesn't necessarily display Roy at his most combative, it certainly establishes a low tolerance for non-Trench behaviour.

You see, when Savage was thinking of leaving Blackburn, there was interest from both Sunderland and Derby. For his part, Robbie says, 'it was an easy choice' as 'Roy Keane couldn't make our meeting. And when I met Paul Jewell, we got on like a house on fire.' According to Keane, however, it's a good job that Savage found a soulmate in Jewell because Sunderland ceased to be an option the moment Keane called Sav and got a voicemail message saying. '"Hi it's Robbie – whazzup!" – like the Budweiser ad. I never called him back. I thought, "I can't be fuckin' signing that."'

Brilliant. We've never loved Roy more.

Believe it or not, Keane claims to have only lost his temper once as a manager. That doesn't quite tally with the anecdotal evidence, as Jimmy Bullard suggests that Keane once launched himself two-footed at a tactics board to destroy it during a rant about tactics meaning 'fuck all in this game' – and that's not the one time Roy admits to. Roy's confession is even better, though. It involves Kevin Dillon again, a man who exists in the margins of this book, drifting through anecdotes consistently being nobody's idea of a good time. Unstoppable force meets mildly irritating object, then – it can only end one way.

Dillon started it, by all accounts (well, Roy's account, anyway), taking the ill-advised step of shouting from the Reading bench to the Sunderland one, 'calling me a wanker'. Keane insists that he remained stoic in response: 'I never got involved with opposition managers or staff – never.' Except, he sort of did afterwards, when he joined Dillon, along with Wally Downes and manager Steve Coppell, for the traditional post-match drink in the office.

Keane went in ahead of his staff, feeling slightly miffed after a defeat, and took umbrage with Downes over a perceived lack of respect in the technical areas. Dillon challenged Keane in turn and, 'I grabbed him, got his head on the table, pulled his tie up.' This act of classic schoolboy violence naturally took the Madejski Stadium office by complete surprise (they've been sponsored by Waitrose, for God's sake – they'll have no trouble here), and once Keane had been pulled away he bid them all a fond 'Fuck yis, anyway,' and went on his merry way.

Dillon was okay, with no lasting damage, and the real victim in all this appears to have been Keane's goalkeeping coach, Raimond van der Gouw, who trotted breezily along to the office hoping for a quick beer and a sandwich, only to find his gaffer had soured the mood somewhat.

All of which paints a picture of Keane as our ultimate hard man, and rightly so. We haven't even touched on that time he walked out of a World Cup because he locked horns with the formidable Mick McCarthy. And yet, whisper it, there's a softer side to him, and after the brutal chapter we've just scrapped through, let's end on that nicer note.

As we can see from the ABBA episode, Keane places great store in dressing-room spirit, and that doesn't always need to be about keeping people in line. At one point in his book he brings us a heart-warming story from his Manchester United days. In the mid-90s, the players had a pool for any fees they earned for club videos, magazines and the like, and come the end of the season they were each due around £800. Not nothing then, but not a fortune either to some of the higher earners. There was a suggestion that all players should put their cheques in a hat, with the last name out winning all of the money. Of the younger players there at the time, David Beckham and the prudent Neville brothers opted out, but Paul Scholes and Nicky Butt went all in.

Imagine the scene, 'great crack in the dressing room. Lads sweating,' before Eric Cantona came out last and won the pot of around £16,000. Naturally, as he was already the highest earner at the club, he took a bit of ribbing, but he then surprised them all the next day when he split the haul between Scholes and Butt 'because – he said – the two of them had had the balls to go into it when they couldn't really afford it'. Roy was impressed, as are we, by the gesture.

Eric himself could have been in the running for our title. He did, after all, kung-fu kick a fan at the height of his powers. Instead, though, we'll leave you with his story of generosity, and the way Roy Keane is so quietly touched by it, as an antidote to all of the mad dogs, shotguns, property destruction and raw violence we've dealt with here. It takes us back to our happy place.

7

Call the Cops
Gracefully spread-eagled

After a few months of reading autobiographies, we noticed a pattern. So we started counting, did the maths and came up with what tabloids would likely describe as the 'chilling figure' that close to 50 per cent of those in our sample have had a proper scrape with the law.

Not all did jail time – indeed, some of the law-brushes ended with the players in question being found innocent. But then again, our statistics don't include incidents that didn't involve the cops when they probably should have done: you know, like fighting, animal cruelty and that time Billy Bonds and Trevor Brooking almost killed someone.

Oh yeah – Bonzo and Boog nearly done a murder. It happened on tour with West Ham. The lads were all celebrating the fact that Peter 'Les' Bennett's wife had given birth back home and, while nicely sloshed, Bill, Trev, Harry Redknapp and Jimmy Lindsay thought the perfect way to crown the celebrations was to throw Les in the swimming pool. Unfortunately, he was much drunker than the other drunk people had realised. Bonds writes: 'Instead of surfacing, spluttering and cursing, he simply lay quietly floating face down on the water, arms and legs gracefully spread-eagled.'

Quite the image Bonzo has painted – it reads like the start of *Sunset Boulevard*. Fortunately, they rescued him, and he was fine, but presumably it put a bit of a dampener on the whole evening. Can you imagine if Sir Trevor had been nicked for manslaughter? He'd never have had that gig on *Match of the Day* after retirement,[19] he'd never have

---

19 He even had his own strand, *Brooking's Brief*, as any MOTD aficionado will recall. Alan Shearer's never had one of those.

been at the FA and he'd never have been a 'Sir'. Truly, like the game of football itself, life is all about fine margins.

To our great relief, most of the law and order issues we read about did not nearly end in death. In fact, many of them were beautifully low level. The most famous example of small-time crime involving footballers is Glen Johnson and his mate Ben May getting fined for nicking a toilet seat at B&Q. Amazingly, though, we discovered that Johnson's not the only football person to get pinched after a mix-up at that particular DIY chain.

Johnson's accidental oversight (on buying a whole bathroom, he and May swapped one toilet seat for another, not realising the difference in price) led to a kind of attempted theft worth £2.35 – but even that titchy figure is comfortably trumped by Sam Allardyce, who spent five hours in a police cell after being accused of nicking a B&Q hosepipe adaptor worth a paltry 69p.

Sam's incredible story is full of delicious detail as to exactly how this outrage came about. The day started like any other non-working day, and Sam decided to wash his car (an activity we're fairly sure Sam performs rigorously every Sunday morning, work permitting), but when he came to use his special spray gun, he realised he needed both male and female adaptors for his hose (presumably he'd somehow lost them after the wash the previous week – easily done). So off he went, possibly in his soapy car, down to B&Q.

Once there, he found the adaptors and screwed them together to check they fitted. This one innocent, and entirely understandable, action was to prove extremely costly: 'My fatal mistake was not pulling them apart again, meaning I only got charged for one adaptor.'

Now, Sam seems like a man who knows his way around a DIY shop. He's probably never asked a B&Q employee in which aisle he might find a *soldiering* iron, for instance, so to make such a rookie mistake must have meant his head was elsewhere – perhaps considering PowerPoint presentations, large measurements of wine or where best to deploy Joey O'Brien that week. We just don't know. Still, the deed was done and, after paying, he was collared by a security guard as he left. (Specifically, Sam says: 'the female security guard'. Surely the guard's gender is irrelevant? He doesn't tell us the sex of the checkout person, after all. We don't know, but we suspect Sam still feels that a male security guard might have been more understanding.) As a result of this grand larceny, he was banged up for a few hours until, we assume, Sammy Lee came to bail him out. If there's a lesson here, it's that we should all be aware that B&Q security guards are extremely eagle-eyed – nary an errant toilet seat nor a craftily bodged together set of adaptors escapes their expert gaze. Test them at your peril.

But Sam is only the beginning. Here, in handy table form, are ten of our favourite low-level crime stories we came across in our research.

	Name	Crime
1.	Paul Cannell	While playing for Washington Diplomats, was arrested at US customs for smuggling. The contraband? Black pudding.
2.	Frank McAvennie	Frank was famously caught at airport customs with cocaine in his suit pocket. He claims in his book that it was simply leftovers from a night out a few weeks previously. He tried to mitigate the situation by hopefully protesting, 'It's only a wee bit of Charlie.'
3.	Tony Adams and Ray Parlour	Caught pilfering a pot plant from a hotel while drunk. It makes more sense than it sounds – Rodders had forgotten to buy his mum a birthday present, so they needed something quickly. Unfortunately, they were not subtle and were easily spotted. The hotel let them off, but they still had to report to a police station a couple of days later. The copper there, Parlour says, greeted them with: 'Here comes Bill and Ben.' And if you didn't get the reference, Ray adds, 'The Flower Pot Men' – but if you didn't get the reference, it's doubtful the explanation helped much.
4.	Chris Sutton	On his leaving do from Norwich, Suts got a bit pissed and dived head first into a random convertible, doing some minor damage. Police were called, but when Sutton saw them looking for him in a club, he decided the best thing to do was turn fugitive, so he legged it out the back and jumped in a taxi. This led to three police cars tailing him and eventually he was banged up, although not arrested. 'I thought it was an overreaction from the police,' says Sutton in his autobiography, reckoning it was his status as a star footballer that led to the heavy-handedness, and not his Dr Richard Kimble act.
5.	Tony Cottee	Along with a few Leicester players, Cottee was landed in relatively warm water for selling cup final tickets. One who escaped any wrath, though, was Icelandic forward Arnar Gunnlaugsson. Cottee says he gave the police '75 made up and untraceable "names" living in Iceland – and got away with it!' Yes, only a true criminal mastermind would think to give names that were both made up *and* untraceable.

6.	Zlatan Ibrahimovic	Zlatan admits in Zlatan's book that Zlatan used to nick a lot of bikes, and Zlatan was also once caught stealing about £120 worth of stuff from a department store. Zlatan adds, confusingly, 'Not that we went out thieving.' Zlatan also details the time Zlatan drove at 325kph in Zlatan's Porsche Turbo to outrun the police.
7.	Harry Redknapp	During his tax evasion court case, Redknapp was grabbed by security guards for, it seems, leaving the supermarket through the wrong exit. In *Always Managing*, he says he shouted at them: 'I'm not a thief, I'm the fucking manager of Tottenham!' – always a cast-iron defence strategy, as David Pleat would attest.
8.	Jimmy Floyd Hasselbaink	Stole a special watch from another player at Dutch outfit DWS. He ended up leaving the club over it. This doesn't stop Jimmy from posing with a massive watch on the front cover of his book, though, as if mocking his victim to this day.
9.	Andrea Pirlo	Slightly odd one, this, as no crime actually took place, but in *I Think Therefore I Play*, Pirlo reveals that he and Alessandro Nesta were so enamoured of Pep Guardiola and his work that they hatched a plan to kidnap him for themselves when Milan went to play Barcelona. In the end, they abandoned the idea: 'To avoid constantly falling out, we'd have needed to saw him in two when we got back to Italy, and that wouldn't have been a good idea. How the poor thing would have suffered.'
10.	Jack Charlton	Stealing trout from River Wansbeck. Of course. Was never caught. Still at large.

We also encountered a couple of instances where the crimes weren't really low level, but the perpetrators seemed to think they were. Stuart Pearce admits to stealing an old Escort with a few mates once because it was late at night and they couldn't find a cab. We've all been there – no cabs about, so you just boost the nearest car, right? Pearce says they talked about ringing the police anonymously once they got home, adding: 'In our weak defence, it was not like modern car theft, which is a serious offence and a real stigma, but more of a minor misdemeanour.' Nicking cars meant nothing back in the day, did it? Bit like pinching bums or smoking indoors.

Former Arsenal and England defender Peter Storey had similar thoughts to Pearcey. Needing money, he sold a couple of cars he had taken on hire purchase – when he later couldn't afford the repayments or produce the cars, he was taken to court: 'Theft makes it sound as if I was going out nicking motors on the streets of north London,' he complains, yet it's difficult to think of a more accurate word to describe selling something that doesn't belong to you.

If you take Mickey Thomas's autobiography as gospel, he's constantly wisecracking his way through life, even at moments of great import. Famously, he did time for forging money – have a read of his version of events when the police came to pick him up:

'And, you've guessed it, there was a joke not far behind with good old Mickey Thomas taking the piss. I opened the door and this copper said, "Are you Mickey Thomas?"

'"Yes," I replied.

'"I'm Detective Roberts," he said. "I have come about the forgeries."

'"Come back tomorrow and I will get you loads," I joked back.'

In the car to the station, one officer asked Mickey if he knew his cousin. And good old Mickey was ready again with a classic one-liner: 'Oh yes, I've given her one. I had no problem taking down her particulars.' If he did say these things – and some might think they feel like after-dinner speech embellishments – they seem pretty ill-judged when you're being investigated for a serious crime. It's not exactly the kind of thing that's going to endear you to officers who might be taking the stand as part of your prosecution, is it?

The major sin among footballers, though, seems to be drink-driving – much of it, but not all of it, occurring back in the 1970s and 80s. Some players, such as Archie Gemmill, are very repentant and regretful about their mistakes, but others almost excuse themselves on the grounds that it was a different time. Mick Quinn, who received a one-year driving ban after being nabbed drink-driving, says 'it wasn't the social no-no it is today', apparently ignoring the whole 'legal no-no' of the thing.

Mick actually ended up in jail for a couple of weeks after twice being caught driving (and speeding) during his ban. He recalls in his book what he said to the press on his release: 'It was silly what happened and I wouldn't advise anyone in a similar situation to do that.' Yep, over those two weeks, Mick had properly wised up, and if anyone ever asked him in the future if they should do a bit of drink-driving and then, if they get banned from driving, to drive anyway, and, for good measure, exceed the speed limit, he'd say, 'No, son. I wouldn't advise that.' Proof that our penal system does sometimes truly reform those that are shoved through it.

Obviously, Portsmouth boss Alan Ball took the sensible steps once Mick returned to the club after his bird: got him back into training, made all the right noises about lessons having been learned, and ensured his striker kept his head down for a bit to avoid any further controversy. Not really. He threw a massive party. Says Ball: 'It may not have been the politically correct thing to do, but we loved the big fellow and all his daftness.'

'Daftness'.

Ball's former team-mate Mick Channon can see the cheery side of vehicular crime too, and in his autobiography tells a light-hearted anecdote about the time Peter Osgood was so drunk that he turned his purple Capri over in a ditch when driving back to Southampton after a night out in London.

'The story goes that the police arrived at the scene and the only reason they knew it was Peter Osgood, as they saw two figures running off across a field, was that the girl was twenty yards in front!' In #2Sides, #RioFerdinand #saysthat 'anything at all that sticks out about someone becomes a thing you tease them about'. And this tale illustrates his point perfectly: even Peter Osgood almost killing himself and a passenger gets reduced to some joshing about how Ossie lost a yard or two of pace in his dotage.

And if we're talking about tales involving booze, then you can be sure there'll be something from the remarkable book of Roy McDonough. Two things, actually. On one occasion he was driving home drunk with a hot kebab in his lap and became so paranoid that police were following him that he crashed his car. Then he found out the police weren't following him after all. And on another occasion he found himself as designated driver during an afternoon session, so laudably kept his drinking down to just the ten pints of Guinness – well, you can't be too careful, can you? As he drove to a pub for one more on the way home, he was hit by a Mini: 'The first thing I did was run in the pub and order another pint to steady my nerves,' he writes. Lucky he was near a pub, really. It's a sad fact that many car crashes occur nowhere near pubs, leaving victims and perpetrators without instant access to the calming effect of decent grog.

No one seems to have more stories about brushes with the law than Peter Storey. As well as his car-selling scam, he was had up before the beak for assaulting a traffic warden (a charge he still denies), financing the purchase of a coin press to manufacture fake half sovereigns ('I will always maintain I was the innocent victim of circumstances beyond my control in the coin conspiracy business'), running the 'Calypso Massage Parlour' with Camilla and Lulu ('I was grassed up after five or six weeks … It led to one of the worst Christmases of my life' – indeed: being done for running a brothel would take the edge off anyone's festive celebrations), and finally – earning him a month in jail – importing porno videos from Holland: he and a mate stuffed them into the spare tyre of his Suzuki Jeep, but were still caught out by customs.

Interestingly, both Storey and Quinn mention that during their time behind bars, the favoured currency among the 'lags' (as Quinn refers to the inmates – he must be the only person left in the country outside of *The Sun* headline writers to still use that term) was Mars bars. Not Marathons, Yorkies or Picnics. Just Mars bars.[20]

Kerry Dixon also spent a bit of time in prison after getting in a fight with a man in a bar who had told him to 'fuck off, fatso'. But he doesn't mention anything about Mars bars, only that he really missed the football banter. In that respect, he's no different to his peers: every player is contractually obliged to say they miss the banter once they've retired. The craic with the lads is the hardest thing to replace. Only if you're lucky, like the boys on *Soccer Saturday*, do you find a decent substitute – a kind of methadone to ease the comedown from years of mainlining purest pharmaceutical-grade banter in the dressing room.

Archie Gemmill was never behind bars, but he was lucky not to have spent time in juvy after an incident when he was a youngster:

'One boy took my ball and wouldn't give it back – big mistake. I seized a friend's air rifle and fired a warning shot. Unfortunately, the pellet caught the boy on the top of his arm. His mother went screaming blue murder to the police and the next thing you know I'm being driven off in the back of a Black Maria with Mum chasing us down the road. It never went to court. Things like that didn't in those days. I just had to go round to the boy's house and make a proper apology.'

Yep, even at a young age, Archie clearly had a decent shot on him. So many things pop up from this one paragraph. Firstly, don't ever nick Archie Gemmill's football. Secondly, a 'warning shot' is pointing the

---

20 No other confectionery seems to have been introduced into the financial system, which seems like a real missed opportunity. A Revel could be worth a penny, for example. Or you might need three Milky Ways to equal one Mars. Or they could have just used chocolate money and made things easier for all concerned. Going purely with Mars bars feels so limiting.

gun to the sky, not in the vague direction of the target, surely? Thirdly, 'these things didn't go to court' – what, shooting a child? Just what kind of judicial system were people forced to endure in the 1950s and 60s? Where did he live? Deadwood? And fourthly, the ending of this anecdote conjures a wonderful image of a young Archie, already at least thinning on top (possibly with a junior beard), standing on a doorstep, self-consciously scratching the back of his head and twisting his toe into the ground, and saying, 'I'm sorry I shot you,' to some traumatised kid with a bandage on his arm who probably never dared kick a football again. Who knows what a loss he was to the Scottish national team. He might have made all the difference in 1978. He must've watched Archie score his famous World Cup goal and wondered how unfair life can be.

THE VICTIMS

Instances of footballers being the victims of crime rather than the perpetrators were much less common in our research, but there were still some startling stories to be had.

Kevin Keegan has had two nasty incidents in his life when he's been badly beaten through no fault of his own. The first occurred back in 1974 when England played Yugoslavia in a friendly. At the airport in Belgrade as they waited for their baggage, Keegan was assaulted by armed guards, apparently for the heinous crime of laughing when Alec Lindsay got into a bit of trouble for pissing about on the luggage conveyor belt. In the end he was released and a diplomatic incident was narrowly avoided. Keegan writes in his first autobiography that he saw the guard at the airport on the way back, too: 'I swear that if I had had a gun I would have shot him,' and it's not hard to understand his anger.

The second time was the awful occasion he was randomly beaten by a group of assailants armed with baseball bats on his return to England after seven years abroad. His account of it in his second book makes for some grim reading – Keegan, tired after a long drive, had pulled into a layby for a nap, only to be in the wrong place at the wrong time.

You can only have sympathy for him. But it all gets a bit odd when Keegan later attends the police station to recover some of his gear and learns that the suspects for his assault have been brought in. Keegan, understandably, is still furious about his ordeal, and so asks the detective constable to just skip the processing bit and let him mete out some good old-fashioned payback with a baseball bat of his own: 'He was very understanding, but told me that, unlike in the old days, criminals now often had more rights than their victims.' He also told Keegan that he couldn't use the term 'Black Maria' for police cars any more 'because of the racial overtones'. You can almost see Kev shaking his head sadly as he writes: 'Things had certainly changed a lot in the seven years since I had left England.'

Now, what happened to Keegan was horrific. But, Kev, if there *was* a time when victims were allowed to beat the living shit out of suspected criminals before they were even tried for the crime of which they were accused, it's probably a good thing that that time has passed. It feels like the sort of justice that might quite easily get abused, because, well, not everyone who has been arrested is found guilty. And secondly, it's absolutely fine to use the term 'Black Maria' when referring to a police car. It's a bit out of date, but it's fine. Archie Gemmill used it in his story about shooting someone, and no one's said a word about it.

Keegan's England colleague Trevor Francis was a victim of crime, too. In his 1982 diary-cum-autobiography, *The World to Play For*, he recalls being mobbed by thousands of excitable fans at the airport when he signed for Sampdoria. And then it happened: 'In the crush leaving the airport and getting to the car, I had a really expensive Yves St Laurent jumper snatched from around my neck.' That's what we want from autobiographies – detail. Not just a jumper, not just a YSL jumper, not just an expensive YSL jumper, but a *really* expensive YSL jumper. Poor Trev!

That's the way to arrive at your new club, though – with a really expensive jumper casually draped across the shoulders. We'd love to find a picture of this, because we're imagining his inevitably immaculate ensemble also included loose but stylish slacks, loafers, and a pair of aviator shades resting in his nest of hair. Sadly, we can't seem to find one – the closest we get is a shot of him and Sampdoria team-mate Graeme Souness wearing swimming trunks so tiny you have to look twice to check they're actually there. You can see the shot in our pictures section; Souey's Speedos must be cutting off the circulation to his thighs. Absolutely living it up, the pair of them, aren't they? You look at that snap and you wonder why on earth more British footballers aren't begging for a transfer to Italy or Spain.

And finally, Terry Curran was once accidentally a small part of criminal history. He was in a hotel late at night, having a bath with a lovely lady (not unusually – see more in the 'Top Shelf' chapter), when they, and everyone else in the hotel, were asked to leave their rooms and assemble in the car park.

'It turned out to be really good news,' writes Curran – the Yorkshire Ripper, Peter Sutcliffe, had been arrested nearby. It's never explained why this necessitated everyone to be evacuated from a local hotel – perhaps that's just how the police got the word out about good news in the days before Twitter.

Anyway, once Curran had processed that information, he started to worry. It was the night before a Sheffield Wednesday match, and he should have been resting, not enjoying a bit of how's your father. He had genuine concerns that one of the coppers, who he recognised from being on regular duty at Hillsborough, might ring his then gaffer, Jack Charlton, and grass him up. That would have been quite the phone call: 'Mr Charlton? Constable Davies here, sir. We thought we should let you know, sir, that this evening, having arrested the Yorkshire Ripper ... yes, thank you, sir, it *is* really good news, isn't it? Um, yes, having arrested him, we began the customary procedure of evacuating all the nearby hotels, sir. And in one of them, sir, I'm afraid we found your lad Terry "Teddy" Curran, in the company of a young lady who we have reason to believe was not his wife, sir ... Yes, sir. Just thought you should know, sir ... Good luck tomorrow, sir. All the boys are right behind you.'

So worried was Curran by this potential conversation that he approached the coppers and asked them not to call his boss. And, being good sorts, they agreed not to. Classic Curran. The scallywag.

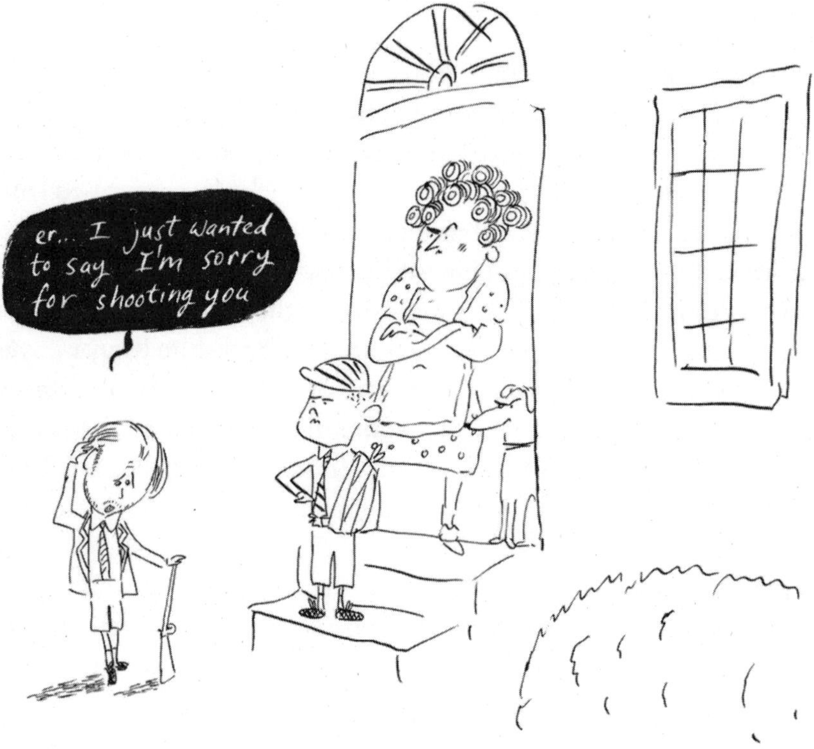
er... I just wanted to say I'm sorry for shooting you

8

The Gaffer
DK – *different class*

Once they cross the white line, the players may be living on their own wits, but up to and including that moment they are in the hands of a rag-tag collection of tactical geniuses, innovators, philosophers, serial failures, incompetents and outright chancers who go under the broad umbrella of 'The Gaffer'.[21]

The gaffers who get it right can become legends: people who enjoy lifelong respect from their charges and from fans alike. They might get a statue built in their image or, better still, a stadium tea bar named after them. Those who get it wrong, however, run the risk of becoming a simple punchline:

'Knock, knock.'

'Who's there?'

'John Carver.'

See?

Maybe this is a little unfair on Carver, who is by all accounts a great coach (the 'best coach in the Premier League', actually – according to, erm, John Carver) and good assistant gaffer. Not everyone is cut out to be the number one. Take Gordon McQueen for example. Paul Merson talks fondly of Gordon during his time at Middlesbrough, where McQueen was on Bryan Robson's staff, saying that he and his wife would even cook a Sunday dinner for himself, Gazza and Andy Townsend ('Gravy?' 'Not for me, Clive.') So a good friend and colleague by all means, perhaps even a steadying influence on what was likely a rowdy bunch. However, when Merson talks about visiting the referee's

---

21 A metaphorical umbrella, not a real one like what Steve McLaren disgraced himself under.

room on a matchday against Aston Villa, we're given the impression that McQueen may not have had his priorities right as the team sheets were handed in: 'Gordon started to shout. His fists were clenched. "GET IN THERE!" he yelled. "Get! In! There!" I looked at him, I didn't have a clue what was going on.

'"What's up Gordon?" I said.

'"Oh, I've got Ian Taylor in my dream team."'

Perhaps not the cut-throat, dog-eat-dog mentality required for managing at the top of the game, and that's why he remained an assistant gaffer. But we're not just here to pass judgement on the ability or otherwise of certain people to do what must be a very difficult job; rather we're here to get under the skin of the bosses, find out what makes them tick and laugh with or at them. We'll leave it to others to decide who is the greatest and what made them that way out there in the deeper waters, while we paddle in the shallows and enjoy moments such as:

- Trevor Francis hiding in the laundry room from a terrifying Brian Clough, as told by Stuart Pearce
- Claudio Ranieri turning up for Christian Fuchs's birthday party 24 hours early and walking into an empty room, according to Jamie Vardy
- Ian Wright telling us that a 'dumbfounded' Arsene Wenger once caught him 'on rollerblades in Highbury's marble halls'[22]
- Martin O'Neill's obsession with true-life crime.

Let's alight there, shall we, and look into that last one a bit further. We're led to believe that managers are married to the job, eating and sleeping football 24/7, and yet here we are finding out that O'Neill passes his time getting knowledgeable about Nilsen, cramming on Crippen and boning up on Bundy. Stan Collymore says that his former Leicester boss routinely enjoyed 'sitting in the public gallery at the Crown Court, watching a bloke get tried for murder. He's a real student of serial killers. He's visited 10 Rillington Place, all that sort of thing.'

Craig Bellamy, meanwhile, says it's a passion O'Neill shares with his long-serving backroom staff John 'Supertramp' Robertson and Steve 'Wolfie' (probably) Walford: 'They loved mass murderers.' Well,

---

22 Given that the later version of Wenger at Arsenal was frequently perplexed by a zip on his coat, this isn't perhaps completely unexpected.

Duncan McKenzie – The Last Fancy Dan. Our proposed Morrissey LP cover.

Mick Quinn.
'Ask your missus.'

Kelly & Eni celebrate winning at Operation or Buckaroo or something.

John Aldridge pictured in one of his top 8 chairs.

Le Tiss – Three Sausage and Egg McMuffins.

Elton & Rod running toward or away from some football chums.

Teacup and saucer on the training pitch. The none-more-English Sir Bobby Charlton.

Trev & Souey in Italy. Visibly shaken by the thought of Gentile.

Jim Smith trying to get his hand up Archie Gemmill's back. 'Three-nil today, Boss.'

Yep, the entire thing. Full of Cabernet Sauvignon.

Hand of Hod. Just weeks later Maradona won the World Cup. Coincidence?

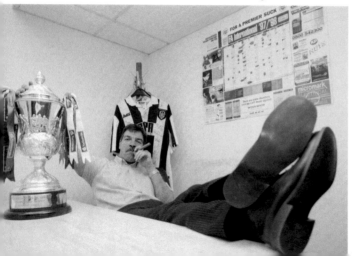

Jack Charlton possibly looking for Ian Brady.

Curran, Ball & McMenemy. Simmering tensions just out of shot.

Ron Greenwood, or Alan O'Dell.   *Alan O'Dell, or Ron Greenwood.*

Shilton & Clemence. Tops off.
Trousers creating an optical illusion.

Steve Harrison – look out below.

Someone's nicked Phil Thompson's tyres. So many people could be in the frame for doing this.

Wright & Collymore in happier times. When Stan was all moustache and no trousers.

Tommy Docherty – not everyone's cup of tea.

Buckets on their heads. What are they like? Whatever next?

presumably as much as anyone really can 'love' a mass murderer. 'They'd get into big arguments about how many people one of the murderers had killed or what method they had used.' Today's results: Jack The Ripper 5 – John Reginald Christie 8 (eight).

Even more curiously, this seems to be something that Young Martin inherited from his mentor, Brian Clough. Terry 'Teddy' Curran says of Clough: 'One of his great loves was the law and on his days off he'd often go to the courts and tell interesting tales of what he'd seen and heard.' We can only speculate who the murder baton has since been handed to, but until we hear otherwise we're going to assume that Emile Heskey is knee-deep in police reports and forensic evidence.

* * *

As we take our ride on the managerial merry-go-round and see what they all get up to, it's important to remember one thing: all managers are liars. It was a penalty; they didn't see it; they haven't spoken to any transfer target; our fans are the best. These guys will say whatever they need to say to look after themselves. Yep, even the nice ones. This is nowhere more apparent than in the job market, where they will look you in the eye and tell you they will stay forever, before jumping ship for a few extra quid and a chance of finishing three places higher up the league.

Take Graeme Souness for example. When at Rangers, he wrote that 'I don't want to leave. Ever. Only failure will move me out of the manager's office at Ibrox.' Well, failure or Liverpool – right, Graeme? That's what you meant. Or Dave Bassett, who claims, 'I might be many things but I have never been a quitter.' Well, apart from that time you quit Wimbledon, or the time before that when you quit Crystal Palace within about ten minutes of agreeing to join them.

But again, perhaps we're being unfair. These guys are swimming in shark-infested waters. If you can win the league and be sacked within months, as we've seen happen to the likes of Ranieri and Mourinho in recent years, then why wouldn't you constantly be looking around for other opportunities – even though it can mean stitching up a pal? And so a giddy whirl of paranoia engulfs the whole coaching community.

Sam Allardyce says that his time at Newcastle was plagued by rumours that Harry Redknapp could take his job – rumours that Sam believes to be true, despite Harry's denials over the phone: 'Supposedly all that stopped him moving was his missus not wanting to leave their home in Dorset.'

Does Harry Redknapp live in Dorset? He should have said. Oh yes, he did, didn't he? More than once. Apparently, 'I'm very popular there. Some people have said, probably jokingly, that before long I'll be Lord Mayor.' No doubt, as with the England job, there will come a time when Harry is claiming that town council members have been texting him to say they want him for the mayoral role.

Prising H away from paddling on Sandbanks can be a difficult thing, but he's been tempted into London on a few occasions, most successfully at White Hart Lane. That being the case, we were surprised to read from him that he wasn't that fussed about getting the Spurs job in the first place: 'It wasn't that much improvement from my salary at Portsmouth … I accepted but more with a deep intake of breath and a resigned sigh than a jump for joy.' Really? You didn't have to take it, Harry. Nobody forced you. You don't have to be polite. It's not a dodgy-looking homemade cake at your auntie's house.

But Harry's not alone in this laid-back attitude to job-seeking. When Newcastle came calling for Jack Charlton back in the 80s, he wasn't particularly keen and successfully resisted the lure of the passionate Toon for some time before relenting: 'So at last I said, "OK, I'll come and talk, but I'm not going to St James' Park. I'm opening a double-glazing firm in Consett in Durham tomorrow, and if you want to talk to me you can do it there."' Apparently this is where the term 'transfer window' comes from.

Even lazier than Big Jack, however, is El Tel. Tony Adams tells us that when he took a job in Azerbaijan, Terry Venables had been offered the job before him but 'Terry seemed to want to do the job by Skype.' We love this. You get some managers who don't spend a lot of time on the training ground with the players, but this is ridiculous. You can't run a football team remotely like Charlie off of *Charlie's Angels*. It seems entirely fair that Adams got the job instead.

Once you do take a new job, of course, first impressions are crucial. Stan Collymore tells us that when Barry Fry took over at Southend before an away game at Sunderland, he met the team coach on the A1 at the services: 'He got out of a Mercedes. I think the number plate was BAZ 1.' Like we say – crucial.

You might expect a new boss to come in and give a speech about a clean slate, how everyone will be given the opportunity to impress and what the team could achieve together if they work hard. When Ron Saunders took over at West Brom, Mickey Thomas says that he went for a slightly different opening gambit: '"Right," he barked, "I'm the new manager. You can call me a c*** if you want but you will have to pick your bollocks up afterwards." Fair enough, I thought.'

A strong start, we're sure you agree, but Saunders (lest we forget a part of that strong run of Albion managers that reads: Johnny, Ronnie, John, Ron, Ronnie, Ron, Johnny, Nobby, Ron, Ron), is not alone in the 'my way or the highway' approach. Micky Quinn brings us news of Larry Lloyd's opening salvo when he took the Wigan job: '"Hello, I'm Larry Lloyd. If you don't like what I'm going to say then I'm going to head-butt you." Everyone looked at one another in amazement.'

What we particularly enjoy about that is the very specific nature of the threat. Ron Saunders is clearly grandstanding, and you wouldn't necessarily believe that you would end up scrabbling around on the floor looking for your knackers; but Larry is explicit that should you not like the content of his words, or indeed the tone in which they are delivered, you will be met with a headbutt. It's worth remembering that headbutts were all the rage in the early 80s, due to a combination of *Boys from the Blackstuff, Auf Wiedersehen, Pet* and Russ Abbot saying 'See you, Jimmy' a lot. You don't see them so much any more.

Threats of physical violence are a sure-fire way of commanding instant respect. Wearing the wrong clothes can do the opposite. Alan Ball remembers his first encounter with Terry Neill in Highbury's marble halls, where he was 'confronted by this fellow in jeans and a denim shirt', which Bally immediately took against. 'He had a bit of a swagger about him,' he adds. You can already tell he doesn't like him, can't you? He's really taken against the double denim there; there were clearly no Status Quo albums in his house.

If arriving at a club and winning over the players is a bit tricky, then leaving a club and saying goodbye can be even more difficult; the way to avoid such a touching scene is, of course, to duck out the back door on your own terms. This is known as 'The Keegan Option'. Long before he was becoming an ex-England manager, realising in a Wembley toilet that he was 'a bit short', Keegan became an ex-Newcastle manager by handing in his 'petrol card and my club credit card', like a rogue cop handing in his gun and badge, and buggering off.

Kev's dramatic flounce set him off on some fairly erratic behaviour. He asked the club to postpone the announcement of his departure until he could flee the city with his family: 'We set off for Heathrow to try to get a flight to Florida before the news hit the headlines. We couldn't find one with four seats together, so we decided to get back into the car and head for France via the Channel Tunnel.'

This strikes us as a bit odd: haring down the motorway to Heathrow, only deciding on America on the way down. Then, not liking the idea of maybe splitting into two pairs on a plane, you abandon that, retrieve your car from the long-term car park, and head for the tunnel. Were there no flights to Spain or France? How on earth did his family pack for this hasty mystery trip? But who are we to judge? It's a stressful job and perhaps your judgement becomes clouded.

What we do know is that once you're in a job, in order to keep it you need to be good at what we've arbitrarily decided to call 'The Four Corners of Football Management'. These four corners are as follows:

Transfers	The Boardroom
The Training Ground	The Dressing Room

We all know what happens once you lose the dressing room. Please, God, don't lose the dressing room.

TRANSFERS

In his memoirs, Paul Merson tells us something very revealing about John Gregory's approach to transfers. In 1998 Villa splashed the cash on the likes of Steve Watson, Dion Dublin, Alan Thompson[23] and Merson himself. Merse was moved to question it: '"Crikey, Boss, spending some money, aren't you?" I remember saying to him.

'"Well, I might as well," he replied. "If I don't spend it, the next bloke in will."' One suspects that Gregory is not alone in this attitude, and who's to say he's wrong?

---

23 That's Steve 'Used to do a flip when he took a throw-in' Watson, Dion 'Spacious semi-detached needing a bit of work in Mablethorpe' Dublin and Alan 'Pretty sure he got an England cap once' Thompson.

Managers live and die by their success in buying and selling players, so who can blame them for looking after themselves as well as indulging in the odd bit of skulduggery here and there? It's all in the game, y'all.

Harry Redknapp tells an interesting tale of nabbing Mark Newson from under the nose of then Maidstone boss Barry Fry when H was in charge at Bournemouth (he lives local, you know) – a story that is backed up practically word for word by Fry himself, so we believe this one. But it's Fry's reaction to the incident that we find so refreshing: 'Having seethed when this happened, I laughed about it the next day because the fact is that I would have done the same. There are no ethics in football; no ethics between managers. We all feel for one another, but if we can nick a good player we will. And have no conscience about it. I may have threatened to have his legs blown off, but we have been mates ever since.'

Yep, you heard. He threatened to have Harry's legs blown off. As we know, this didn't happen and it was many years later before Redknapp started complaining of knee trouble affecting his work.

So what if a bit of underhand dealing, or, at the very least, thorough groundwork, goes on before transfers take place? Didier Drogba tells us in an anecdote full of portent that the first time he met Jose Mourinho (at a Porto v Marseille game) he possibly looked deep into his eyes and told him, 'One day, when I can afford you, I will sign you.' This obviously worked, and whatever your feelings about The 'Whatever He Is This Week' One, you can't deny that he inspires fierce loyalty in some of the players around him. Or at least he used to.

Mourinho also tried tugging at the heartstrings of Zlatan Ibrahimovic when he left Inter for Barcelona. The following exchange is from the extraordinary *I Am Zlatan*:

'He came up to me: "You can't leave!"

'"Sorry, I've got to take this opportunity."

'"If you leave, I will too." My God, what can you say to that? That really hit me. If you leave, I will too.' Presumably this would have really hurt Jose as Zlatan was running into the arms of Pep Guardiola, so it's a bit like Ken Barlow finding Deirdre in Mike Baldwin's arms in what has since become Manchester's second greatest rivalry. Zlatan left anyway, but discovered that he and Pep were far from a match made in heaven, and he eventually returned to Jose's warm embrace on the red side of Manchester for one more, brief fling.

It would seem that a better United gaffer, Alex Ferguson, was particularly thorough in his transfer scouting (though how you explain Bebe is beyond us). Chris Sutton says that when his own move to the Red Devils was mooted, he heard that 'a couple of former SAS men followed me around for two weeks to check on my behaviour. They returned to Sir Alex with a good enough reference.' Although perhaps not, as Sutton ultimately never went to Old Trafford.

One man who did was Lee Sharpe, who joined as a young man from Torquay in very hush-hush circumstances: Torquay manager Cyril Knowles told Lee 'he had been leaving the ground late … The lights were off and nobody was about as he walked out the front. A Jaguar was parked there, on its own with no lights on, and as he came alongside it, the door swung open and a voice said: "Get in, we'd like a chat with you."' It was Ferguson, possibly about to make Knowles an offer he couldn't refuse.

The manager-and-player relationship seems crucial in making a transfer happen. Players will jump at the chance to work with a boss who will value and nurture them – it stands to reason. Contrary Mary Roy Keane, however, is once again the exception to the rule. It appears that he joined Celtic out of spite after Gordon Strachan told him he wasn't fussed about Keano signing as they were all right either way. 'So I said to myself, "Fuck him, I'm signing."' We're not psychologists, but this doesn't seem like the soundest basis on which to make a decision about a new career path. Unless, of course, Strachan was employing some kind of genius reverse psychology.

Where there is competition for a player's signature, though, the boss man has to pull out all his best moves – literally in the case of Jimmy Melia when he was trying to lure Mickey Thomas to Brighton. Thomas paints a vivid picture: 'Jimmy Melia took me out to see Dr Hook. He even brought his dancing shoes and wore a white suit. I couldn't stop laughing. He shoved more than a few drinks down my neck and in a moment of weakness I agreed to sign.'

If there's another example of this specific approach working, we're yet to come across it. We may have questioned Roy Keane's 'I'll show you' motive when signing for a new club, but being enchanted by a couple of light ales and a white-suited manager jiving to 'You Make My Pants Wanna Get Up and Dance' doesn't seem like the soundest reasoning either.

One final word on managers and their transfers. For Pat Van Den Hauwe's autobiography, *The Autobiography of the Everton Legend*, Pat Van Den Hauwe asked former boss Howard Kendall to write a foreword. Kendall obliged, duly penning a few lines about who his greatest-ever signing was. As you might expect in a book by Pat Van Den Hauwe about Pat Van Den Hauwe, Kendall writes: 'When I look back at every signing I have made at all the clubs I managed, one stands out head and shoulders above any other – Neville Southall.'

THE BOARDROOM

A strong and stable relationship between the manager and his employers can be as vital as any between players out there on the pitch. Think of the powerhouse that Arsenal was when Arsene Wenger and David Dein worked in tandem. It's important to get along. Tony Cottee tells us that during his brief stint as Barnet manager, he got along so well with his chairman, Tony Kleanthous, that even when he was sacked the chairman invited TC into his office for a game of Subbuteo first: 'For the record, Everton beat Arsenal 10–8.'

It will surprise nobody to learn that Barry Fry has a lot to say about the boardroom and those in it. In his earliest days of management at Dunstable, he worked for a man named Keith Cheeseman. Cheeseman was a convicted fraudster who used some of his ill-gotten loot to lure the likes of George Best to turn out for the Bedfordshire club, before getting himself in such a tangle that at one point Fry got a call from the police asking if he could identify a headless corpse they believed to be Cheeseman.

With such close proximity to Cheeseman's nefarious activities, working with those bongo merchants David Gold and David Sullivan at Birmingham must have been tame by comparison. And yet between Barry, the two Daves and their trusted lieutenant Karren Brady, there is enough material there for a sitcom – one of those bawdy, sexist sitcoms of the 70s, but a sitcom nevertheless.

From the very first dealings between Fry and Brady, he called her 'love' – that's only to be expected – but he has nothing but praise for his new boss, saying: 'She is a clever woman and made untold millions for Sullivan in his sex empire.' That's Sex Empire. However, the respectful acceptance of a woman as his boss in the macho world of football could only last so long. Eventually, the unreconstructed male chauvinist within Barry exposed himself – almost literally.

After mouthing off about his diminutive chairman, Mr Sullivan, and suggesting he didn't know a goal line from a clothes line, he was anticipating a post-match telling off from Brady, and got one when a staff member had to drag him out of the shower: 'I got out, and dripping wet, put a towel round me. She gestured me towards the boot room. "Bloody hell", I thought, "my luck's changing here. She's going to say 'Well done, Baz, brilliant 4–0 win, great crowd … how about it?'" Instead she slammed the door shut and shouted at me in no uncertain terms.'

Oh Barry, you were doing so well. We may dislike Karren Brady for everything she's doing to football on behalf of the 'sex empire', but we resolutely defend her right not to be objectified by tubby, wet, naked employees. Plus, it was never really likely, was it?

Simon Jordan is very good on his efforts to forge a bond across the boardroom table with Steve Coppell, who you'll remember was Palace manager about 17 times, one of which coincided with Jordan taking over the club. The chairman arranged for the pair to travel to Southend together to watch a player, only to find the sullen Coppell annoying him with his gloomy demeanour and lack of sparkling repartee.

'I had just spent £11.5 million and counting in three weeks, to listen to this negative, dour, unresponsive football manager do me a favour and sit in my car grunting at me.

'As the journey continued I persevered, just to receive more of the same. In the end I remarked that he was so negative he was interfering with the signal strength on my phone.'

Very bold of mobile phone impresario Jordan to call into question the quality of his own product. Just goes to show how strongly he feels about Steve 'Eeyore' Coppell's lack of good chat.

Possibly in a search for a manager he could share a pleasant road trip to the seaside with, Jordan rattled through several bosses at Selhurst Park, including cheeky scamp Neil Warnock, who seemingly wrapped him around his finger, asking him if he thought he was the best boss in the division: 'Innocently, I said: "Of course you are, Neil."

'"Well, how come Dave Jones at Cardiff is getting paid more than me?"

'"I guess he won't be any more!" was my response. That was the quickest £250,000 pay rise Neil ever got.' That would have raised eyebrows. Well, some anyway. Not Neil's, of course.

Crafty old Dave Webb was another who knew how to work the system. Harry Redknapp says that when Webb was Bournemouth manager he used to get the hotel reception to announce a phone call in front of the directors, saying there was a Mr Bates on the line, so that the directors would panic and think it was Ken Bates headhunting him and jack his wages up. Well played, Dave Webb.

THE TRAINING GROUND

The training ground is where the magic happens. Reputations can be made, bonds forged, teams built and occasional fancy free-kick routines practised. A manager needs to be the master of the training ground, whether getting in amongst it himself or instructing trusted cohorts to mould a team in his image. Lasting impressions can be made out there on the fields.

It's fair to say that Mick 'Not Mike' Duxbury was not a fan of Ron Atkinson. This is a rare example of a player taking against a manager even though he picked him a lot. Part of his problem with Big Ron was his continued involvement in training: 'It was becoming more and more like he was setting it up for himself sometimes. All managers joined in the five-a-sides but he'd still be participating in the drills.'

We like this image of Ron, like Brian Glover in *Kes*, running round dictating play amid a squad of seasoned internationals. We can only imagine what Arnold Muhren thought of it all. Atkinson's behaviour clearly rankled with Mick (Not Mike), though. When Big Ron was sacked to make way for some Scottish chap we can't quite recall, he threw a party for all the players, but Mick (Not Mike) wasn't having it: 'I can't speak for who went or didn't, I just know that I didn't turn up. Why do it? It didn't make any sense. I wasn't particularly disappointed that he'd gone and wouldn't have attended one of Ron's parties anyway.'

At least Ron had a grip on his sessions, though. Vinnie Jones talks of Chelsea training under Ian Porterfield as being 'pretty shambolic', which is a mild description of what assistant manager Stan Ternent describes as more like anarchy. According to Stan, Porterfield kept out of the way while Dennis Wise and his gang resisted Stan's futile attempts to get them to do anything other than play small-sided matches.

But while Wise was trying to get out of doing any hard work, Paolo Di Canio was asking for more when he moved to West Ham. He arrived to find an unsatisfactory, lax arrangement under Harry Redknapp, and according to Jimmy Bullard he complained bitterly to his new boss: '"We are supposed to be stretching and Razor Ruddock is talking about drinking last night. He's talking about shitting! This is not right!" Before long, Paolo had brought over his own fitness coach from Italy to put us through our paces.' So you can say what you like about Di Canio with his fascist sympathies and Mussolini worship, but he did at least make the training run on time.

One of West Ham's favourite sons dipped his toe into management, as previously discussed. For Tony Cottee, it wasn't all playing Subbuteo with the chairman. Sometimes he was out on the training ground trying to rally his troops. Barnet were not alone in having a special bib in training for the worst performer that week, and, worrying that it might undermine his authority, Cottee banned his players from voting for him: 'Anyway, after about three weeks, John Still told me that a few of the players had approached him and said that they didn't feel it was right that they weren't allowed to vote for me.' Guess what Cottee did? Yep. And guess what the players started doing again? Yep. And this is why Tony Cottee was not a successful manager: he fell down on the training ground element of the 'Four Corners'.

One man who must have fallen down on a different corner because he sounds like he's got this training ground lark nailed is Colin Murphy, who was briefly Stan Collymore's boss at Southend. Stan says he had a few strange methods, our favourite of which is undoubtedly 'all the players standing around him in a circle while he held a cricket bat and smacked a ball at us. If you dropped it, you did ten press-ups.' We can see how this might pass for team bonding, at a pinch.

It could have been worse, though: Murphy could have picked his team based on who caught or dropped the ball. We know that sounds daft, but it's not wildly different to what Uwe Rosler describes Gary Megson doing during the German striker's loan spell at West Brom[24]: 'Gary got us together and told us we were to go with the fitness coach,

---

24 No. We didn't remember either.

run around the perimeter of the university pitches and the first 11 back would start the game later that evening!' Quite what Megson would have done if there was no goalkeeper in the first 11 back we don't know, but it is certainly one way of doing it; it cuts down on the admin, after all.

THE DRESSING ROOM

The Dressing Room can sometimes refer to a figurative place: a collective state of mind for a group of players under the guidance of their gaffer. Losing this figurative dressing room can often be followed soon after by finding a figurative job centre. Imperative to maintaining a harmonious dressing room is motivating your players in the right way. Too aggressive and you lose them, too soft and they will run rings around you. It's a delicate balance to achieve and every manager has their own approach. Here are a few – pick a favourite:

- Sam Allardyce says that, at Coventry, George Curtis would 'grab players and try to bite their noses'. He never tried it with Sam, of course.

- Cyrille Regis says that Ron Atkinson 'would do absolutely anything to wake you up and get you buzzing. He'd put Vicks Vaporub ointment in your face or dip your head in cold water. He would even give you a dig in the stomach to get you to tense up – just to motivate you.'

- Ian Holloway confesses he 'told the lads they had to have the constitution of a police horse. For me, horses are amazing beasts as they are trained to deal with stress or noises and bangs which are against their nature, because they are naturally flight animals.' Clearly he was hoping to gee, or, if you will, gee-gee his players up. They must have been champing at the bit etc.

- Luis Suarez says that 'Brendan Rodgers used to motivate his team by reading out a message from an anonymous player's mum and they would all guess "whose mum is it this week?"'

As we say, approaches are varied and only time can truly tell if any or all of them are successful. We like to think that given a combination of all of those – having our nose bitten, being punched in the stomach, having Vicks rubbed on our face, and being told to be like a police horse all to the lilting soundtrack of a letter from our mum being read aloud – would have us right up for the big game.

These are all generic approaches, though; one size fits all, whether you're Lionel Messi or indeed Fitz Hall. To really examine the dressing room, we have to shake off the figurative and get right into the actual inner sanctum; because sometimes a Dressing Room just means a dressing room – you know, where people get changed and that.

Tony Cottee remembers a time when Martin O'Neill decided to simplify the game of an overreaching Robbie Savage by dissuading him from trying the fancy stuff, and telling him, 'When you get the ball from our back four, you pass it 10 yards to someone who can play.' It's fair to say that, in the long run, this advice has not deterred Robbie from showing off a bit.

Similarly, Bobby Robson felt the need to bring a mouthy Craig Bellamy down a peg or two in what must have been a lively Newcastle dressing room at the time, as Bellamy remembers: 'Ronaldo, Romario, Stoichkov, Hagi, Guardiola, Luis Enrique, Gascoigne. These are the people I deal with. Who are you?' To which Bellamy admits he thought 'fair enough' and duly kept quiet. Quiet enough to hear the soul of Russell Osman crying out for being excluded from Robson's list of greats, no doubt.

Osman had his own problems as a manager. Leroy Rosenior recalls one unnamed hero piping up at the end of a half-time rant from the one-time Bristol City boss, when they were 2–0 down: 'From the corner of the room came a small voice, "Come on lads, we can still win this."' Anyone who quotes directly from *Escape to Victory* to a star of *Escape to Victory*, as they are being balled out by said star of *Escape to Victory* is all right by us. Quite rightly, Leroy says, 'it brought the house down.'

Les Ferdinand says that Kevin Keegan's trick was to insist he wouldn't single anyone out for criticism in the dressing room, before doing just that, while Trevor Francis says that after being sent off for Man City, John Bond told him, 'if it had been his son, he'd have taken him behind a hedge and given him a good hiding. I didn't think that was the right thing to say'. As we've seen, threats of physical violence are common, but quite where the hedge comes into it we're not sure. Odd, certainly, but John Bond is far from the most eccentric manager to set foot in a dressing room.

On that front, Tony Cascarino might make a case for Glenn Hoddle – the man who really puts the 'odd' in Hoddle. Cascarino can never forget 'the morning Paul Elliott arrived in our dressing room wearing an immaculate leather trenchcoat and stood there, stunned, as Hoddle the manager ran to the "cover" of a bin in the corner and started shooting him with imaginary bullets – "Pshhhh, Pshhhh" – like a five-year-old with a cowboy pistol set.' Evidently, this was an attempt at a gag from 'probably the unfunniest man I have ever known', so maybe we can forgive him. We know he'd forgive us.

The Finger-Pistol-Packing Sheriff Hoddle doesn't, however, make our top three dressing-room incidents involving one of our gaffers. What does make it, you say? Well, it would be rude not to, wouldn't it:

3. The Cream of Brian Clough

Brian Laws, in *Laws of the Jungle* (nice), brings us the tale of the time that Cloughie was so blasé about Forest's prospects pre-match, that his thoughts turned to his own 'distinctly blotchy' red face. The managerial genius asked the physio for some cream for it and proceeded to grab a tube, squirt it all over his face and start rubbing it in.

Far from finding a soothing balm, however, Cloughie had picked up the Deep Heat instead and started screaming for help in getting it off, as his head must have felt like it was on fire. 'All the lads were trying not to laugh but inwardly we were pissing. Whether this scene was by accident or design – and I believe it was the latter – it certainly relieved all the tension.'

This was before a game at Old Trafford, so it is possible that Clough performed the whole charade as a complicated ruse to settle nerves, but we can't help thinking that a lesser manager wouldn't be given the same benefit of the doubt on this one.

2. Sergeant Wilko Grasps the Nettle

Jason McAteer, in that odd present tense he employs throughout his book, brings us news of an inspirational speech from Howard Wilkinson during his brief, spectacularly bad spell as Sunderland manager. Wilkinson is not alone in the 'Managers That Have Failed at Sunderland' Hall of Fame, but he might be alone in his unique attempt in getting his players to play without fear.

'Howard's way of showing us to grasp the moment is to put his hand in a plastic bag of stinging nettles, which he tells us won't sting him if he grabs them firmly. His face goes bright red and his hand comes out red raw with white dots all over it where he's been stung a hundred times by the nettles.'

Had we been there, we probably could have told him that was going to happen.

1. Catch the Pigeon

Top of the shop in the gaffer-going-nuts stakes, however, is the late John Lambie at Partick Thistle. As recalled by Chic Charnley, Lambie was deeply dissatisfied after a poor Thistle performance and was working his way around the dressing room making a series of points to a series of players, before getting to a youngster named Declan Roche: 'He pointed at him and astonished us all by suddenly pulling out a pigeon from somewhere inside his coat. He fixed Declan with a stare that would terrify the devil and said, "See you, you Irish bastard, you're as useful as this doo." He then wrung its neck and threw it at the player. Declan just about passed out! It could only happen at Firhill.'

Now, we confess we've never heard of Declan Roche, and it's possible that could be because of our underwhelming knowledge of the Scottish game. Alternatively it could be because Roche fled the scene that very day and never set foot in a football stadium again – or slept again. Charnley's justification for this outrageous act by Lambie is that 'the doo hadn't been taking its feed and was dying, anyway. It was the kindest thing to put it out of its misery.'

We have so many questions. Why did he have it? Was it always the plan to use it as a prop? At what point did he put it in his coat? What would he have done with it if Thistle had won and Roche played a blinder?

* * *

How successful this made Lambie in terms of maintaining a loyal and harmonious dressing room we can't say; but, despite all the evidence, he probably wasn't the worst at keeping his players onside.

Brian Clough is pretty scathing in his book about his boss at Sunderland, Alan Brown. Clough says of him that 'he used to stride down corridors thinking he was the most important man on earth', which seems a bit rich to us, but then again Brown didn't have the currency that league titles and European Cups bring you. What he did have was a religious fervour and an 'organisation called Moral Rearmament', which he tried to get some of his staff and players on board with. But it didn't wash with Cloughie: 'Somebody once told me, "Don't be fooled by Browny. He'll give you all the stuff about living right and not stepping out of line but he's been knocking off his secretary for eighteen months." I'm told he admitted it when he joined MR.'

Aah, getting involved in a sexual relationship at work. That really is a sure-fire way of losing both the dressing room and the job, as both Tommy Docherty and Redacted Redacted could tell you. Keep it in your pants, guys. Or if, like Graeme Souness, you insist on not keeping it in your pants, at least be careful what you do with it. We mention this because a recurring theme across several of the books we read was Graeme's tendency to let it all hang out around his players.

Jason McAteer can clearly not wipe from his mind the time he was summoned to a showdown meeting in the gaffer's office, where Souey 'was sitting with his feet up on his desk and this tiny, I mean tiny, towel wrapped around his arse. His knackers were hanging out of the towel, staring me in the face. It was like looking at a grandfather clock.' Absolute scenes, as the kids say.

If this was an isolated incident, we'd brush them, oh God, we mean brush *it*, aside – but it's not. Keith Gillespie recalls Souness arriving in the 'canteen wearing just a towel around his waist and a pair of smart, black suit shoes. He puffs his bare chest out and sits down to tuck into lunch. We knew our new manager was a vain man, but this is taking it to the extreme.'

Clearly, flashing his body at players was one way in which Souness sought to inspire them. Or maybe he was just showing off. In looking for the root of all this, we discovered in his own book that he once won the 'Body Beautiful' contest on a family holiday to Butlin's. 'The prize was a week's holiday the following year, so my mum and dad had to save up to take me. I put them under some pressure there.' And so presumably the cycle never stopped. Go to Butlin's – win Body Beautiful – win a week's holiday at Butlin's – win Body Beautiful, and repeat. Skegness,

Minehead, Filey, Ayr and Bognor Regis all surely got the benefit long before the boys at Blackburn Rovers.

By his own admission, Souness has always taken good care of himself, in spite of suspicion about it from some of his gaffers. As a young player at Middlesbrough, his then boss Jack Charlton tried to mock his grooming regime. 'I used to turn up with the shampoo, the conditioner and the hairdryer and Jack would laugh at that. I'd be sitting in the bath after games and Jack would say, "Shampoo? I've never washed my hair in my life."' As Souness quite rightly says, though, the '10 strands coming out of the top of his head' were hardly the best advert for being a stranger to the tea tree and jojoba, and Graeme decided to ignore his boss's advice on this one.

Jack Charlton had perhaps grown too casual about maintaining his hair, as he could rest easy that he didn't have the shittest hair in the game as long as brother Bobby was around; and then, when he was really losing the good fight up there, he made a virtue of it by becoming one of the most famous flat cap wearers in the world. You see, knowing your strengths and covering up your weaknesses are the kind of traits that took Charlton a long way in the game – all the way, lest we forget, to international management and a World Cup quarter-final with the Republic of Ireland.

Early on in his time with The Boys in Green, Wor Jackie came in for some criticism from discarded striker Michael Robinson for messing players' names up. Here's Jack's response to such accusations: 'It's possible that I may have called Liam Brady, Ian, on a couple of occasions. All my life I'd been accustomed to dealing with Ians and Tommys and Bobbys, and suddenly I've got Irish names like Liam and Niall and Pat! And when you think of it, it's not that difficult to confuse Liam with Ian when you meet a person for the first time.' Come on guys, it must be really tough getting to grips with those notoriously tricky Irish names like Pat, right? And anyone could confuse a great footballer with a notorious child killer. We've all done it.

Charlton wasn't the only boss on the international scene at that time causing confusion among his players. Before Toshack was being told by Robbie Savage that he could 'stick it up your arse'; before Bobby Gould was grappling on the training ground with John Hartson (see 'Fight! Fight! Fight!' chapter for further details); back, even before Terry Yorath's playful tap on the back of the head to greet Pat Van Den Hauwe was met with an international-career-ending 'Don't you ever fucking do that to me again' – Wales were managed by a man called England, which was confusing enough for us as children. It seems that Mike England would baffle his own players, according to Neville Southall: 'He'd go around and tell you that you were "DK – different class"; I don't know how many times we told him that class began with a "C" but it never seemed to register.'

Some of the greats have managed Scotland, and none greater, perhaps, than Jock Stein. So we were surprised to find that most of his mentions in charge of the Tartan Army involved players moaning about him. Ray Stewart insists that being critical of Jock meant that 'maybe I spoke my mind too often for his liking' and that was why he didn't get the caps he felt he deserved. Ordinarily we might put this down to sour grapes and we'd just assume that Stein had better players to pick in his position, but a recurring story does lend credence to the idea that if Jock took against you, there was only one way your career with Scotland would go.

These days it's hard to think of Alan Brazil as anything but a talk radio host who really likes horse racing, but once upon a time he was a very talented footballer ... who really liked horse racing. Even in an era when Scotland were spoilt for choice, Brazil was certainly worth more than the meagre 13 caps he got; but that was all he ended up with after getting on the wrong side of Jock over a horse called Teenoso.

Teenoso, as our more equine-savvy readers will know, won the Derby in 1983. Alan Brazil, with his connections and by being even more equine-savvy than most, had an inkling way in advance that this was a possibility and managed to get '£100 each way on it at 33/1'. However, once it was announced that the legendary Lester Piggott was going to be on board, the odds tumbled until Teenoso was hot favourite, and a miffed Jock Stein had missed the boat. With us so far, yes? This is categorically not Alan Brazil's fault, right? So you'll be as surprised as Alan was when Stein came sniffing 'for "a bit of your bet at twenty fives". I genuinely thought he was joking. I couldn't believe he was seriously trying to muscle in on one of his players' bets. I just laughed, shook my head and said, "No chance."

'The following day the manager pulled me at training. Looking very stern, he said, "Have you had a chance to think about what I said? Maybe we could agree on sixteens?"'

Brazil refused; Stein asked for 12/1 as a final offer – once again Brazil refused. Brazil enjoyed his own winnings – and Stein never picked him again. Now, as with Ray Stewart, we'd be prepared to believe that the player might be laying it on a bit thick and in fact they had just lost their place for footballing reasons, except for the fact that this story is corroborated in detail by both Spurs team-mate Graham Roberts and John Wark, so we're inclined to believe it.

We're certain none of that sort of thing goes on with the Three Lions, even if the England team have had their fair share of oddballs at the helm. Let's take a look at a few of them:

SAM ALLARDYCE

Perhaps it passed you by because you were on a short holiday or involved in a box-set binge watch, but Sam Allardyce was briefly England manager a while back. He breezed in, claimed he 'fit the chair', won his only game (100 per cent record), got involved in a bit of business he probably regrets, and left again. But it could have all been so different had he been given his chance much earlier, when Steve McLaren got the gig; and he would have got away with it too, if it hadn't been for the pesky lack of PowerPoint facilities.

Allardyce insists that he was denied a chance to give of his best at the interview by the fact that he prepared his presentation on PowerPoint, but had no way of showing it to the FA panel, beyond printing it all out and handing it round. 'So much for the progressive FA,' says Sam, while the harsher among us might say that he could have checked what facilities were available first and that if you fail to prepare then you prepare to fail, Sam.

ALF RAMSEY

Sir Alf will always have a place in the hearts of the nation after winning what looks increasingly like our only World Cup, and yet he remains an enigmatic figure. Famous for his elocution lessons, Ramsey had an apparent desire to bury his Dagenham roots behind a façade he created. Another England manager, and another Dagenham lad, Terry Venables, remembers the time as a player when 'I had met a former neighbour of his and when I saw Alf at training I mentioned that Sid passed on his best wishes. Alf didn't say a thing but turned and walked away.'

This aloofness is a recurring theme with Alf, but we found an alternative view in the course of our research. Bobby Charlton, a man who got to glimpse behind the curtain more than most, speaks warmly of Alf as an 'engaging and funny' man, adding: 'In the right setting, and in the right mood, he was happy enough to do his version of the Lambeth Walk.' Now hold on, that we would have liked to see. One wonders what his own version of the popular classic involved, and what occasion he would have deemed suitable for busting it out, if not becoming world champions.

DON REVIE

The Don of Elland Road eventually replaced Sir Alf, and while there's no sign of a Lambeth Walk, he certainly had his own ideas about maintaining a happy squad.

Peter Storey, a man not averse to making a sly pound note on the side, says that he and other England players were unimpressed at Revie's initial gathering of potential England players when he told them he had got their 'appearance money raised from £100 to £300'. This didn't wash with an old traditionalist like Storey, who insists that playing for England was 'all about honour and pride', accuses Revie of 'banging on about money' and says that Don was 'a strange character, a bit suspect, with a dark side to him'. It will come as a surprise to nobody upon hearing this that Don Revie never picked Peter Storey to play a game under him.

Trevor Brooking also recalls that first gathering under Revie, at which 'The Revs' summoned 81 potential players for a chat. That's 81. Try making a list of 81 potential players for England now. It may take a while. Brooking's recollection of that meeting isn't the money, but rather that Revie 'announced that he'd adopted "Land of Hope and Glory" as England's anthem'. Really? Did this happen? Can this even happen? If an England manager can choose the anthem, does that mean Gareth Southgate could have chosen 'God Save the Queen' by The Sex Pistols?

SVEN-GÖRAN ERIKSSON

Jack Charlton says of Revie that 'he tried to talk us out of having sex on Fridays. He said that it weakened you.' Well, there was certainly none of that nonsense under the free-thinking Sven.

Jamie Carragher says that Eriksson had his own take on both the hanky and indeed the panky after a story broke early in his reign about girls getting into the team hotel. '"There's no need to have girls in the team hotel," Sven told us. "If you see someone you like, just get her phone number and arrange to go to her house after the game. Then we will have no problems."' He goes on to say, 'Looking back, I think he was being genuine. He was giving us his best tips.'

This sauciness is a recurring theme of Sven's stewardship of The Golden Generation. Both Rio Ferdinand and Ashley Cole recall a story that is similar enough to be the same incident, though slightly different in the details (which is the beauty of reading so many of these autobiographies). What they both agree on is that a few players were relaxing around a TV watching a show that was either discussing Sven's love life in graphic detail or parodying it with actors. Both agree that the players were discussing the TV without realising that Sven was stood in the doorway behind them. Rio suggests that it went down like this:

'I was going, "Look at her! I bet Sven … I mean can you imagine? I bet he was throwing her all over the gaff!" All of a sudden I notice it's very quiet and Sven, standing behind me, goes, "Well, it wasn't quite like that"; he then starts to laugh, says "Good night" and walks out.'

Ashley Cole, meanwhile, insists that it was a Channel 4 parody show which had 'this scene showing "Sven" having sex with some woman over a pool table. All of us started hooting with laughter: three players and two masseurs, belly-aching with laughter, roaring the place down.' Then he has Sven arriving with Steve McClaren, Sammy Lee and Ray Clemence in tow and catching them laughing. 'Sven looked at us, started to smile and then, as calm as you like, laughed it off and said: "My taste isn't that bad."'

Now either Sven constantly wandered around the England camp delivering saucy quips like Roger Moore, or this is the same story remembered slightly differently. For what it's worth, we prefer Rio's version because the presence of Sammy Lee in Ashley Cole's makes us uncomfortable; but either way, you didn't get this with Sir Alf or The Revs.

KEVIN KEEGAN

Keegan has frequently had to answer suggestions that he was somewhat tactically naïve as a manager, and that is borne out from his time as

England boss, with some players suggesting that Keegan never worked on tactics. Gary Neville even says that on one occasion when Les Reed was giving a talk on how they might counter their next opponents, 'Kevin fell asleep. He was sitting on the front row and we could see his shoulders sagging, his head nodding forward. He woke up with a start and all the lads burst out laughing.' And that's why you see Gary Neville on Sky with a shiny floor and a massive TV screen to play with these days, not Kevin.

GLENN HODDLE

Any field with Kevin Keegan in it is a competitive one, but a hill we are prepared to die on is the claim that Glenn Hoddle is, hands down, the oddest man ever to manage England. Before you start, this is not just about his faith healer Eileen Drewery – Paul Merson, for example, speaks very highly of her and the help she gave him in a troubled time. Although, it is a little bit about her.

It would seem that Glenn feels that her powers rubbed off on him, possibly literally – and that he could heal players himself. Gary Neville recalls him 'doing his usual pre-match routine of moving around the players, shaking their hands and touching them just over the heart', while Merson says he did the same to him before the penalty shoot-out v Argentina. He touched his heart, looked him in the eye and told him he wouldn't miss. It's just a shame he didn't have time to get to Paul Ince and David Batty isn't it? To be fair to Glenn, there's photographic evidence of him doing this to Diego Maradona just weeks before he won the World Cup in 1986[25] (see picture section), so you can't blame him for thinking he might have the magic touch.

This idea of Glenn's that his hands are healers reached a peak when Michael Owen got clobbered in a World Cup warm-up game against Morocco and there were worries that he might swallow his tongue until a quick-thinking Dion Dublin span him over. Amid a flurry of medical staff, Glenn says, 'I just felt that I wanted to go out there and do something positive so I put my hand on his body and said a quick prayer … eventually he came round.' Yep, it was probably you, Glenn.

Gary Neville also recalls that the 1998 Argentina game saw Glenn asking 'the staff, including the physios, to walk around the pitch anticlockwise during the game to create positive energy for the team'.

---

25 This was at Ossie Ardiles's Tottenham testimonial game.

Just to clarify, this is a man who openly said that there was no point practising penalties to help on such an occasion, believing all the time that we would be okay because he'd touched everyone above the heart and he had John Gorman moonwalking round the pitch.

Glenn's most infamous episode is dropping Gazza from his World Cup squad, then watching Gazza smash Glenn's hotel room up, all to the strains of Kenny G. In hindsight there may have been a case for leaving a disruptive and past-his-best Gazza at home, and arguably the bigger scandal was not taking Matt Le Tissier, but we can probably all agree that whatever the decision, there was a better way to handle it.

Early in his World Cup diary, Hoddle boasts of Gazza that 'I know how to treat him – with the right mixture of love and discipline'. Oh, Glenn. That right mixture clearly should and could never involve Kenny G, but Hoddle had it playing 'because I felt that some of the players might be a bit nervous walking into a silent room'. Of course they would have been. Each player was asked to walk into a huge, posh hotel room, with just Glenn sat there like Robert De Niro in *Angel Heart* (if you haven't, please do), waiting to give them the thumbs up or down on their World Cup dreams. The G wouldn't calm your nerves – it would put you even further on edge. And so Gazza didn't go to the World Cup and Glenn was left picking lumps of Corby trouser press out of his elegantly coiffured hair while 'Songbird' played on relentlessly behind him.

Appropriately for a French World Cup, Hoddle insists 'Je Ne Regrette Rien' about the selection process. Instead he says that 'the biggest mistake I think I made was in not getting Eileen Drewery out to join us from the start'. That's right, Glenn: the only thing that stopped us winning that World Cup was insufficient mumbo jumbo.

LAWRIE McMENEMY

We know what you're thinking – Lawrie McMenemy was never the England manager. And you'd be right, but perhaps he should have been. He was apparently in contention when Ron Greenwood got it, played a pivotal role in that hilarious Graham Taylor documentary as assistant manager ('He's not even give a fuckin' penalty!' / 'Oh, I don't believe it!' etc.) and, according to his players, was well versed in taking superstar footballers abroad. Alan Ball says of their Southampton days that 'Lawrie was big on lucrative foreign tours. He took us to Malaysia on one trip. Kevin, Mick Channon and myself were the attractions.' Frank Worthington also alludes to this, and Mick Channon confirms that 'we were forever jumping in a plane to go off for a friendly'.

McMenemy was also at one point the England under-21s gaffer, and we love this story of him teasing a young Andy (Andrew) Cole by telling him that he wouldn't be selecting him for a game and having him think he'd done something terribly wrong to be treated in this way: 'I told him the decision had been made; I was not going to pick him. I dragged it out as he continued to protest before then telling him: "Go pack your bag." After another delay and more anguish I added: "You're going with the first team."' With patter like this, maybe Lawrie was a bigger loss to *X Factor* judging than he was to coaching England. Pack your bags – you're coming to boot camp.

* * *

Elsewhere, in a classic of the 'needless to say, I had the last laugh' genre, Lawrie tells of an argument with his great rival Ron Atkinson. Like two rutting stags, the pair were taunting each other when Ron told him to 'Put your semi-finals on the table.' They were in company and Lawrie says, 'He must have forgotten Southampton had won the Cup. Everyone knew that he'd laid himself open and I could have knocked him down with a feather if I'd wanted to. I said nothing.' This is the late 70s, but were it 20 years later we believe this is what was known as 'mugging him off'.

Putting your semi-finals on the table, or even, should we dare to dream, your finals. When all is said and done, for a gaffer, it's the measure of the man. And how you handle those big days and special occasions can make or break you. Lawrie Mac, as we know, had Freddie Starr in tow for one of his finals at Wembley. Atkinson did similarly at Sheffield Wednesday, inviting comedian and professional Scouser Stan Boardman on to the coach 'to do his cabaret act. I wanted every member of that team to feel he was part of a special event.' And nothing says 'special' like a man repeatedly saying 'Fokkers' and 'They bombed our chippy', as you're edging through the crowds towards the twin towers.[26]

---

26 If having comedians on coaches is such a masterstroke, though, why don't teams do it more often, even for run-of-the-mill away games? There's a real gap in the market here: southern-based comics with gigs up north could earn a bit extra on the side by doing a set on the coach while also getting a free ride into the bargain. Everyone's a winner.

Having a comedian to rally the troops on the coach with their act is all well and good, but why bother with all of that when you can do it yourself, like Jim Smith? The Bald Eagle is a gaffer who seems to inspire a lot of loyalty and devotion in some of his players, but the fact that he doesn't mention the following episode in his own autobiography suggests that he might have some regrets about the way he handled taking QPR to Wembley for a Milk Cup Final showdown with his previous team Oxford in 1986.

Leroy Rosenior remembers an astonishing journey this way: 'When we reached Wembley Way, Jim [Smith] stood up at the front of the bus and produced this monkey puppet on the end of his arm for what would be the strangest team-talk in the history of team-talks.' That's right: in his finest hour, on the cusp of his biggest game, Jim Smith went with a monkey puppet. 'Then the monkey started to talk as Jim put on this weird, croaky voice. "Three-nil today, boss. It'll be easy!" Cue very awkward laughter and shifting on seats. That monkey was right, though. The thing is we lost 3–0.'

Tough room. Poor old Jim (and his unnamed simian partner) fell a bit flat here, it would seem. We do love that even the monkey called him 'Boss', not 'Jim', though.

At least, at the very least, Jim had ensured that all of his players were on the coach with him that day, which is more than can be said of Jack 'no shampoo' Charlton. When he took his Sheffield Wednesday side to the FA Cup semis in 1983, 'we set off for the game against Brighton at Highbury without Gary Megson, one of our key players – we didn't discover he wasn't on the coach until we were in the ground'. This seems like quite the oversight, doesn't it? It's one thing for Jack not to notice, and it's ultimately his responsibility, but it doesn't say much for Megson's sparkling personality that all his team-mates failed to notice he wasn't with them. The best thing about this is that Charlton never explains what had happened to Megson, why he missed the coach and what he was up to instead. It's just one of life's mysteries.

It's not all about the coach ride there, though. It's about preparation and relaxing before the game. Vinnie Jones remembers vividly that Bobby Gould had gifts for his Wimbledon squad before their famous FA Cup win. Homemade dolls from Mrs Gould, 'in Wimbledon colours, blue and yellow, and wearing black boots'. A nice, if slightly odd thing for her to do, and naturally it wasn't appreciated by the players. "We all collapsed when it came to the No. 9. She'd knitted Fash's doll in black. Brilliant.'"

A good, racially ambiguous laugh will do its bit to relax a squad, as will a night out, which is why Ian Branfoot took his Southampton players to see the musical *Buddy* before the Zenith Data Systems Cup Final (ask your dad, someone with a better memory than you, or the internet) – a move that Matt Le Tissier describes as 'one of the best things he did as a manager, which tells you a lot about his football decisions'.

A West End show is all well and good if you're in London, but, as the saying goes, 'when in Rome do as the Romans do, and when in Amsterdam head straight for the red light district'. Before a Forest game against European giants Ajax, unconventional management duo Brian Clough and Peter Taylor thought a sightseeing trip was in order. Taylor led the way, as described by Peter Shilton: 'We came across a window where a young woman of some considerable size was sitting, eating a bun. She must have weighed 22 stone and her bottom and thighs were enormous. To a man, we stared at her voluptuous form in both wonder and amazement.'

Whatever gears you up for the game, lads. Who knew that the domination of English teams in Europe was once upon a time built on staring at big lasses in Amsterdam windows?

Shilton received a further taste of Clough and Taylor's big-game preparation once the team reached the final against Hamburg in Madrid, in 1980. The meticulous Shilton was worried that he didn't have a suitable grassy area near the hotel on which to practise, so Clough sent the England keeper, led by Taylor and trainer Jimmy Gordon, to 'a grassed area that's perfect for you, Peter me lad'. Shilton followed Taylor expecting to find a local park, when, on the outskirts of town, Taylor stopped: '"There you go," said Peter. "There's your grassed area." I couldn't believe what Peter was pointing at.

'"Give over. You can't be serious," I said – but he was. Brian Clough and Peter Taylor never believed in pampering their players and I certainly wasn't an exception. We were standing in front of a traffic roundabout, and on it was a perfect circle of grass. Jimmy and I dodged the cars and climbed on to the roundabout. He put two tracksuit tops down as makeshift goalposts and I set to work.'

We know that the past is a different country and all that, and that older football seems like a very different game from the slick product we enjoy these days, but stop to think about this for a moment. The England goalkeeper, on the eve of a European Cup Final, was training in the middle of a roundabout with jumpers for goalposts. But once again, it clearly worked. Shilton kept a clean sheet and Forest retained the European Cup. And that's why Clough is one of the masters.

Alex Ferguson is also clearly in that bracket, due in part to his fearsome reputation in the dressing room – the hairdryer treatment and all that – but we also know he had his subtler moments in there, such as the famous rallying war cry, 'Lads, it's Spurs.' Gary Neville also recalls his team talk before the 1996 FA Cup Final, when United faced Liverpool and their infamous 'Spice Boy' white Armani suits. Despite Liverpool players such as Robbie Fowler insisting that the whole suit thing was blown out of proportion, Neville remembers it forming a cornerstone of the pre-match chat from Ferguson, who told them to 'keep playing the ball around their area because David James will probably be waving at Giorgio Armani up in the directors' box'. You will almost certainly recall that Man United lifted the trophy after David James punched weakly out to a waiting Eric Cantona, who scored the only goal of the game.

That team talk is only topped as our favourite by what Joe Fagan said to Graeme Souness and that fine Liverpool team before they beat Roma on their own ground in the 1984 European Cup Final: 'It was as if Joe was talking to himself. "Big team, big match, must be a good team," he mumbled. "Some good players, some of them have won the World Cup, but I tell you what, they can't be as good as us. Now the bus leaves at 5.30, make sure nobody is late."' That did the trick.

For everything we've learned, and however much we may laugh at the boss man, we can't deny that if you're good enough at it, you go down in history as a legend whose every word is treated as pure gold; Clough, Ferguson, Paisley, Jewell and, of course, the king of the soundbite, Bill Shankly, are all regarded as sages in the game.

Duncan McKenzie tells a very touching and revealing tale of Shankly post-retirement, when he couldn't let go of the game and could often be found loitering around the Everton training ground, which was near his house. McKenzie took a moment from his incessant Mini-jumping and golf-ball-chucking to take on board a nugget of wisdom from Shanks, when he overheard the Liverpool legend addressing a bleary-eyed Terry Darracott as he arrived for training one day. "Morning son, how are you?" Terry said, "Fine Bill, no problems." Shanks, razor sharp as ever, snapped back, "No problems, what do you mean, son? You've got problems and I've got problems. It's when you've got no problems that you have your biggest problem.'"

Which goes to show that not everything Bill Shankly said was pure undiluted wisdom and anecdote-worthy; some of it was just bollocks. And we think every other gaffer can take some comfort in that.

9

Fight! Fight! Fight!
Stramash! Kerfuffle! Schemozzle!

'You won't believe what the fuck's gone on here.'

That, according to Jamie Carragher, was Stevie G's opening gambit when reporting to the Liverpool lads that a slightly unreasonable Craig Bellamy had belted John Arne Riise on the arse with a golf club on that night in Barcelona.

Stevie's wonderfully succinct phrase, brutally direct yet deliciously tantalising, is a line we could have used on many pages in this book. Just chuck it on the front of any of these revelations we uncovered during the course of our reading:

'... the gaffer's ripped the head off a live pigeon!'

'... Mark Dennis's dog's eaten the neighbour's cat!'

'... Gazza's hitting chickens with bars of soap!'

And so on. Feel free to try it with your own examples, or even in everyday life when something remarkable happens: 'Next door have just parked a tank on the drive!' or 'Next door have just put a ruddy great EU flag up a giant flagpole!' or whatever it is your weird neighbours get up to.

Bellamy thwacking Riise ('Ginge' as Craig refers to him) is a wonderful example of the footballer fight, with its involvement of a comical weapon elevating it to the upper tier of football folklore. His explanation of how he came to tee off on his petrified team-mate is enjoyable because of its banality. Turns out, it all started when Bellamy repeatedly asked or told Riise to do some karaoke, and when John eventually snapped and shouted that he wouldn't, Craig was not best pleased, deciding that 'I wasn't going to let it go, especially after a drink'

– because if there's one thing the Welsh take seriously, it's singing. So, based on someone not wanting to belt out 'New York, New York' in front of his peers, and with Steve Finnan at first trying to stop him, then giving up and just deciding it was all too good to miss, Craig went to Riise's room and spanked his bottom through the duvet with an eight iron.

Incredible, really. But footballers live in a pressurised, masculine, testosterone-fuelled world. This kind of thing is inevitable. As fans, we love stories about training ground scraps and we love fights on the pitch. Commentators and pundits always say things like 'We don't like to see this kind of thing' when players start throwing down; but that's nonsense, isn't it? A proper derby, for example, should feature at least a couple of goals, a hotly disputed penalty, a game-changing injury-time goal (or, preferably, two), a row between the two benches and, most importantly, a fight and a couple of red cards. *That's* a derby.

Footballer autobiographies are not shy in reporting the details of fights precisely because footballers, like us, are fans, or were once fans, and they know that deep down we like to see a punch-up and we want details. Very few autobiographies will get from page 1 to page 300 without the juicy red meat of a scrap chucked into the mix.

And what variety there is, too. At one end of the scale you have Sam Allardyce detailing a vicious epic between Bernard Mendy and Akin Bulent at Bolton that started on the training ground and culminated in Sam's office: 'Suddenly, the office door flies open and Bulent comes through the air Eric Cantona style, his right leg fully extended, and bosh! He takes Bernard out at the neck, sending him flying clean off the desk and onto the floor with a smack.' Amazing. Like a scene from a Chuck Norris film. Bulent, by the way, without pausing to utter a kiss-off line like, 'Sorry, I forgot to knock' or 'Hope you're soon on the Mendy', pegged it to the car park after that, as it didn't take long for Bernie to rise menacingly to his feet. Sam must've nodded in appreciation at the scene – in his playing days, he too wasn't above a bit of angry door-smashing, as we know.

And at the other end of the scale, there's John Aldridge's visceral description of an absolute tear-up at Liverpool between Phil Thompson and Wayne Harrison: 'One day I was injured in a training game and had been walking around the pitch when I had to break them up. They were getting ready to thump each other. I don't know what caused it.' Heart-pounding stuff. To recap: two people nearly had a fight, but didn't, and John doesn't know what the non-ruck was about. Wouldn't open with it on the after-dinner circuit, Aldo. If that's the worst he saw, no wonder he doesn't offer up a Top 8 Fracas list.

Mendy, Bulent, Harrison. Three names never mentioned again in terms of scraps in the books we read (or, for that matter, in any other context). Some players, though, barely seem to be able to get through a season without some sort of fisticuffs. Six names in particular come up again and again, always apparently ready for one more round.

STAN COLLYMORE

DETAILS: A lover and a fighter. To be fair to Stan, he doesn't shy away from his fights and details most of them himself in his book. He's had some kind of to-do with (at least): Mark Bright, Geoff Thomas, Alf-Inge Haaland, Andy Todd and Trevor Benjamin. Plus, he once tried to storm into the Sky studio at a Bradford game – in full kit, mind you – to get at Keysie, who'd said something about him on the telly. That would have made an interesting confrontation – one suspects that Richard would have had more than his back doors smashed in.

However, he doesn't even mention a brawl he had with goalie Tony Warner at Liverpool, despite the fact it's gleefully reported in the books of Jamie Carragher, Jason McAteer and Collymore's apparent nemesis, Robbie Fowler. One of the lovely things about fight stories is the intrigue – no two people ever have exactly the same version of events – but the gist of this one seems to be that the Liverpool lads were having dinner in a hotel, but there was no chair in Stan's place. So Stan asked – or told – junior squad member Warner to give up his seat for him. When Warner refused, there was an almighty melee. From there, while trying to keep the peace, boss Roy Evans got a smack, either on the nose or mouth. McAteer reckons there was 'blood all over the hotel dining room'. Blimey. Seems a big enough deal for Stan to remember, but when you've had as many fights as he's had, maybe they all blur into one.

BEST PUNCH: A set-to with Leicester team-mate Trevor Benjamin. It starts when Benjamin doesn't take kindly to Collymore offering some coaching during a reserve game and it kicks off in the dressing room, with punches thrown: 'Everybody scattered. Chairs and tables went flying and it was a real kerfuffle.' Eventually, but probably only after a good look, some team-mates broke it up. Bonus points for use of the word 'kerfuffle' – a fluffy word for a bit of violence.

DAVID SPEEDIE

DETAILS: It doesn't look like Speedo's committed his life story to paper yet,[27] which is a shame because we'd like to get his side of a few events found in other books. One thing seems sure, though – he wasn't afraid of a bit of physicality. Mickey Thomas writes: 'Speedie was volatile with a capital "V". Joey (Jones) said the little man had twelve fights in his career – and never won one.'

Surprisingly, it seems Speedie and Kerry Dixon (another one happy to let his fists do some talking) didn't get on despite their profitable partnership up front for Chelsea: 'I didn't like David Speedie,' says Dixon, before recalling the time he punched him in the face after they'd had a row on the pitch. Speedie also lost out to Paul Canoville – Thomas recalls that one as 'a real belter', but we get little more than that.

BEST PUNCH: Speedo once had a scrap with the genuinely terrifying Terry Hurlock while at Southampton – now that is a fight we'd all pay to see were they to be thrown into a UFC cage together. You know it was a good one because both Dixon and Matt Le Tissier bring it up in their books.

It took place during a bonding session on the Isle of Wight, instigated by manager Ian Branfoot in an effort to sort out their sorry season. However, during a team meeting, alcohol was taken and soon the battle began: 'Very few people would ever dare tangle with Terry Hurlock but David Speedie didn't worry about that. There were a few punches thrown and a bit of blood,' recalls Le Tiss. But then comes the kicker, from Dixon: 'As the fight was breaking up, Terry picked up a glass ashtray from one of the tables and hurled it at Speedo (who ducked), hitting Mickey Adams on the side of the head. There was blood everywhere.' Dixon says Hurlock and Speedie spent the night in cells; Tiss reckons poor Adams had to join them, despite being an innocent

---

27 'A Speedie Story'? Maybe. 'The Speedo Files'? Probably not.

victim. A sorrier sight it's hard to imagine – innocent Adams, with his resemblance to poor little Ralph Wiggum from *The Simpsons*, sporting a cut eye, huddled in a corner of the cell, trying to persuade Speedo and Hurlo not to go one more round.

Speedie never played for Saints again.

KEITH GILLESPIE

DETAILS: Despite his infamous super-fast sending off after elbowing Stephen Hunt seconds after coming on as sub while turning out for Sheffield United against Reading, Gillespie doesn't immediately feel like a serial scrapper. Yet in his own book he mentions rumbles with: a fan in a nightclub, his Blades boss Kevin Blackwell, an irate husband (see 'Top Shelf' chapter), Alan Shearer and Blackburn reserve boss Alan Murray. Plus, Robbie Savage reckons he got 'his nose splattered' by Nicky Butt when they were all kids at Man United.

BEST PUNCH: It's worth seeking out Gillespie's book to enjoy the full glory of his falling-out with Blackwell, which ends with them swapping brilliant insults: '"That cunt over there," he said, pointing at me. "Fuck off you cunt." "You're a fucking cunt." "You fucking egg." "You're a fucking egg."' Weird that 'fucking egg' seems to be a threat level up from the C-bomb, but anyway.

Still, his well-known fight with Shearer just edges it. The Newcastle squad are in Dublin and Gillespie starts to annoy Shearer by pinging bottle tops at him. Things deteriorate after Keith knocks some cutlery on the floor, they argue, and then: 'For some reason, I asked him if he wanted to take it outside. Madness … We emerged to a busy street, where Sunday afternoon shoppers were going about their business. It didn't deter me from the battle-plan. I took a swing at Shearer but I was punch-drunk and inaccurate.

'He responded with a blow that sent me flying backwards against a plant pot. I cracked my head and entered the blackout zone.' Beautifully told, with all the sense of a sober mind looking back at the crazily muddled thinking of a booze-addled brain. Although he's misunderstood the phrase punch-drunk there, hasn't he? That usually describes a boxer looking groggy after taking a few heavy punches. Gillespie wasn't that yet – just proper drunk.

ZLATAN IBRAHIMOVIC

DETAILS: Never far from a fight is Ibra. Even his best mate at Ajax, Mido, once chucked a pair of scissors at his head, only narrowly missing. ('Of course I went over and gave him a smack, a slap.' Of course.)

There's a thing Zlatan does in his book quite a lot – he likes to jump into stories towards the end, at a point where he's being wronged, but as you feel sympathy for him, his instinct to be truthful kicks in, and you get the fuller picture. For example, when relating a story about his early days at Malmo, he laments that an 'idiot father' of one of his team-mates got a petition together to get him out of the club. 'It was mental,' he says. Sounds it. Then he admits: 'Okay, I'd been in a fight with that dad's son. I'd taken a load of nasty tackles, and I went off on one. I'd headbutted him, if I'm honest.' Oh, right – that's called 'burying the lead', Zlatan. To be fair, Ibra did apologise to the kid – while he was in hospital.

BEST PUNCH: Ibrahimovic had a decent skirmish with Jonathan Zebina, but his grapple with American defender Oguchi Onyewu (aka 'Gooch') at Milan sounds epic, as the kids like to say. Onyewu had annoyed him by 'shushing' him during training, so Zlatan launched a nasty tackle on him the next chance he got – just the standard response to a shushing. He didn't quite make the contact he wanted, but it didn't matter, because seconds later, after a blow from Onyewu, it was *on*: 'I headbutted him, and then we flew at each other. I'm not talking about a little scrap. We wanted to tear each other limb from limb. It was brutal. We were two guys who each weighed over 14 stone, and we were rolling round, punching and kneeing each other, and, of course, the whole team rushed over and tried to separate us. That wasn't easy, not at all.' Like trying to get between The Hulk and The Thing, we shouldn't wonder. 'It was like life and death. And the weirdest thing happened afterwards. Oguchi Onyewu started praying to God with tears in his eyes. He made the sign of the cross, and I thought, "What is this?" I got even more furious. It felt like a provocation.' Never pray in front of Zlatan.

ROBBIE SAVAGE

DETAILS: Sav's career was (is) probably one long argument, just with different people in front of him for different intervals. We already know he had physical altercations with Simon Royce and

Alan Birchenall, but he also swapped blows with Nico Vaesen, Clinton Morrison and Rio Ferdinand. Then there's also the bizarre chocolate-cake-smearing-on-face incident with Dennis Wise, which hints that his willingness to resort to the fists may be because his verbal game is a little lacking.

BEST PUNCH: Sav doesn't seem to have any truly great fights, but his wrestle with Morrison at least has a nice premise: Robbie had a new phone, Clinton liked it, Savage got hold of one for him, Clinton seemed to avoid paying him, and, well, one thing led to another. 'We were in the canteen, and I ended up diving on him. We were wrestling on this collapsible table, and David Dunn split us up … I outmuscled him that day – and I never got the money.' This is a bit much, isn't it? Slamming each other through tables like they're in a WWE No Disqualification match? All over a phone? Even if it cost a grand, that's the equivalent of your two authors laying the smack down over a fiver.

PAOLO DI CANIO

DETAILS: The thing about Paolo is that while he probably did have the occasional dust-up with other players, in the main it was authority he raged against (surprising, since he seems to quite like dictators). There was referee Paul Alcock, of course, who he shoved to the deck for sending him off. And then there were the managers. Paolo had rucks with Giovanni Trapattoni, Fabio Capello and most brilliantly, Big Ron Atkinson.

BEST PUNCH: Big Ron is a large man, and even though he was in his late 50s when managing Di Canio at Sheffield Wednesday, he would certainly have presented an intimidating figure, yet you get the impression Paolo Di Canio wouldn't be intimidated by an angry grizzly. This fight occurred after a 3–2 defeat at Bolton. Atkinson, uncharacteristically according to PDC, was fuming at the final whistle. He called Paolo a 'fucking prick', accused him of being scared and told him he should be ashamed to pick up his wages.

Accusing Di Canio of not caring, or of letting the fans down, is a bit like telling Marty McFly he's chicken. They faced off: '"Who the fuck do you think you are, talking to me like that?" I screamed. "You're the one who should be ashamed! You come to training once a week! Once a week! You, of all people, should be silent! Even if they paid you one pound a week, you would still be a thief!"'

This, as you might expect, did not improve Ron's mood: 'By now, his face had gone from red to purple. He was shaking, hyperventilating. I could see foam and saliva drooling out of his mouth.' This reminds us of an old clip we once saw of a press conference when Ron was at Man United. He had a blob of tea nestling in the corner of his mouth throughout. Still makes us feel queasy. 'He just kept repeating, over and over, in a hoarse whisper: "You fucking prick! You fucking prick!" I leaned towards him and said, as calmly as I could: "Come on, come here. I'm right here, who's fucking scared now?" It went off immediately. I was still standing on the bench when the punches started flying. He looked like a man possessed.'

Amazing. What a ruck that would have been. Apparently it took several people to break it up, but why people break up fights has always been beyond us. Let them get on with it, particularly if it's two absolute bulls on the rampage, like with this pairing.

We'd love to be able to compare this with Ron's version of events, but in his recent autobiography, while listing his thoughts on 'foreign players I've managed', all we get is a dismissive 'Paolo Di Canio was simply mad.' Well, he was after you repeatedly called him a 'fucking prick', Ron.

THEY SHOULD'VE SOLD TICKETS

Remember the days? Saturday nights, ITV. The glory years. Benn, Eubank, Watson. Great boxers all. And millions watching. These days it'd cost you upwards of £30 to watch boxing of that quality on your telly. Those stone-cold classics were shared sporting experiences. The problem with footballer fights is that, unless they're during a game, the 'crowd' often barely reaches double figures and, as we said, bloody do-gooders keep breaking them up. We saw none of these doozies below – but we wish we had.

John Hartson v Bobby Gould

This one was so bizarre, so utterly jaw dropping, that it was passed around joyfully between football fans and made it into football folklore long before it ever appeared in anyone's autobiography. For the uninitiated, it took place when Gould was managing Wales, and, well, there's no sugarcoating it, he decided the needle that had developed between him and Hartson needed to be sorted out the old-fashioned way – by wrestling.

Craig Bellamy was an open-mouthed spectator as Gould instructed Hartson to 'vent all his frustration to rid himself of all the resentment he was feeling by expressing himself in the wrestling. I suppose it was the equivalent of getting a kid to hit a punchbag, except in this case the punchbag was the manager of the national team.' One of these men was hurled to the floor like a rag doll. But who did the throwing? Well, Hartson obviously. 'When Gould got to his feet, he was holding his nose and looking aggrieved. Blood was streaming out of it.'

Just to be clear, this was the manager of the national team fighting with his star striker. It's like Hoddle offering out Shearer, Bobby Robson taking on Gary Lineker, Giggsy (assuming he doesn't pull out of the Wales get-togethers with a minor knock) putting up against Bale. Incredible. But this is how it should be: everyone standing in a tight circle, just like at school, creating a makeshift gladiatorial arena. With any luck, Barry Horne, Ceri Hughes and Karl Ready were all chanting 'Fight! Fight! Fight!' in time-honoured fashion as Hartson showed Bobby who was boss.

Roy Keane v Peter Schmeichel

It's barely worth hating Man United these days, but back in the 1990s most of the population of Britain was, well, united in despising the not-yet-knighted Alex Ferguson, his team, and in particular their smug hordes of fans born, raised and still based in the home counties, who'd only been to Old Trafford once, and then only for a guided tour of the trophy room as a tenth birthday present. Anyway, where were we? Oh yes, United.

Well, everyone had their particular player to dislike, whether it was Steve Bruce, Paul Ince or Paul Parker (only joking – everyone loves Paul Parker). But pretty much all fans loved to hate Keano and Schmeichs. Therefore, watching these two – the temple-vein-throbbing psycho versus the red-nosed Viking behemoth – pitilessly whale on each other would have been a particular pleasure.

Keane says that trouble had been brewing between them for a while because he didn't like the way Peter would shout at the defence all the time – Keane felt like he was playing to the fans a bit; fair point. Anyway, it all came to a head in a hotel after a bit of … wait for it … *banter*. On leaving Nicky Butt's room after a bite a little later, Roy found Pete waiting for him, anxious to do some air-clearing, as it were: 'So I said, "Okay." And we had a fight. It felt like ten minutes. There was a lot of noise – Peter's a big lad.' Sadly, we don't get much more than that, although Keane adds Schmeichel wore shades on the flight home, 'and it wasn't very sunny'. True to form in what, we cannot lie, is a pretty dull book, Schmeichel doesn't even mention this epic. So Keane probably won.

The footnote is that they were had up before the beak, well, Fergie, when they got home after Sir Bobby Charlton himself grassed them up. Turns out they woke the poor bugger up as they went pell-mell in the hotel. Keane sniffs: 'Peter took responsibility for the fight, which was good. I admired him for it. But Sir Bobby could have tried to break it up.' Imagine Bobby Charlton, even then a man of advanced years, trying to stop Keane v Schmeichel! He'd have been crushed! Plus, he had just woken up: he'd have been trying to stop it in his silk pyjamas, or the hotel's terry towelling dressing gown. Not ideal attire for a spot of peacekeeping. We like to picture him in that big woolly hat he wears in the stands in the winter, and we wouldn't want to see it knocked off in a stramash.

Stuart Pearce v Brian Clough

This didn't quite turn into a fight, but it is weird enough for us to want to have seen it. The back story is that Clough had substituted Pearce for Brian Laws (in Pearce's book he admits he can vividly remember each of the few times he was substituted by Clough – he did not like being hooked at all), and Clough had then made a show of praising Laws for his performance. Laws picks up the story back in the dressing room: 'He (Pearce) stood with his arms stretched out like metal rods. His fists were clenched and he was staring right through Cloughie.'

Arms stretched out like some sort of angry robot? Terrifying. Laws continues, and it's worth quoting this in full: 'Cloughie said: "Have you ever been punched by a manager?" Still Psycho stood with his arms outstretched. We're all thinking: "Oh God, something's really going to kick off here."

'Cloughie moved in very quickly with a rabbit punch to Pearcey's stomach. Stuart never had so much as flinched as we all held our breath. Then Cloughie took two steps back and said: "You're the nearest thing in football that I can call a friend – and a friend will never hit a friend! You wouldn't hit an old man, Stuart, now would you?" At this point, Cloughie stood away. Psycho was still glaring. If looks could kill! I'm sure at that moment Stuart wanted to fight back. But he didn't. He had too much respect for Cloughie. But one thing he insisted on doing was standing his ground. And as we all went for a bath, still Psycho stood there. It was a moment in football that I will never forget.'

And now you know why they called him Psycho. If only someone had had the balls to hang a couple of towels on his arms to make him resemble an avant-garde towel rack. Props to Clough for risking a punch in that situation – it's a step up from cuffing those lads on the pitch as they ran past him back towards the stands.

Stan Ternent v Kevin Blackwell

Keith Gillespie says in his book that Kevin Blackwell enjoyed referencing the time he knocked out Stan Ternent, but as Blackwell hasn't written a book, all we can go on here are the words on that encounter from Stan himself. And it's a good-un. Stan's furious at the end of a Sheffield United v Burnley match – Ternent and then Blades boss Neil Warnock are not exactly best buds. He's just taken his player Paul Cook to the referee's office to show him an injury from a challenge, when an unimpressed Blackwell yells at him: "'You're always at it, you!" I call that red rag to a bull. I shouted "We'll have it now."

'I ran up, smacked him in the face and nutted him for good measure, banging him hard. He hit me back and my nose ruptured. Here we go. I jumped on him and we fell to the floor, shoving the door to the ref's room wide open. From all sides, stewards and United staff pounced on to my back and tried to pull me off Blackwell. Eventually, they dragged me away. I'd given him a quick crack and a couple of follow-ups. I hadn't had an option. He offered me out, so I hit him.'

So if Blackwell *did* knock Ternent out, Stan isn't admitting to it. More importantly, what is Stan going on about at the end there? By his own telling of this story, Blackwell absolutely didn't offer him out. He raised an objection. Of course you had options, Stan. *Not* headbutting him was another, quite obvious, option for starters.

Stuart McCall v Dean Saunders

The authority on this story is Dean Windass, and it occurred in the aftermath of Bradford's 5–4 defeat by West Ham in the Premier League, after they'd been 4–2 up. Saunders apparently tried to shoot to make it 5–2 instead of passing to Windass for a tap-in, but hit the post. It would have been game over, but instead West Ham rallied for a memorable comeback. Stuart McCall was not happy with Saunders's perceived selfishness, and told him so after the game. Windass remembers:

'Dean wouldn't back down and told him: Shut it, you prick. Then it all went off. One thing Stuart didn't like was people calling him a prick and Dean said it a couple of times. They were at each other's throats and everyone had to jump in the middle. It was like the fight at the OK Corral.'

So, not much in the way of detail, then, but two lovely bits from Windass. First, that McCall particularly did not like being called a prick. Really grinds his gears, that does. And second, how was it like the fight at the OK Corral? That was five cowboys against four lawmen; they used guns (30 shots in 30 seconds, apparently), not fists/heads/feet; and that fight was outdoors, not indoors. And Wyatt Earp's team hadn't just lost 5–4 to West Ham either.

John Burridge v Ossie Ardiles

John Burridge's book is a fascinating read – from the title (*The Autobiography of Goalkeeping Legend …* that's probably for others to say, John) right to the end, it's a breathtaking tour de force of often comical hubris, characterised by his ability to fall out with almost every manager he played for, plus many players besides. But he has a particular dislike of Ossie Ardiles, which dates back to a Southampton–Spurs game.

This is Budgie's story, but he doesn't come out of it as well as he seems to think he does. It starts with Spurs 1–0 down and Burridge trying to time-waste by not giving Ardiles the ball for a corner. Then, as Ardiles runs off, Budgie admits to shoving him, and says Ardiles goes down claiming an elbow. This annoys Burridge and now he's spoiling for a fight: 'Because people used to try to stand on me at corners all the time, I used to retaliate by breaking the metatarsal bone in the top of their foot. I used to work on my back studs – filing them down so they were like arrowheads … I'd bring my left or right boot down on the striker's metatarsal – BANG!' Burridge explains this violence away by claiming a striker would do the same to him if he got the chance. So, Budgie was merely getting his retaliation in first. He went for it as Spurs took that late corner: 'Ossie tried to get in a sneaky stamp, trying to tread on my feet. There was only one thing for it – I gave him the old two-studs combination on the metatarsal, and he went down in absolute agony.'

Ardiles doesn't mention this incident in his fairly dry book, so it's difficult to be sure, but the chain of events is: Burridge time-wastes; Burridge pushes Ardiles; Ardiles complains, possibly exaggerating; Ardiles tries but somehow fails (is that possible?) to stamp (or tread – two very different words, there) on Burridge; Burridge stamps on Ardiles with sharpened studs.

Yeah. So far, we're on Ardiles's side.

After the game, Ossie was still angry, possibly justifiably so, and was shouting at Burridge as the teams left the pitch. At the Dell, there was a set of stairs going down just inside the tunnel and Budgie claims Ardiles gave him a shove down the first few steps: 'I tried to control my temper, but he was still gobbing off at me, so I smacked him … Britain had just been at war with Argentina over the Falklands, and I lost it at that stage, shouting: "We've just beat you in the Falklands, now I've just beaten you here, now fuck off!"'

We tracked down this game based on Burridge's details, and it can only have been played at Christmas 1987. So, 'just been at war' equates to, you know, just the five years after the Falklands conflict. Never forget, eh, John?

Burridge later claims that Ardiles took his revenge by getting rid of him when he became manager of Newcastle. But while he doesn't come out well of his own anecdote, we have found that he wasn't the only footballer to have taken against Ardiles. We've always fully bought into his charming 'in the Cup for Totting-ham' shtick, but it seems he's quite adept at getting people's backs up.

- Graham Roberts fell out with him when Ossie became Spurs manager: 'Manners were never his strong suit at the best of times,' Roberts sniffs.

- Neil Ruddock was upset by comments Ardiles made about him after he (Ruddock) left Spurs.

- While at Torquay as a teenager, Lee Sharpe nutmegged a Spurs player in a cup game: 'Then the ball went out for a throw, and as I went to pick it up, I was shoved in the back, and I turned round and Ossie Ardiles was in my face, wagging a finger, shaking his head, going "tut, tut, tut" … I think he was saying you shouldn't go around nutmegging people when you're only 16, that it isn't respectful.' Yeah, all right, Ossie, was it respectful to do that rainbow flick against the German in *Escape to Victory*, mate?

- This shouldn't really count against Ossie, but he rubbed referee Clive Thomas up the wrong way too: 'I have thought of him as an excellent player, yes. But Ossie, a little man, can still manage to look down at you.' Ouch.

- Pat Van Den Hauwe, similarly to John Burridge, reckons Ardiles wreaked sweet revenge on him when he was manager of Spurs because of a challenge earlier in their careers: 'I went in hard on Ossie Ardiles and he was rolling around on the ground squealing like a baby. I stood over him and told him he was a whining Argie bastard and to get up. It was a comment that years later came back and bit me on the arse big time.' Pat says Ossie, with his long memory, didn't pick him when he was Spurs boss. The professional thing to do when out of favour might be to knuckle down, work hard in training, and prove your worth. Pat had no truck with that sort of nonsense: 'I booted his door open, I almost took it off its hinges and he shit himself!' Fairly understandable, as Pat says he then threatened to chuck Ossie out of the window. 'One wrong word from him and I'd have given him a proper hiding there and then.' Well, it's one way of putting in a transfer request.

So there we go – the dark side of lovely old Ossie. Who knew?

There is a fight, however, that we genuinely could have bought tickets for: Graham Roberts v Frank McAvennie. They famously had a bit of needle dating back to an Old Firm game in which the latter was sent off. Roberts's memory of that skirmish is crystal-clear: 'Sensing Big Terry (Butcher) would probably have killed him I grabbed McAvennie by the throat and tried to haul him out of the way.' Yes, because when you're trying to protect someone the first thing you always reach for is their throat, isn't it? Check that one out on YouTube and see if you think Roberts is remembering it accurately.

Anyway, this pair ended up having a couple of actual boxing matches after their playing careers ended. The first ended in a draw, while the second was officiated by special guest referee and actual boxer Steve Collins, who apparently told Roberts before the bout: 'There's no chance of a former Rangers player winning while I'm the referee.' Roberts was up against it, then. He says he won easily as Frank was 'in even worse shape than me', but nevertheless Collins still raised the former Celtic man's arm at the end. 'It should have been a bit of fun but I stormed out of the ring in a right huff because I was so disgusted.'

But what about this concept of legalised scrapping between middle-aged out-of-shape ex-sportsmen? Either it should not happen at all or it should happen a lot more often and be televised by the BBC at Christmas. We're not sure which.

So, delve into almost any footballer autobiography and you'll likely hit a juicy scrap at some point – amazingly, all the above is merely the tip of the fight-berg. We haven't even mentioned:

- A furious Paul Jewell shutting an equally angry Jimmy Bullard's head in a door.

- Graeme Souness breaking the jaw of Dinamo Bucharest's Lica Movila in two places – as retaliation for some shirt-pulling (well, it is annoying).

- Lee Sharpe's revelation that at Torquay they invented a sort of football/Fight Club hybrid called, accurately, 'murder ball', where they'd play training matches with no rules: 'Everybody piled in, volleying the back of people's legs, scraping trainers down their thighs, booting their calves; it was kill or be killed.' Bloody hell.

- The time Tommy Docherty got roughed up by some fans on a train. This was after the scandal about Docherty getting involved with Mary Brown, the wife of the Man United physio. He was on his way

170

to Stockport and was spotted by some rowdy Man City fans who duly reeled off a few naughty songs about his indiscretions. The Doc bravely told them off and assumed that was the end of the matter. Only it wasn't: 'About a couple of hours earlier, Denis Law, who was also travelling north and sitting a short distance away from me, had come up to say hello and we had passed the time of day. As the train came to a halt and I put down my suitcase and leaned out of the window to open the door, I received a violent blow on the back of the head. As I turned round I could see this same group of City supporters were right on top of me.'

Terrifying, but he's mentioned Denis Law there – surely the appropriately named Lawman would step in and help out his old boss? Granted, they weren't BFFs after The Doc told the press about his free transfer from Man United, but still. The man needed help. 'There were about four or five of them and before I knew it I was on the ground and they were kicking hell out of me. But I was on my own as the boots came piling in.' There was a devil of a schemozzle with people shouting and screaming. Only when the hooligans had gone off, leaving me lying there on the platform, did some of the other passengers come up and give me a hand.' Oh. Well, maybe Law had got off at the previous stop.

- This, from Kevin Keegan, in relation to his iconic punch-up with Billy Bremner: 'Perhaps it was my fighting spirit, or my Irish ancestry showing itself.' Because the Irish love to fight, don't they? Fighting and booze, that's the Irish. And blarney. Keegan also muses, while discussing the longevity of Gordon Strachan and Billy Bremner's playing careers: 'They say all redheads are freaks.' Do they, Kev?

- And a bizarre story from Alan Ball about pinning Portsmouth chairman Jim Gregory up against a wall because he'd just slapped athlete Ron Jones in the face. He'd slapped Ron Jones in the face because he'd brought him to his office and asked him to play a song on his guitar and Gregory didn't like the song. It's a tale as old as time, isn't it?

But we can't sign off this chapter without our favourite fight story – one that comes complete with samurai swords and traffic cones. Not surprisingly, because his book is full of crackers stuff like this, this is a

Chic Charnley tale and it happened while he was enjoying one of his 20-odd spells at Partick Thistle.

Unlike the rest of our fight stories, it wasn't with other players, but with a couple of herberts who had been heckling the squad during training. Charnley had sent them away with an offer to discuss things further later, and was a bit surprised when they returned – and this time they were tooled up. Not with a standard flick knife or a set of knuckle-dusters, either – one went for a carving knife, while the other was wielding an actual sabre, 'one of those curved Japanese-type weapons that would terrify the life out of you'. To complete the picture, they'd also enlisted an angry dog for added intimidation.

Fight or flight duly kicked in; and for Chic and the Partick boys, flight was not an option: 'We started to run in their direction and, amazingly, the first thing to scarper was the dog! ... As I raced towards the moron with the Samurai I picked up a traffic cone. It didn't look like a fair fight, but there wasn't anything else handy ... I was waving the traffic cone above my head and was startled when he stopped abruptly and, as I got closer, swung the sabre at me. I instinctively put out my hand and I felt the blade slash through my palm.' Christ, it's like a scene from a Kurosawa samurai epic. Only with, you know, a bit more football training paraphernalia than you'd usually find in 16th-century Japan. 'I was raging, to say the least, and I dropped the traffic cone. I wasn't going to back out, though. I whacked him with a right-hander and down he went in a heap, thankfully releasing his weapon as he did so. We were now on a level footing both unarmed. I won't go into the gory details, but, suffice to say, we never saw those guys again when we were training.'

No gory details? You might as well, Chic, you left in the bit about almost having your hand sliced off. You're lucky you weren't literally unarmed, mate. What a story, though, and there's even a lesson in there too: there's no point taking a knife to a gunfight, but you might be able to get away with taking a traffic cone to a swordfight if you're hard enough.

10

Banter, Tomfoolery and Hi-Jinks

Keen mooner

Few things are more important in the life of the average footballer than good, solid banter. We know this because when ex-footballers talk about what they miss about the game, it's not scoring goals, winning trophies or having a job that effectively involves two hours of advanced PE a few days each week. No, what they really miss is The Banter.

This may not always have been the case. Did Wilf Mannion mope about after retirement, missing the sheer, visceral adrenaline rush of cutting up someone's shoes? Did Billy Wright struggle to contain the urge to set off and aggressively wield a fire extinguisher every time he stayed in a hotel while on holiday with his Beverly Sister missus? Was Tom Finney continually disappointed at his wife's failure to 'take a joke' after he'd laced her best knickers with Deep Heat? We simply have no way of knowing.

But somewhere along the line, banter became big, and there's no doubt the misty-eyed longing for the golden-hued days of top, top 'bant' by ex-pros has been around a long while. Garry Nelson was already reporting on the phenomenon in his groundbreaking book of 1996: 'Ask any ex-pro what he most misses about the game and I'm sure that without a moment's hesitation he'll answer "the changing-room banter".'

We found corroborating words in many other autobiographies. Ashley Cole says that 'good banter is part of a healthy dressing room' (note the use of 'good' – just an inference there, that 'bad' banter can, and indeed does, exist[28]). While Sir Alex Ferguson comments, 'Of course I'll miss the banter of the dressing room.' Now, he probably just means he'll miss the thrill of some sharp verbal jousting with Mike Phelan or Patrice Evra, but to us it conjures images of Fergie hilariously setting fire to David May's new Armani suit. And that raises an important point. When ex-players or retired managers talk about missing the banter, what, exactly, are they referring to? After all, the dreaded word has taken a fairly dramatic shift over the last few years. Is it just, as Jimmy Greaves charmingly calls it in his autobiography, 'tomfoolery and hi-jinks'? Or is it something more complex?

These days, 'banter' can mean innumerable things, but it wasn't that long ago, certainly well within our lifetimes, that it had nothing to do with pranking, forced nudity or bodily fluids. Instead, 'banter' was humorous, clever discourse – the sort of thing done with aplomb by what we might term the Oscar Wildes of this world when in relaxed mood with other well-educated, intelligent young men wearing cravats and, possibly, knickerbockers. It was smart word play; cutting put-downs; fast-paced, witty repartee between two or more eloquent wordsmiths. That sort of thing.

But by the early 2010s, if not before, the word had widened its remit quite spectacularly to encompass things like pranks, crude insults, politically incorrect chat and sundry 'laddish behaviour'. The poor word finally reached its nadir when it became the standard defence when a public figure texted something racist or was caught saying something sexist, Keysie. Even the Leader of the Free World himself, Sir Donald Trump, believed it to be the correct term to use (with the mandatory American prefix of 'locker room', natch) when trying to explain away his apparent bragging about actual sexual assault. Rarely has a single word been laid so low, so fast.

While there's not a lot of Trump-level horror in footballer autobiographies (thankfully), there is a ton of laddish banter. In fact, we've sort of been dreading this chapter a bit, because we feared we might drown in the torrent of slurry released once we decided to crank open the figurative Thames Barrier holding back all the mega-bantz found within the books we read. Because it really is *absolutely everywhere*.

---

28 Like shooting a young intern with an air rifle, for example.

There's no denying that some of it is very enjoyable, and some of the best anecdotes concern the camaraderie between the players and what they get up to away from the game. But some of it is pretty awful. As Tony Cascarino writes, 'In English football a black humour pervades and at times borders on the depraved.' The Crazy Gang wouldn't have been for Cas, then (although, conversely, his style of play would have suited Wimbledon perfectly), because they truly were the original banter merchants – so Crazy it's a wonder it wasn't spelled with a K. To demonstrate what Cas is driving at, here's a quote from Crazy Gang ringleader Vinnie Jones, comparing the banter that existed in each of his two spells at the club: 'Back then, cars would be smeared in Vaseline, car tyres let down, potatoes wedged up exhaust pipes … New arrivals this time round had their bootlaces cut and dodgy clothes removed and burned, and they were rugby-tackled, stripped and flung into a patch of nettles and into a river.'

That's right; The Gang had a kind of checklist of things that new signings had to endure on arrival, ranging from vehicular inconvenience to exposing them to the possibility of contracting Weil's disease. You can almost imagine Wisey or later Peter Fear (or is it Warren Barton? So tough to tell) standing there with a clipboard, joylessly ticking things off to make sure nothing gets missed. There's a real sense that after a while they simply started getting bogged down in the admin of it all and completely lost the spontaneity they once had.

Such Crazy Gang antics might make your heart sink or soar depending on your sense of humour, but it would take someone with a particularly strong constitution to avoid a groan of dread at this quote from Mick Quinn as he reminisces about his days at Pompey: 'I had an unofficial role as first officer of dressing-room banter.' Quinn's book is an astonishing read in many ways, stuffed with eye-opening anecdotes about his prodigious drinking and varied sex life, but this line gives the impression that he's the type of guy who'd be photocopying his arse at least once a week if he had an office job. He sounds like the evil spawn of *The Fast Show*'s Colin Hunt and Harry Enfield's Scousers.

Or there's this, from Teddy/Terry Curran, recalling the first time he met Alan Ball when arriving at Southampton: 'I walked into the dressing room wearing a short leather Christian Dior jacket I'd paid a cool £400 for and light blue jeans. Bally shouted out: "Where's your motorbike?"

"It's outside," I replied. The banter had started straightaway.' And what banter! This is what we mean by the wide scope of the word. Somehow, throwing someone in a river and making a vaguely comic comment about someone's clothing choices are both comfortably covered by the huge banter-brella.

So, in an attempt to truly understand the real lifeblood of the game, the thing that glues teams together and leaves ex-pros with a giant hole in their life after retirement, we'd like to explore the many faces of banter. Let's drill down into the dread word and discover exactly what footballers mean when they hail the tomfoolery, the hi-jinks and the banter of the dressing room. And once we've done that, we'll reveal who we consider to be Football's King of Banter. (Spoiler alert – it's not Garth Crooks.)

TYPES OF BANTER
1. The Verbal

This is your basic banter and usually involves some kind of riposte, rejoinder or put-down. We'll also allow the use of the occasional prop in this section.

Examples: Jimmy Case tells a lovely story in his book concerning Kenny Sansom. They were overseas on a veterans' tournament, and around the hotel pool Kenny kept asking Case how many England caps he'd won (Case is not the only player, incidentally, to report on Sansom's eager glee to ask this question, and even Sansom's book is called *To Cap It All*). Jimmy, you may know, didn't win any. 'I shouted "Three" and stuck three fingers up as I lay back on the sunbed, a beer in my hand … Anyway, after about five minutes he suddenly piped up, "Hey Casey, are you sure you got three England caps?" and so I replied, in my best Cockney accent, "Sorry, Ken, I thought you meant European Cups … now fuck off!"' Boom.

Brian Clough's reputation for one-liners is legendary, and Archie Gemmill remembers the great one burying Bobby Robson after Forest had thrashed Ipswich 5–0 in the 1978 Charity Shield: '"Well Done Brian", he [Robson] said, "but I don't think the scoreline reflects the performance of both teams today."

'"You're quite right, Bobby," the Boss shot back, "and if we hadn't been playing at half-pace, it would have been ten-nil."' Burn. Mic drop.

Another manager who brought unexpected success to the East Midlands, Claudio Ranieri, also has a nice line in cutting humour. When Jamie Vardy scored for a record 11 games in a row, he says that Ranieri 'presented me with a signed Leicester shirt at the training ground a few days later. I turned it round to look at the back. It said "9. Wanker".' A bit route one, but the joy comes from it being so unexpected from such an urbane, elderly Italian gent. And they say the 'foreigns' don't understand the British bantz.

A lot of ex-pros make a few bob from the old after-dinner circuit, but the crossover between footballers and genuine stand-up comedians must be fairly low. A few comics are pretty handy at football – Russell Howard (Basingstoke Town) and Noel Fielding (Sutton United) were both on the books of non-league sides – but footballers becoming stand-ups is even more rare.[29] Still, in Duncan McKenzie's book we discovered that Blackpool and England legend Stan Mortensen did become a turn after retirement. This, according to McKenzie, was his opening line: 'Good evening, you might wonder why a person who has scored a hat-trick in an FA Cup Final is billed as a comedian. Well, when you have scored a hat-trick in an FA Cup Final and it's named after somebody else, referring to Sir Stanley Matthews, you can stick the game of football as far up your arses as you can get it.'

Excellent. From the time we were old enough to learn about the great cup finals of yesteryear, it's always struck us that the 1953 final was named after the wrong Stan, so we're glad someone pointed it out. Ideally, however, that someone needed to have been around when the mystical discussion took place as to what to name the final after Mortensen had just scored a hat-trick in it. To be fair, it could have been an admin error: 'Shall we just name it after Stan?'

Not all verbal banter hits the spot, though. Jimmy Bullard says that when he joined up with the England squad he quickly spotted that Fabio Capello looked a lot like Postman Pat. Now, since the age of the internet we've been bombarded with footballer lookie-likeys to the point where many of us would be happy to never be shown one again (indeed, we have to look for richer fixes outside the game – like Elton John and Nicola Sturgeon's mum for example; go on, treat yourself) but this is actually pretty good, isn't it? That observation would probably

---

29 There was Bob 'The Cat' Bevan, of course, but we're not convinced he was ever a real goalie.

be enough for most people. Jimmy isn't most people, though, so he organised a competition between him and David Bentley to see who could say 'Postman Pat' the loudest in Capello's presence.

You may have done something along these lines at school – daring your mates to say a swear word at risky volumes in the presence of a teacher. Bentley, however, has little truck with the accepted way of doing things. Bullard writes: 'He would walk straight up to the boss and scream "Postman Pat!" in his face before adding "And his black and white cat!" for good measure.'

If you were wondering why Bentley's England career was so brief for someone so talented – now you know. It's stuff like this that really makes you start to comprehend the struggles the England manager faces just during a standard mid-season get-together for a friendly with a minor European nation, let alone what they put up with during actual tournaments. Would the Italians have done this? Would Andrea Pirlo have walked up to Capello and screamed, 'Il Postino Pat!' in his face? It seems doubtful, but we'll get to Pirlo's particular line in banter later.

2. The Set Piece

Planned banter, usually more of a physical sort of comedy, more about actions than words.

Examples: Our favourite instance of this sort of banter seems like it belongs in some kind of French art house comedy film. It stars three members of the England squad during Italia 90: Chris Waddle (a set piece this good would have to), Terry Butcher and Gary Stevens. Stuart Pearce remembers arriving for dinner to find the three of them already sitting at a table, hair slicked back and dressed in clothes worn either inside out or backwards: 'They ate their meal backwards, starting with coffee, dessert, main course and soup while quaffing bottle after bottle of 'wine' … At the end of their meal they stood up and said, "Thank you, gentlemen, and goodnight." As they emerged from the shelter of the long tablecloths, we could see that they had nothing on, apart from G-strings, from the waist downwards.'

They received a well-deserved ovation for this outstanding piece of comic theatre. Somehow, you can't imagine David Bentley matching this performance, at least not without stopping halfway through to scream at Steve Hodge that he looks a bit like Sport Billy (one for the teenagers, there).

Nicky Butt once pulled off a prank that was less subtle, but it must have required superb timing, pinpoint positioning and outrageous courage. According to Gary Neville, Butty stood close to a naked Peter Schmeichel in the dressing room, holding a piping hot teapot in such a way that when he eventually turned round, Schmeichel Junior (not Kasper) received a serious scalding.

As far as we know, Alan Hansen was not one for singeing the pubes off of Bruce Grobbelaar's ballsack, but Ronnie Whelan tells us he pulled off a particularly decent set piece after the shock news that Kenny Dalglish had resigned as Liverpool boss in 1991. Hansen, with the help of Ronnie Moore and Roy Evans, convinced the lads he was going to be the new manager:

'Jockey stood up and said, "Right, there's going to be a lot of changes round here. No more days off. Mondays we're all in. Thursdays we'll be looking at videos of the last game. Fridays we'll be looking at videos for the next game." Then he looked around at a few of us and said, "I know where you all drink in Southport, them pubs are off limits from now on."' Hansen carried on laying down the law before turning on his heel and leaving, followed by his trusty lieutenants. Whelan reports: 'No sooner had he walked out than the bitching started. More training, no drinking, videos, new regime, what's all this shit about? Someone said, dead vicious, "I never liked that Scottish twat anyway."' And that's how easily and quickly footballers can turn once one of their number moves upstairs. Absolutely beautiful simmering anger in that final sentence. Bravo to Hansen for pulling that off with a straight face. It's lucky he didn't take the job, too – he'd have spent years trying to win things without kids.

But for real innovation and commitment to planned banter, we go to Kevin Drinkell's autobiography, *Drinks All Round*. Despite its excellent title, this isn't in our top ten most riveting footballer books. In between his memories of goals and the details on contract negotiations, there's not a lot of room for fun, but one story from his Norwich days did stay with him (and us) forever, thanks to Disco Dale Gordon going the extra mile.

At the Christmas party one year, the squad decided to do a bit of fancy dress. Drinks went as a snooker player. Sensible, effective, no chance of embarrassment. Kevin says the rest of the squad were more ambitious, but reserves special praise for Dale: 'He went out dressed as a giant Tampax.'

Of course he did.

'He was unbelievable. He wore a white doctor's jacket and painted his body all white. He then wore a red hat, had a string up his back and had all these red tampons all over his outfit. He had put a lot of thought and effort into his attire.'

We'll wait here while you re-read that.

An actual tampon, yes.

With bloody bits and everything.

And Drinks's reaction to this stunning set piece, this courageous costume that, it must be said, is not readily available in the majority of fancy dress hire outlets, is beautifully measured. He's not shocked, necessarily, nor appalled. We don't even know if he thought it was funny. No, his overriding emotion seems to be one of admiration. Above all, it's the 'thought and effort' that went into Gordon's attire that impresses him the most. Dale had clearly spent hours crafting and grafting, working to turn his bold vision into a tangible, terrifying reality.

3. The Friendly Nonsense

Nice banter. Lovely banter. No-one-gets-hurt banter. Light joshing among good friends.

Examples: Jamie Vardy says at Leicester they would sometimes roll up a sock, dip it in the bath to get it nice and wet, and chuck it at someone. Nothing wrong with that. Good healthy hi-jinks.

Also at Leicester, Tony Cottee reveals that in pre-match warm-ups they invented something called 'The Shambles'. They'd stand in a circle and then coach Steve Walford would call a player to the middle, and whatever sort of exercise he did, the rest had to copy. Except no one did a proper exercise: 'I did the "Mick Channon", imitating his famous windmill goal celebration. Matt Elliott did his impersonation of Baloo from Jungle Book, jumping with his legs tucked behind him. Muzzy [Izzet] laid down on his front and did the "caterpillar".' Sweet, harmless fun – they're the kings of that at Leicester.[30]

---

30 Unless they're on tour, obvs.

We also discovered that footballers, just like us mortals, love a good mimic, and if you start reading autobiographies in bulk, it won't be long before you find somebody saying that Peter Taylor (the winger and England manager for one game, not Cloughie's assistant) does a great Norman Wisdom. Having read dozens of lines of praise for this particular impersonation, we're desperate to see it. Sir Trevor Brooking remembers everyone enjoying it while on England duty: '[Don] Revie, and all the players for that matter, enjoyed his company because he was a funny guy in the dressing room and his Norman Wisdom impression used to have us all rolling about on the floor with laughter.' The idea of The Revs ROFLing is a particularly strong image – a real testament to the quality of Peter's mimicry.

Kenny Sansom also has a reputation for a strong Wisdom[31] and Bobby Robson positively rhapsodises about his voice skills: 'He would take off Alan Ball, Sir Stan Matthews and various others, but his best was the fall-about style of Norman Wisdom.' Glenn Hoddle agrees, saying, 'If we are having a drink after a game, he will stand up and put on a show.' No wonder Sir Bobby picked Sansom (86 caps) so much – who could compete with a left-back who was quick, skilful and moustachioed *and* could do a turn to keep the lads happy at the post-match drinking sesh? It's the total package. Poor Alan Kennedy (two caps) never stood a chance with no Pitkin shtick.

Man United and England winger Gordon Hill was another who apparently excelled at this particular skill. Judging by how much players still go on about it, it seems being able to do a decent Wisdom could really ingratiate you to any set of footballers back then.

It's probably different now, but until the young tyros of today publish their memoirs, we won't know whether they enjoy the kind of innocent banter that kept footballers amused back in the 1970s and 80s. Which brings us to what the Liverpool lads of that era did to assuage their boredom while on tour. Phil Thompson vividly remembers the time Terry McDermott bought a trick ten-dollar bill in a joke shop, then used it to prank travellers in 'Alaska Airport' (although our research shows no such airport exists, throwing a dark veil of doubt over the

---

31 Glenn Hoddle adds that his Prince Charles was great too. But then, everyone did Prince Charles voices in the 80s. You don't see them so much anymore. It was one of the Holy Trinity of classic comic impersonations of the era that almost anyone could pull off: Charles, Margaret Thatcher and Mavis from *Corrie*.

whole anecdote). The way it worked was that the cash was attached to a wire, so Terry would place it on the floor, then when some unsuspecting schmuck bent down to pick it up, he'd press a button on the device and the note would be yanked back to his hand, leaving the traveller hilariously nonplussed. Sounds like it would pass the time nicely, for a while. Thommo adds: 'It's amazing how such a simple toy kept us all amused for about two hours.'

Two hours? Imagine how they would've felt if someone from the future had turned up and given them an iPad. They'd probably still be in the airport playing on it today. Two hours!

4. The Physical

The rough stuff. The sort of banter that might leave marks.

Examples: Some of the hardcore, physical, almost bullying type of 'banter' is meted out against new signings, but the main targets are what were once known as apprentices or youth teamers but are now known only by the age group in which they 'ply their trade' (under-23s, under-21s, under-18s etc.), or by the catch-all term favoured by fans, 'youngsters'.

Some of the abuse these poor young men faced is genuinely eye-popping. Take what was known at Manchester United as 'The Bong', a phenomenon reported by both Lee Sharpe and Keith Gillespie. It's not complicated: someone would (somehow) shove a football into a large sock, then swing it on to the top of the head of some poor soul. Bong. Sharpey adds: 'I think they finally stopped that one when one lad had a bong too many, six of the best I think, nearly fainted and they all thought he'd suffered serious damage to the neck.' Christ.

Footballs, in fact, seem to be regularly used not only as tools to improve skills, but as weapons. Gary Neville says that another type of torture at United was to hold a player's head over a treatment table so that a ball could be repeatedly booted into his face; Everton in the 1980s sounds like some form of dystopian nightmare. This is from Neville Southall's *Binman Chronicles*: 'Sometimes Howard [Kendall] would get all the apprentices and line them up in the goal. We'd all smash balls at them and they had to stop them going in. They'd all be trying to impress Howard by throwing their faces at the ball and all that. They'd be covered in blood or half knocked out and the first team would just be pissing themselves laughing.' That's right, a bit like stocks in medieval times, Everton players would blast footballs at the kids until they were *covered in blood*. This was obviously before Big Nev became the social conscience of Twitter and just liked belting footballs at kids.

Was this sort of thing going on everywhere? When West Ham boast about the historical magnificence of their famed Academy, we imagine some paradise of football schooling, a sort of precursor to Barça's La Masia. But is that what it was really like? Or were senior West Ham pros just spending their days hammering balls as hard as they could at the faces of terrified teenagers until they hardened up and turned into Alvin Martin?

It's not only footballs that are used to torment the boys, though; there are other common dressing room items that are adaptable beyond their primary purpose. Like boot polish, for example. Perfect for polishing boots, but also useful for dishing out sadistic punishment.

Back at United, Keith Gillespie says one of the worst forms of torment was 'having the design of a United kit rubbed onto your body in boot polish with a sharp brush'. We thought he must be exaggerating about the whole kit, but Gary Neville backs him up: 'the shorts, the shirt, even the number on your back ... I can still feel the sharp bristles ripping my skin'. Yet we're still struggling to properly picture this – how exactly was this piece of living art achieved? Did United employ a particularly skilled boot polish artist who could pick out the complicated United badge? Was the whole body covered in boot polish, then to get the detail, was it rubbed off where it needed to be – so the number, for example, would be clean skin? Or was boot polish carefully etched into the skin with a needle for the detail, as a tattoo artist might apply a new tattoo? We need answers on this. We feel a *One Show* segment coming on. One for Tuffers to tackle, perhaps.

Worse still, both Sam Allardyce and Dean Windass painfully recall their ordeal of having their testicles roughly blackened with boot polish. 'I'd come home with a black dick nearly every day. It sounds cruel but that was all part of the education,' says Deano. Yeah – it was all about the education: 'All right, lads, today we're going to be practising set pieces, then Don will be doing some offside drills, and afterwards we'll take you over to see the senior pros, who'll be offering a practical workshop on the best way to blacken someone's gonads with boot polish, OK? Right, let's do some stretches.'

Big Sam starts with what you'd say is a reasonable response to this sort of hi-jinks: 'It took ages to scrape it off and it didn't half hurt.' 'Scrape it off'? It sounds like he removed it with a chisel. Bang out of order, really. 'Nowadays, if the police heard about that, they'd have six good squad cars round to the training complex which would be sealed off and the protagonists charged with sexual abuse.' Ah. Of course. There are very few occurrences in life that Sam can't relate back to some sort of dig about political correctness going absolutely bonkers. He'll have been furious when he arrived at Everton to discover that Idrissa Gueye and Seamus Coleman weren't having target practice against the under-18 boys on a weekly basis because of some sort of bullshit health and safety concerns.

Meanwhile at Fulham, Rodney Marsh says they had a slight twist on the old boot polish torture back in the day: 'When one young lad joined, we put him in a cold bath, then whitewashed his bollocks, and chained him outside to the pitchside railings for an hour. Stupid, but in those days good fun, only this time the poor lad almost caught pneumonia.' So that made it less fun, probably. For him, at least.

So: raw ballbags, severe neck injuries, faces smashed in and pneumonia. This is pretty hardcore banter – we're a long way from Norman Wisdom pratfalls now. But none of these are quite as bad as what happened to Stan Ternent while he was coaching at Chelsea. Playing golf against a pairing of Andy Townsend and Vinnie Jones, Stan played a hole and jumped into his buggy: 'I confidently floored the accelerator to take us to the next tee.

'Slam! ... Instead of nudging forward, the buggy shuddered backwards over a cliff.' Bloody hell. 'Along with the wildly revving buggy, I plunged into a ravine, clutching the steering wheel with a look of puzzled horror fixed on my face. While I'd been holing the ball, one of the bastards we were playing had fucked about with the gears and switched them from forward to reverse. I landed neck-deep in clumps of razor-sharp brambles.'

Stan says his body was sliced and battered and bruised, but when he yelled for help it took a while coming because 'Skip' and 'Jonah' were too busy laughing their arses off. Incredibly, despite Stan Ternent almost plunging to his actual death, this whole episode doesn't even merit a mention in Jones's book. Then again, when the bar in your book is shoving a shotgun up Howard Wilkinson's nose, not everything is going to make the final cut.

5. The Rubbish

Banter that is just not very good.

Examples: Fertile ground for referee autobiographies here. Let's go straight to housemaster David Elleray, who is quite keen in his book to show off some of his droll wit: 'There was some good-natured backchat with Arsenal supporters about my booking of Bergkamp. "You mean I should have sent him off," I retorted to their amusement.' Slayed them in the aisles, that did.

Surely Sir Alex Ferguson can do better. Apart from when United lost or when they wore grey shirts (and lost) or were losing in injury time (and lost) he seems to have a pretty dry sense of humour, which comes across nicely in his books. And there's nothing at all wrong with this memory: 'All my players would call me "gaffer" or "boss". Lee Sharpe came in one day and asked, "How you doing, Alex?" I said: "Were you at school with me?"'

Nice. We can imagine a young Sharpey's big bombastic bubble being pricked by that retort. But Sir Alex can't leave well enough alone, adding: 'Even better, a young Irish boy, Paddy Lee, saw me on the stairs of the Cliff, as he was coming down, with Bryan Robson behind me, and said, "All right Alex?"

'I said: "Were you at school with me?"

'"No," he said, perturbed.

'"Well don't call me Alex!" I get the giggles now recalling these moments.'

How is this 'even better', Sir? It's the same story, almost word for word.

It didn't take much for Glenn Hoddle to be tickled by his England boss Ron Greenwood, either. Apparently, Ron used to look very much like the FA's administrator, Alan O'Dell (we've checked, and there's something (although not much) to this, although in the early 80s most men over 60 looked like Ron Greenwood and Alan O'Dell – see our pictures section for the evidence). As you can imagine, this situation was ripe for some top-class bant: 'On one trip, Ron got into the swing of the mix-up and took over Alan's job of handing out the tickets. We all thought he was going to let Alan pick the team! On another occasion, when asked for his autograph, Ron signed "Alan O'Dell".' And players say being on international duty can be boring.

Comedy and banter is very much about taste, though, and footballers don't always agree on what is and isn't funny. At one stage in the late 90s, for example, the England squad did a thing where they would try to mention song titles during TV interviews. It was just a little game they played to try to lighten the chore of having to talk politely about 'the mood in the camp' to Gabriel Clarke or Ray Stubbs. Paul Merson, who is very much a fan of banter in almost all its forms, was not impressed, though: 'Personally, I didn't find it funny,' he writes. The Merse is not having it.

6. The Weird

Banter we can't quite explain.

Examples: By now you'll be starting to appreciate just how vast an area the word 'banter' manages to cover. And while much of it can be pigeonholed into handy categories, we have found examples of things that are undoubtedly banter, but don't really seem to fit anywhere at all.

Take John Burridge. Along with coaching in the Middle East, Budgie did some media work, and in his book he tells of the time he decided to prank a new pundit, the former Palace defender Gary O'Reilly, by pretending to have Tourette's syndrome. He got the whole crew involved, so O'Reilly thought they were on air when Budgie started to act up: 'I put on my maddest face (and believe me, it is a mad one) and said: "Why don't you just go and fuck off!" I then stood up and started rocking the set, calling everyone bastards and shoving anyone who came my way. We got a couple of security guys to come and cart me away.'

Really strange, partly because John doesn't seem particularly au fait with the symptoms of Tourette's, confusing it as he does with some kind of violent schizophrenia, and partly because Budgie didn't let O'Reilly in on the gag until after they'd recorded the actual show. He remembers that Gary 'took it well enough', a phrase that makes us pretty certain the poor man was as bewildered as we are by the whole ordeal.

Then there's the sort of banter that if you heard about players at your club doing it you'd be right to feel a bit annoyed because of the flagrantly obvious risk of injury. For instance, for Pat Van Den Hauwe and his Millwall mates Keith Stevens, Alex Rae, Gavin Maguire and Andy Roberts, a simple game of darts just didn't have enough jeopardy to make it interesting. So, they added a twist where one of them would put their hand on the board and the others tried to throw darts between the fingers: 'but we were so pissed we'd throw them like spears! You could not move your hand out of the way as you would lose too much face.' Losing blood is fine, of course, but never, ever lose face. 'Sometimes all three darts would be embedded in your hand and we were forever going into training with them bandaged up. It was a stupid idiotic game but we loved it.' Indeed, who can resist a game that usually ends with a tetanus shot in the bum at one in the morning?

Many of these activities do seem to emerge out of sheer boredom. Take a story from Graeme Le Saux, who recalls a group of Blackburn team-mates whiling away a journey to Crystal Palace with the help of the hammer sometimes found in coaches that can be used to break a window in the event of an emergency: 'The crux of the game was that each player took a turn hitting the window. You had to hit it as hard as you could without breaking it and each player had to hit it harder than the last one. You can guess the outcome of that particular game.' But who lost? The players, Le Saux says, were Shearer, Newell, Warhurst, Sherwood and Batty. It might have been Shearer, but presumably if anyone grassed him up he'd have threatened to retire from international football. We reckon Paul Warhurst is a strong contender – he'd have been equally adept at smashing the window at the back of the bus as he would be at the front, of course.

Still, for properly weird banter you have to go to the maestro: Kevin Keegan. Who else? This story occurred during his Southampton days, when he liked to hang out with Mick Channon and Alan Ball (Channon says they called themselves 'The Three Musketeers', which straight away lets anyone know that these boys are well into their banter).

The three of them are out for a drink in Brighton. Channon recalls: 'With us having a drink there was a fifty-year-old, peroxide blond with a green streak in her hair who had been at the races. She must have been about fourteen stone and was well known for being a local character.' They decided to bet Keegan that he couldn't carry this lady on his shoulders to another pub half a mile away: 'It was never a good thing to offer Kevin a bet on anything because he wouldn't let anything beat him,' says Channon. And he didn't. In fact, Kev carried her to that pub and back again. 'It was a hilarious sight to see Britain's most famous footballer haring along a quiet street in Brighton with an old dear on his back, Alan Ball chasing along behind as the referee and the old lady's face going the colour of the green streak in her hair.'

Seems a bit harsh to call her an 'old dear' when she's only 50. Poor woman.

7. Classic Bantz

For some footballers, when they talk of banter, it's this subset of banter to which they are mainly referring. It encompasses the Holy Trinity of classic banterous elements:

- clothes and shoes
- fire extinguishers
- nudity and human waste

This is the kind of banter central to the footballing lives of most footballers, and the sort present in about 90 per cent of footballer autobiographies ever written. This is biblical banter. Garry Nelson claims this kind of thing was particularly bad on April Fool's Day: 'When it's on a normal training day the strain of being on your toes non-stop becomes insupportable. Salt in the teapot, mentholatum smeared around the toilet seat, knotted together shoelaces, toes cut out of your socks, underwear up on the roof. Alan Bennett would be totally out of his depth.' It sounds exhausting.

Let's take these elements in turn. First, footballers are absolutely obsessed with the destruction of clothes and shoes. Rare is the British footballer, if one even exists, who has gone through an entire career without having either had their shoes or clothes cut up, or cut up someone else's shoes or clothes. It's particularly common for new signings to have their stuff ruined in this way, but it can happen at any time at all.

The instances we found are too innumerable to mention. Merely as a taster, though: Rio Ferdinand talks about sawing Paul Robinson's shoes in half (innovative use of a saw here, admittedly); Ian Snodin remembers having his entire suit ripped to shreds when he made the mistake of falling asleep on the coach back from a game; and Paolo Di Canio laments that the West Ham lads (Neil Ruddock in particular) used to slash his long socks and put spiders in his shoes. That last one sounds inventive – but how did they get the spiders to stay there? Copydex? There you go – another *One Show* segment sorted.

You have to feel sorry for players, because the rules, such as they are, are baffling. On the one hand, your shoes or clothes might get ruined because they're quite nice or look expensive. Take Joe Jordan. On joining Leeds United, he says he had two items of clothing he particularly loved: 'One was an oilskin coat … I was rather proud of it … The other much-valued item was a sweater of the finest Arran wool knitted by my mother.' But when he wore them to Elland Road, both were dumped in a rubbish bin. Come on, lads – his mum knitted that!

You'd think, therefore, that the secret is to not wear any flashy gear. Keep it simple. Blend in. That may have been Ed de Goey's plan at Chelsea, but it turns out that doesn't work either. Jimmy Floyd Hasselbaink remembers, 'At one point we noticed he was wearing the exact same tracksuit each and every day. He probably had several of the same tracksuits since the one he wore was never dirty.' Apparently annoyed by this, the Chelsea lads (not named, but it was probably Wisey, wasn't it?) cut up his tracksuit and his boots. So how are you supposed to win? Turn up in flashy gear – it gets ruined. Turn up in average stuff – it gets ruined. How exactly do you tread that precarious middle ground? Such are the complexities of football's inner sanctum.

Next, fire extinguishers. It seems likely that when footballers first walk into any public building – hotel, restaurant, massage parlour – they make sure to clock where the nearest fire extinguisher is. Not because they're safety conscious, but because fire extinguishers are prime banter material.

Stan Collymore, for one, famously indulged in some vintage extinguisher action in a bar while on tour with Leicester and in his book he remembers the place resembling 'Santa's grotto' with foam everywhere. Afterwards, every glass in the place had to be individually cleaned, and Stan had to pay the bill – a cool £700 for a few seconds of frothy entertainment.

Even Graeme Le Saux, the thinking man's left-back, was not above fun with fire extinguishers in his younger days, and says one trick was to unscrew the eyepiece in a team-mate's hotel room door, shove the nozzle through and send a torrent of liquid shooting through the hole.

And then there's Jimmy Bullard – much more on this top banter merchant in a minute – but the simple random squirting of fluid was not enough for him. No, Bullard had science in mind as he attempted to find out just how slippery the marble-floored corridors at Fulham could get. So, he went into the dressing room and annoyed a few team-mates until, still in their boots, they got fed up and started to chase after him, no doubt to give his cheeky grinning face a satisfying punch. Out in the corridor, Bullard discharged his weapon: 'The resulting scene was like watching a cartoon as, one after the other, they slipped on the wet, marble floor and fell arse over tit on top of each other.'

Finally, to nudity and human waste. Footballers are supremely comfortable with getting naked in the name of having a laugh. The thing about indecent exposure, though, is that however funny it might be, it can backfire. Don Hutchison, for example, was caught on camera doing his party trick of placing a Budweiser label on his knob in front of some young students, but while Neil Ruddock claims 'It was hilarious and everyone took it in good spirit, even the parents of the girls who got an eyeful,' Robbie Fowler says that it was this incident that finally convinced Roy Evans to boot Hutch out of the club.

Similarly, Keith Gillespie says Lawrie Sanchez[32] never picked Gerry Taggart for Northern Ireland again after this disgrace on a plane: 'Just after the food was served, Taggs pressed his call button and the air hostess came to his seat. "Is this supposed to be in this sandwich?" he asked. She looked down and Taggs had taken out his cock and placed it between two slices of bread.' Some might say Sanchez overreacted, but others might say that's less 'banter' and more 'sexual harassment'.

Dave Bassett got himself into trouble during a speech he made at a testimonial dinner: 'I dropped my trousers simply to illustrate a point,' he says, without elaborating on what that point was, but *The Sun* found out and made a fuss and in time he saw the error of his ways: 'I had been a keen mooner and used any excuse to drop my trousers at parties or dances just to get a cheap laugh. Christine [his wife] hated it, of course. She would get very embarrassed and we had many rows about it. Now I realise how stupid and degrading it is.' We'd never heard the phrase

---

32 The least krazy member of the Crazy Gang, it seems. Dave Bassett says: 'He wasn't a hardcore Crazy Gang member, more on the fringes of things – although he did once take down a Christmas tree in a hotel foyer.' Nice to know the entry level of bantz required for the Gang.

'keen mooner' before. People say they're 'keen fishermen' or 'keen gardeners' but not 'keen mooners'. Makes it sound like a hobby anyone might take up to give themselves something to do at the weekends, or something Buzz Aldrin might claim to be.

And then there's the obsession with bodily functions. We've already seen in 'Be Our Guest' that Merse (the man who didn't find the 'song titles in interviews' game funny, remember) liked to take a dump in the pillowcase of a room-mate. But there's more where that came from.

At Liverpool, Robbie Fowler claims that Steve Harkness enjoyed a bit of playful poo-play, saying Steve 'was the joker in the team ... One of his favourite tricks was to leave a little piece of shit in your toilet bag. He'd done it to me, done it to everyone, and you just bided your time and got him back.' Lovely. Fowler admits that Stan Collymore was entitled to be a bit upset when it happened to him 'because let's face it, it's pretty disgusting', although it's worth reading Stan's book for a bit more on 'joker' Harkness, because he reveals that Harkness's brand of unpleasant behaviour went far beyond the old shit-in-a-bag routine (see 'Why Can't We All Just Get Along?' chapter).

Fowler also says that the Anfield lads were forever pissing in each other's pints – to the point, apparently, where the taste became normalised: he says that once he urinated in Neil Ruddock's pint but Razor 'didn't bat an eyelid'.

Elsewhere, Dean Windass admits he once pissed down Ian Ormondroyd's leg while they were in the shower (and that's a whole lot of leg): 'He took it in good heart to be fair, and still laughs about it, but it was just my way of welcoming him to Hull,' writes Deano. Well, at least Ormondroyd was already in the shower, but still, we'll never quite understand Dean's 'just my way of welcoming him'. It's as if he believes everyone has their particular ways of welcoming people to new jobs, and his is just as valid as any other. And what did Ian think? Was it, 'Why is this weirdo peeing on my leg?' or 'Oh, someone's peeing on my leg, I'll take that to be a friendly welcome to my new club?'

The Holy Grail of banter would involve ruined shoes, a turd and a fire extinguisher. We haven't quite found all three in a single anecdote, but Dave Bassett does say that at Wimbledon one player did defecate in another's shoe, which is at least two out of three. Bassett adds: 'The poor victim was forced to go home in trainers after committing an otherwise perfectly good pair of shoes to the incinerator.' Yes, such was the intensity of banter at the Wimbledon training ground in the 80s that the club was forced to install an incinerator on site to help dispose of all the shit-covered shoes and clothing.

8. Papal

The rarest of all banter.

It's not often players get to indulge in a bit of papal banter, but Sven Goran Eriksson was on hand to witness a classic of the genre when he took his Roma side to meet the Pope. The players all bowed as they met the Pontiff. Well, all except Polish living legend Zbigniew Boniek: 'Instead, he looked the Pope in the eye and said, "Allora, who is the most famous Polack in the country? You or me?" The Pope did not answer.'

Absolutely tremendous work. As audacious as any goal he ever scored.

* * *

Hopefully that lot gives us a much broader understanding of what players mean when they reminisce about the banter that they so miss. And yet, despite it all, we still have absolutely no idea where we would place the kind of banter Mick McCarthy references in his foreword to Jason McAteer's autobiography: 'there was always that flippant side to him as well, the come-a-day, go-a-day, here comes Sunday banter'. Maybe it's a Yorkshire thing.

We've seen opposite ends of the banter spectrum, then – from harmless vocal tomfoolery to the sort of hi-jinks that almost tips over into manslaughter. But surely, somewhere, there is a line? There must be limits on banter? Well, obviously there are, as Malky Mackay, Keysie, Andy Gray etc. could all attest. But what are those limits, exactly?

Luckily, Eamon Dunphy offers us a handy rule of thumb that we're calling Dunphy's Law: 'It's all right if it stays within the group,' he explains. 'It's when it starts involving outsiders – waiters, or other guests, or the public – that it becomes bad.' So, with that in mind, coupled with our own sense of basic decency, let's try to lay down the law a little between examples of acceptable and unacceptable banter:

BANTER, TOMFOOLERY AND HI-JINKS

Type of Banter	Acceptable	Unacceptable
Making a mess.	Dave Bassett's story of the Crazy Gang lads putting talcum powder inside Dave Beasant's motorcycle helmet, so that when he put it on, he was covered in white powder. Fair enough. Minimal mess made in a dressing room that would have needed to be swept anyway.[1]	Neil Ruddock's tale of Paul Gascoigne going to his seat in a cinema before faking a trip and throwing an enormous bucket of popcorn all over the place: 'You should have seen the poor cleaner's face as we fell about in hysterics.' Yeah, the poor cleaner. Minimum wage to clean up the sticky debris of some 'hilarious' hi-jinks perpetuated by millionaire footballers. This clearly falls foul of Dunphy's Law.
Convincing a team-mate something is true, when it is not true.	Robbie Savage impersonating an FA employee and ringing David Bentley to tell him he's made the England squad. Fine.	Phil Thompson, Alan Hansen, Graeme Souness, Kenny Dalglish and the Liverpool lads convincing Steve Nicol that Dalglish had leukaemia. This resulted in Nicol giving Dalglish a heartfelt, private eulogy, which Phil Thompson says Kenny found really funny until Nicol said: 'I thought something was wrong with you because you have been playing so badly.'
Beneath-the-belt banter.	While a youngster at St Mirren, Frank McAvennie received a painful shot into what commentators like to call 'the lower abdomen'. The coach came over sympathetically and offered him some ointment for the area. Frank did as he was told. It was Deep Heat: 'The heat built up slowly to start with then took off like a bloody steam train.' Painful, but no lasting damage. Frank didn't mind.	Tony Cascarino being confronted at non-league Crockenhill just before his big move to Gillingham with a pink dildo and threats of sexual abuse: 'As soon as the game ended, I was grabbed by both ankles and upended in the showers. They split my legs, splashed soap on my bum and switched the plastic penis on. When I close my eyes, I can still hear the guffaws of Maloney and Johnny Hibbitt ...' '"Come on, you hairdresser poof!"' '"You are getting it my son."' Too far, that. Way too far.

1 Still, we don't quite get how this worked. Either the helmet was hole side up, in which case how did Beasant not see the powder? Or the helmet was hole side down, in which case, how did the powder stay in the helmet? Confusing.

Causing pain.	Alex Ferguson on Paul Scholes: 'He was such a brilliant long passer that he could choose a hair on the head of any team-mate answering the call of nature at our training ground. Gary Neville once thought he had found refuge in a bush, but Scholesey found him from 40 yards.' Great – banter with genuine skill.	Graeme Le Saux tells a couple of tales about Blackburn coach driver 'Stoney' that fall foul of Dunphy's Law. Once Mike Newell and Tim Sherwood were messing about trying to see how long they could dangle a spoon off their nose: 'Then they asked Stoney to do it, too ... I think Alan Shearer had been heating the spoon while no one was watching. Stoney grabbed the spoon and put it on the end of his nose and then started screaming.'
		Not acceptable. The Rovers boys also used to make him drink a disgusting potion of things like Tabasco, eggs and milk before they'd give him the cash from a whip-round after away games.[2]

For some, almost all banter is unacceptable. Lou Macari, namechecked in more than a couple of books as something of a Banter Lord, found this out while at a British journalists v Italian journalists friendly match: 'I nipped into the Italian changing room and cut their socks in half. They didn't see the funny side. That particular practical joke was lost in translation.' Well, that's one way of looking at it. The other is that it's simply not that funny, just annoying.

But that does bring us to another facet of bantz: the belief that foreigners just don't get it – well, at least according to some. Stuart Pearce was writing way back in the 90s that: 'This aspect of team bonding is dying due to the influx of foreign players who don't often share the traditional British lavatorial and sarcastic sense of humour.' And while reading these books, we often felt that the view of many British players was in sync with Pearce's thoughts.

Yet how much truth is in that assumption? Matt Le Tissier says of his Norwegian team-mate at Southampton, Claus Lundekvam, 'He completely got that humour, our banter and the drinking culture. The best tribute I can pay him is that he was the most English foreigner we

2 Le Saux, justifiably, makes a lot of his treatment at the hands of the Chelsea banter merchants in his book, but there's no sign he offered to drink the potion in Stoney's stead as an offer of solidarity.

ever had.' That final sentence alone shows you what foreign players were up against, particularly in the earlier days of their 'influx'. Le Tiss's 'best tribute' is not that Lundekvam was a top-quality centre-half; nor that he was an outstanding club servant for over a decade, often as captain; nor that he was a regular international for his home country. No, his best tribute is that Claus understood the British banter. Saints could have signed Brazilian Ronaldo back in 1996, but if he'd turned up and hadn't got on board with the drinking culture, or known his way around a towel fight, Le Tiss presumably would've turned his nose up.

Ray Parlour relates a tale involving a few of the Arsenal players shoving the club chef's face into a cream cake. He says that Arsene Wenger found it funny, adding: 'That was the sort of episode the manager, and the foreign players, hadn't really experienced on the Continent but they thought it was brilliant. They had never seen anything like it before.'

You start to wonder just how special British footballers think British humour is, because we're pretty sure most people in most countries are fairly aware of basic slapstick humour – and pie-in-the-face is about the most universal demonstration of humour that you can possibly get. Had they *really* never seen anything like it? Or was Ray just assuming they hadn't, because they were foreign?

Granted, overseas banter can be different from country to country, but it's no less crucial to team building. Graeme Souness remembers a particularly bizarre incident during his time managing in Turkey: 'The players went to the games room, put some pillows and cushions at one end, got their guns out and created a shooting gallery 30 metres long with a target in front of the cushions and fired live rounds at it for their Saturday night entertainment. Even in Istanbul, I had to discipline them for that.' Makes Gazza taking pot-shots at Jimmy Five Bellies' arse with an air rifle look tame, that.

In Italy, Andrea Pirlo used to love to wind up Gennaro 'Rino' Gattuso, who, Pirlo hints, is not the brightest. Now, admittedly, some of the banter was not typical 'British-style' – the Milan players adored correcting his comically inaccurate use of verbs, for instance, and Rino would retaliate by stabbing them with his fork (they even missed games because of the injuries). The closest we'd get to that is Jeff Stelling and the boys laughing at Merse trying to pronounce Michu on *Soccer*

Saturday. But there's much more: 'I'd nick his phone and send a bunch of texts to Ariedo Braida, our general manager. This one time, Rino de Janeiro, like me, was waiting for his contract to be renewed. I did the negotiating on his behalf by means of a single message. "Dear Ariedo, if you give me what I want, you can have my sister."' Surely even Ray Parlour would be proud of that?

Or how about this tale from international duty, where Daniele De Rossi would hide under Gattuso's bed and wait for him. Look out for the gorgeous zinger early on: 'Gattuso would come in, brush his teeth, stick on his leopard-print pyjamas, get into bed, take out a book and look at the pictures.

Just as he was about to fall asleep, Daniele would reach up from under the bed and grab his sides, while I'd burst out of the wardrobe like the worst kind of lover, making horrendous noises … Another time we gave him a soaking with a fire extinguisher.'

A fire extinguisher! Definitive proof that Italians, at least, really do love their banter.

So, we already know Norwegians (Lundekvam), French (Wenger) and Italians (De Rossi, Pirlo and Ranieri – thanks to that 'Wanker' shirt) were all up for laughs and even Stuart Pearce admits that the likes of Peruvian Nobby Solano and Swede Andreas Andersson got involved with comedy gift-buying at Christmas. But what about the Dutch? Or, more specifically, the iceman himself, Dennis Bergkamp? Doubtlessly this most cold-blooded, most sensible of footballers did not demean himself by getting involved with the 'traditional British lavatorial and sarcastic sense of humour'?

You'd think not, but it turns out that Dennis Bergkamp is a full-on Baron of Banter. Ian Wright fondly remembers the time Den made him put on all Martin Keown's clothes after Keown had gone out on to the training pitch. 'When Martin saw me, he started saying, "I've got a jumper like that … I've got trousers like that …" I'm sure he was just about to tell me that his fitted better than mine when he realised what had happened. Dennis had suddenly gone from being completely straight-faced to killing himself.' Great, harmless banter there – and it involves someone's clothes too. Classic.

Ashley Cole says that while most of the Arsenal dressing room got plenty of mileage out of his relationship with Cheryl Tweedy

(Cole, Fernandez-Versini, her off *The X Factor*), Bergkamp was one of the ringleaders: 'I'd be in the treatment room with him and he'd be lying back reading a copy of *FHM* or *Loaded* and he'd suddenly start going, "Mmmmmmmmmm … Mmmmmmmmmmmm … Look at this woman in here!" and, of course, it was Cheryl. Then he'd look at me, act all surprised and say, "Sorry Ash, didn't see you there!"' Bantz about someone's wife? That is top, top work.

And finally, and this really did come as a shock to us, Bergkamp was a huge fan of pulling people's shorts down at unfortunate moments. Or, as Dave Bassett might say, he was a keen pants remover. Ray Parlour tells us that Dennis once embarrassed him as he prepared to go on as a sub in a friendly, but one of his most memorable was when he pantsed kitman Vic Akers in front of a group of female representatives from L'Oreal: 'His shorts were around his ankles and the women looked completely shocked, didn't know where to look … It was one of the funniest things I've ever seen.' And Ray Parlour has seen someone's face pushed into a cream cake.

So, overall, the whole idea that foreign players didn't or don't understand British bantz doesn't seem to stack up. But while we can say Dennis Bergkamp is undoubtedly the most surprising banter merchant we came across, he's not the most prolific, or the best. So, who is? Well, after much research, we have a top three list of banter lovers, topped by our undisputed King of Banter.

There were many names we considered. Neil Ruddock, Robbie Fowler, Rio Ferdinand, Vinnie Jones, Dennis Wise, Wally Downes and almost anyone from the Crazy Gang were in the running. There should certainly be an honourable mention for John Moncur, namechecked in many books for his bizarre behaviour (he once ran out on to the training ground wearing just a blown-up surgical glove on his head and a jockstrap), but here are our top three:

3rd PLACE
RAY PARLOUR

Ray's autobiography is a really good, funny read that gives the impression of a man who appreciated not just his football career, but all the perks and fun he got to have because of it. It's a book chock-full of banter. He must really miss it now.

Ray's Highlights: Ray showed his potential as a future banter Jedi when he had the courage as an apprentice to sing 'Little Donkey' at Christmas in front of Tony Adams. Rodders may have chased him around the training ground after that, but he later still welcomed Ray into the infamous Tuesday Club, essentially a drink-fuelled banter society, where together they had all kinds of scrapes.

What gives Ray big points is that he's an all-rounder. He's had a fight abroad while on tour; he was part of the Arsenal eating competition; he had a nickname for his boss (Inspector Clouseau, because Arsene is apparently quite clumsy); and once, when some Spurs fans were continually rude to him in a restaurant, he soaked them with a fire extinguisher as he left. Any banter legend worth his salt will always have at least one fire extinguisher story up his sleeve.

Even the title of his book is a bit of banter. It's called *It's Only Ray Parlour's Autobiography,* because immediately before he scored the opening goal in the 2002 FA Cup Final, Chelsea fan and (then) host of *Soccer AM* Tim Lovejoy had commented on Sky's Fanzone, 'Oh no, he's put him through! Oh, it's all right, it's only Ray Parlour.' So not only did Ray answer that banter with the perfect riposte of a goal, he then further hammered Lovejoy by using the quote for the title of his autobiography.

The following year, when Arsenal won the cup again, and with no Lovejoy quote to enjoy, Ray decided to fill that banter vacuum by hiding the FA Cup underneath his table during the celebration banquet. After a while, Arsenal chief executive David Dein started to panic, so before an emergency call for Pickles (the incredible trophy-finding dog) could be put out, Ray stepped in and placed the trophy in a corner to be discovered: 'The great FA Cup mystery was solved.' Well, it wasn't solved, Ray. You just allowed them to find it. You didn't own up to it, you little scamp.

Ray's cheeky-chappie charm didn't save him at Middlesbrough, though. Up there he delivered some classic verbal banter when Gareth Southgate took over as the new boss. The future England manager got the lads together and explained that obviously there needed to be changes now he was management and all that, and asked them not to call him by his nickname, 'Gate', any more. 'I went, "What about Big Nose?" It all went quiet. Steve Harrison started laughing even though he was the coach. Lee Cattermole's pinched me. Everyone heard it but there was no reaction at all from Gareth, not the tiniest hint of anything.' Well, not then, but Parlour says Big Nose stuck him in the ressies after that. When bant goes bad.

Ray also once set fire to the duvet of Tony Adams's counsellor, Steve Jacobs, while he was asleep in a hotel room. This seems against Dunphy's Law, as well as being, you know, really dangerous, but Ray protests, 'we put it out pretty quickly'. We bet you did – it's any excuse to use a fire extinguisher with you lot. Still, when you get up to as much hi-jinks as Parlour, the odd misjudgement is bound to occur.

2nd PLACE
JIMMY BULLARD

We agonised over this. That he only comes second is a real testament to the man who beats him to the top spot, because Jimmy Bullard is an undisputed Bantersaurus Rex. If he was a prime minster he'd be Banthony Charles Linton Blair. His capacity for mad pranks and crazy antics is legendary throughout the game. Listen to this: Rangers' Kris Boyd loved Lee McCulloch's Bullard stories so much that he decided to grow a big moustache purely because McCulloch told him that was the sort of thing Jimmy would do – 'That was all Boydy needed to hear,' writes McCulloch. Imagine your banter having that kind of influence! It's like chaos theory in action: if Jimmy Bullard craps into a pillowcase (which he has done), someone in Scotland will grow a comedy moustache.

So, let's immerse ourselves in a warm bath of Bullard banter. There's a lot of bant to decant.

Impressively, if we go back to our elements of banter, he pretty much has them all covered. He's not afraid of a properly planned **Set Piece** – witness the aforementioned fire extinguisher gambit, for example. And he loves a bit of **Friendly Nonsense** – you may no doubt recall the time he celebrated a goal for Hull by re-enacting Phil Brown's half-time public lecturing of his acutely embarrassed players for the sin of getting beaten by Manchester City, for instance.

Jimmy doesn't much go in for the **Physical** banter – there are no stories about him Bonging terrified youngsters – but that's not to say he doesn't enjoy a more visceral laugh. He loved, for example, simply soaking his team-mates with a bucket of water when staying in a hotel before a game: 'As soon as they opened the door, all ready for their din-dins, bosh! That bucket of water goes all over them,' he explains.

Nothing cerebral about that (and some might even argue it's so route one that it could be classed as **Rubbish** banter), but Bullard could be inventive too. One of his tricks was the *Beano*-worthy prank of covering a team-mate's towel in Pritt Stick glue so that when they dried themselves after a shower they'd be covered in tough-to-remove sticky fluff, giving them the appearance of, in Jim's words, 'a fucking sheep'.

As you'd expect, he always made great use of Ralgex or Deep Heat. After Michael Brown made the grave error of applying Deep Heat to Bullard's pants, Bullard went all out for revenge – replacing Brown's face moisturiser with Ralgex and somehow managing to top up his toothpaste tube with the same. Hell hath no fury like a banter legend who's had his balls burned.

And no one quite does **Weird** banter like Jimmy Bullard either. He has a particular affection for animal impressions. By his own admission, he found mealtimes when away with the squad boring, so he used to enjoy 'hiding under the table as the poor waitress was coming with food, and then leaping out like a dog, barking, and pretending to bite her arm. The food would always go everywhere, except on the table.' A clear transgression of Dunphy's Law.

His canine impressions didn't end there. Lee McCulloch, whose entire life would have been so much greyer had he never played with Jim at Wigan ('Easily the worst hair in football but a lovely guy and the best banter in the game,' says Lee, admiringly), remembers his behaviour before games in the tunnel: 'He used to shout at the top of his voice to the opposition, "Don't come in the Bullard dog house because you'll get bitten,"' and he'd beg the other players to bark like dogs in response. They didn't, obviously.

Perhaps Bullard's *pièce de résistance* (he'd probably call it a *penis de rèsistance*) is the time he terrorised a relaxed Papa Bouba Diop while he was on the massage table. Fulham team-mate Michael Brown persuaded Bullard to 'get little Jimmy out and stick him through that hole into Pap's face'. It didn't quite work out that way, however, because the angle was just too tricky: 'so I made a spur-of-the-moment decision and put my nuts on top of his head instead. He was still mid-massage so I said something like, "How does that feel, Pap?"' This is almost the perfect football banter story – it's in the massage room, it has cocks and balls and it has a foreign player as the butt of the joke who no doubt 'didn't quite understand English lavatorial humour'. What we admire here is the on-the-spot improvisation to change things up mid-gag. He's mercurial. No pre-prescribed Crazy Gang-style tick list abuse here. All on instinct, honed over years of mischief-making. If only he'd met the Pope and asked him if his head went all the way to the end of his hat, then he'd have a Grand Slam.

1st PLACE
STEVE HARRISON

As far as we know, Steve Harrison, former Watford manager and former Middlesbrough, Villa, Palace, Wolves and England (among others) coach, does not have a book out about his life. But we wish he did. Because Steve Harrison is Lord Bantabulosa. He's the Banter King. The Bantmeister General. The Monarch of the Bant. The Maharajah of Bantah. The Duke of Banterburgh. The Bantichrist. Napoleon Banterparte. Nelson Bantela. William the Banterer. The Archbishop of Banterbury. The Bantom Menace. Eric Bantona. And so on. You get the gist.[33]

His legend is so large that your authors had heard rumours about one particular party trick of his many, many years ago. It was shared in feverish whispers between football fans, but no one seemed totally sure if it was really true. We were only dimly aware of who Steve Harrison even was (there's a snap of him in our pictures section – see if you could have picked him out in a line-up), but he became a name to us purely because of his alleged special talent. It was only finally confirmed to us by Stan Collymore: 'He had been sacked by the FA when he was a coach under Graham Taylor for sitting on a banister and shitting into a cup ten feet below.'

The way we heard it, Steve did it from squatting on top of some kind of wardrobe, but it's essentially the same thing. What a party trick. How do you even find out you can do that? Did he start from a lower level and work his way up? It's incredible whichever way you look at it – a clear step up in class from the Merson/Bullard bant of shitting in pillowcases. Anyone can do that. This is genuine skill – and there's no victim either. Not really. Simple fun for all the family. Imagine what

---

33 Rejected names: Bantman, Robant Hood Prince of Bant, Banthony Hopkins and Bant and Dec.

that kind of thing could do for dressing-room morale. You've just lost four on the trot, everyone's moping about, unsure where the next win is coming from, then suddenly Steve smiles, grabs a small plastic cup and starts ascending a set of stairs or hoisting himself atop a nearby wardrobe. Everyone grins and jostles for position to watch the show. He shoots, he scores, and the players forget their woes and go out and win 4–0 the next week. Amazing.

But don't just take our word for the genius of Steve Harrison. Here's some praise we can only describe as glowing from John Barnes: 'Our coach, Steve Harrison, is the funniest man in football.' Told you. 'Steve will never be short of work because people in football know he is very good at coaching and lightening the mood in a dressing-room.'

Paul Merson says he 'has a reputation in the game as a very funny man, which I knew first hand from his time as Graham Taylor's assistant with England.' And Stuart Pearce said he was at Newcastle 'for his banter as well as his coaching' – imagine that! The guy's banter was so good it was part of his CV. Pearce adds: 'The boys loved him. The stunts he would pull were fantastic.' Collymore says that Harrison's dad was something of a vaudeville act, and clearly that's where Steve's comic sensibilities came from and what sets him apart from his peers.

Some of his repertoire was as simple as throwing himself fully clothed across muddy, puddle-filled pitches. But Paul Merson reveals more of Harrison's vaudevillian roots as he remembers a couple of carefully honed routines: 'We met in the hotel lobby to go to the game and heard this commotion at the top of the stairway. This figure came rolling down the 20 or so carpeted stairs all of a sudden, past two ladies who were making balloon figures for a wedding, got up, dusted himself down and just walked off. Everyone was shocked. Everyone except the lads, who were laughing loudly. It was Steve Harrison.'

And: 'As we were all eating, on a raised part of the dining room, four steps up from the main dining area, Steve Harrison came through all the business people eating and fell up the stairs. He had the whole room in stitches. It was a variation on his celebrated Norman Wisdom walk.' Yes – 'celebrated'. Having thought we were desperate to see the Norman Wisdom impressions of Messrs Taylor, Hill and Sansom, deep down we know that Harrison's would be the definitive one.

Stuart Pearce recalls another Steve Harrison joint: 'One morning we were leaving the hotel for training when we heard someone shouting: "The bells, the bells," and throwing gravel at us. We looked up and there was Steve on the hotel roof playing Quasimodo.' The man's a born performer.

In early 2018 you probably heard the story that Soren Andersen, formerly of Bristol City, made a claim on a Danish podcast about Burnley manager Sean Dyche's distinctive raspy voice: 'Maybe the voice comes from eating rainworms, because every time we trained, he used to eat rainworms … It was horrible,' he said. Dyche subsequently denied this wicked slander, although we're not sure why. Surely it's better to make people think you might eat worms? Gives you some mystique.[34]

Anyway, this is actually one of the few clear-cut examples we've seen of a foreign player not understanding the unique banter of British football, but it turns out Dyche was far from a trailblazer in this trick because Steve Harrison was there before him. Merse remembers: 'During my warm-up, he started coughing violently. When I looked at him, he started bringing up … a worm.'

Pearce reckons Harrison went even further while on the team coach at Newcastle: 'He had been round the hotel garden in the morning collecting worms and it was only after about 15 minutes he opened his mouth and let one of the worms crawl out, followed by the others. It was thoroughly revolting but memorable. Hence the saying "soppy as a bag of worms".' You know, that saying.

With his respect for garden wildlife far exceeded by his commitment to eliciting chuckles from the football community, Harrison really is a cut above the other pretenders. In the Great Royal Hall of Banter, he takes his rightful place. While the likes of Bullard and Parlour might be on the dais, scrapping over a seat at the top table, Harrison is up in the rafters, pants down, waiting to do his party piece. All hail King Steve.

---

34 We've always felt that Dyche has the calm but gruff, no-nonsense demeanour of one of those men you have to go and get in the arcade when the machine has swallowed your money. He looks like he should have a big bunch of keys hanging off his belt.

11

The Man (or Woman) In Black (or Green or Yellow or Red)

Believe

One sharp blast of the whistle and we're in and we're off, delving into the Dark Arts of that most enigmatic of species – The Match Official. They live among us, but who are they? Where do they come from? What do they eat? And what drives them? In this special chapter, we're leaving the players behind and focusing on these curious entities. Evidently these guys grew sick of being background artists, always the bridesmaid, never the bride, and decided to take centre stage in their own books; and, once again, we've done the research so you don't have to.

As kids at school, most of us wanted to play up front and get the goals and the glory. There were others, perhaps with a deeper appreciation of the game, who were happy to play a more withdrawn role and pull the strings in midfield, even if it was with a sodden tennis ball on a crowded playground. Fewer still were happy to be defenders – usually the rougher kids who saw tackling as a natural extension of duffing kids up for their dinner money. If you were lucky, there might even be the odd one or two who'd volunteer to go in goal. But, try as we might, we can't remember a single boy or girl desperately wanting to be the ref.

So how do refs happen? Do they appear fully formed at the age of 16, shiny whistle wrapped around hand, cards in separate pockets, disappearing spray attached awkwardly to waist, several watches strapped about their person, just to be on the safe side? We can't really know for sure. But what we can do is explore the phenomenon together in the hope of greater understanding of this most peculiar of breeds.

There can be only one place to start, and that's at Anfield for Jeff Winter's account of his last game in charge. Winter, who won the race, presumably amid stiff competition, to call his book *Who's the Bastard in the Black?*,[35] was feeling the emotion as his career of annoying fans the length and breadth of the country was winding down. He admits to milking things slightly, and adding time until play was in front of the Kop before finally blowing his whistle: 'The fans behind the goal burst into spontaneous applause. It was longer and louder than normal, even for a big home win. Did they know it was my final visit? Was the applause for me? They are such knowledgeable football people, it wouldn't surprise me.'

To be honest Jeff, it really would surprise us. We shouldn't think anyone behind that goal even knew it was your last game at Anfield, much less gave a flying one; and applause after the final whistle isn't spontaneous, it's cued by the game ending – that's when people applaud, isn't it? Especially after a 4–0 home win, which this was. Quite honestly, the hubris, the sheer puffed-up egotism on display here is breathtaking, but it does lend weight to an idea that we just can't shake – that most referees do believe that it really is all about them.

If your experience of referees is anything like ours, you'll probably have no idea who is in charge of your team's game until some time late in the first half when they give one shoddy decision too many against your lot, and you frantically grab up your programme to give a name to your pain, while muttering something along the lines of 'Who's this tosser?'

With that in mind, it makes you wonder who would read the autobiography of a referee. Well, that's where you have us, because we did – several, in fact. Here, then, is a potted history of some of the not-so-much-loved characters and their greatest hits. A quick 'get to know you' for those men in the middle who have no doubt upset some of you at one point or another in their career.

---

35 Actually, we assume it's called that. On the cover, it's: *Who's the B*****d in the Black?*, with asterisks instead of letters, so it could be something else. Bighead. Bandaid. Badland. Baffled. Bustard. Not ideal for a title.

JEFF WINTER – *WHO'S THE BASTARD IN THE BLACK?*

- Winter was a 'boot boy' as a teenager. He's at pains to say that is different from a hooligan, because the Middlesbrough boot boys were 'more bravado than violence'. The distinction seems to rest on the fact that the boot boys left those who had the wherewithal to travel to matches on official club coaches alone, but still might have attacked anyone else – the lovable rogues.

- Jeff clearly still fancies himself as a bit tasty, a bit naughty, or whatever the kids are calling it these days, because he says this of a celebrity encounter with Ray Winstone: 'We talked of our days as young fans, and I wondered whether we had ever squared up to each other on the terraces at West Ham. I reckon it would've been an even-money scrap, for he looks as if he can take care of himself.' If there was genuinely even money on offer for Ray Winstone to beat Jeff Winter in a fight, no wonder Raymondo does all those betting adverts. There's clearly easy money to be made. Get On It. Cash Out. Have a Bang On That. When the fun stops, stop. Although if the fun we're talking about is watching Ray Winstone duffing up Jeff Winter, that fun could last for ages.

- Jeff tells of his relief when Keith Hackett replaced Philip Don as Chief Grand Poobah of Referees and lifted the sex ban before matches. Quite why the ban on referees having sex the night before a game was in place and how it was enforced are both mysteries to us, but it seems that both Jeff and Mrs Jeff were cock-a-hoop with the decision. By all means do your own 'Winter is coming' gag at this point, because we're not touching it.

CLIVE THOMAS – *BY THE BOOK*

Now fair's fair; you have to hand it to him for that title. His nickname was 'The Book' so it really works. It's a beauty. However, if we're honest, that's about all the nice things we have to say about Clive Thomas. Let's take a look at his best bits:

- As a young ref, Clive officiated an under-16 match halfway up a Welsh mountain. The game was supposed to last 30 minutes each way, but Clive ended up playing an hour and 35 minutes because he religiously stopped the watch every time the ball went down the hillside, all the time knowing that everyone was going to struggle for their last train home. A stickler for the rules, then.

- When you're making things up, taxi drivers are always good to slip into your story, aren't they? Just ask Ben Fogle. The very nature of the cabbie–passenger relationship is transient. You couldn't be expected to remember detail and you can't be called on it. Quite why this comes to mind now, we can't rightly say. Oh yes, Clive tells us that he wasn't well liked by Everton fans due to some controversial decisions he gave against them, yet when he found himself in Liverpool, an Everton fan accepting his fare had this to say: 'I'd like to show you the longest way round. But because deep down I respect you, the quickest way is …'

Never happened, did it?

- Clive Thomas constantly talks about Clive Thomas in the third person, does Clive Thomas. Clive Thomas also displays a rampant paranoia seemingly common among referees. For an example of both, look no further than this: 'I am sure in some circles the knives were out for Clive Thomas in the hope that he had made the biggest mistake of his career.' Told you.

- Clive Thomas thinks that neutral fans came to see games he was refereeing because he was refereeing them. He talks about a European tie in Belgium between Waterschei and Paris Saint Germain that a load of Chelsea fans turned up at. 'They had read that I was taking the game, had intended to watch a European Cup game somewhere and decided this was as good and near as any.' For a start, nobody has ever taken the referee into account when choosing which game to travel abroad to see. For seconds, we'll venture that a wandering group of Chelsea fans on the continent in the 1970s were more likely looking for some kind of international dust-up than hoping to see an officious Clive Thomas referee a game to within an inch of its life. This hubris is on Jeff-Winter-at-Anfield levels.

- Further fuelling the idea that Clive Thomas thinks the world revolves around Clive Thomas, he has a chapter entitled 'TV Thomas' in which he describes himself as 'an entertainer, a performer who refuses to accept that there are on the field only twenty-two players'. He also talks of being 'unashamedly delighted' when he knew a game of his was being televised. He even developed an idiosyncratic little showbiz kick as he blew to start a game, which he is convinced the cameras loved. He got it from his great showbiz mate Frankie Vaughan, who used to do it in his act. Kick his leg up, we mean, not blow a whistle.

- Clive Thomas was dead against over-zealous goal celebrations. He worries that players kissing one another 'gives me and the game a bad name among the less understanding and heterosexual rugby enthusiasts in the Rhondda', as well as expressing concern that jumping on a player's back could cause 'physical as well as mental problems for the future'. Aside from the homophobia on display here (which, diplomatically, we might put down to it being 'a different time'), we can't help thinking he's overstating the potential damage of celebrating a goal – unless you count Steve Morrow, of course.

- Disappointingly for Clive Thomas, this one's not about Clive Thomas. Clive Thomas tells us that during World Cup '74, Clive Thomas and his referee chums visited Rudi Kreitlein. Does that name ring a bell? It should. He's the referee who sent off Rattin during England v Argentina in 1966 for 'the look in his eye'. We all grew up accepting that, but it's nonsense, isn't it? Sure, the ref did England a favour, but people shouldn't be getting sent off at the World Cup for funny looks, otherwise where would the likes of Proper Ronaldo be? Especially when he had that dubious half-moon hairdo. Anyway, confirmation that Kreitlein is a wrong 'un comes as Clive Thomas reveals that 'Rudi's house was covered with photographs of his sendings-off – a sort of black hack museum'. He clearly delighted in it. One suspects they all do.

GRAHAM POLL - *SEEING RED*

Poll's book is the gift that keeps on giving. From the almost incessant hand-wringing over his three-card trick at the World Cup, to his tales of drunken antics and their fallout, there's plenty to enjoy. Another ref pun for a title, too – Mark Clattenburg's 'Clatts Entertainment' surely can't be too far away.

- Poll's foreword is by Sir Alex Ferguson. Mark Halsey's is by Jose Mourinho. Make your own minds up about that.

- Poll is a deplorable banter merchant. Hiding Philip Don's shorts, putting mud in people's boots and other similar acts were all par for the course for a self-proclaimed 'young buck having a laugh'. He freely admits, mind, that 'my jolly japes became just too much' and that he was the most complained-about referee. Tiresome, Graham. Tiresome.

- If you ever sang 'You're not fit to referee' at Graham Poll, it didn't hurt him because Graham is incredibly literal in his thinking and he knew that he had passed all physical fitness tests and was probably fitter than most of those chanting. So there. Ditto, 'Who's the wanker in the black?' because, as Graham so rightly points out as he wilfully misses the point, 'I didn't always wear black.' But if you ever chanted at him about his mistake at the World Cup when he booked the same player three times, well, Bingo! He concedes that hurt. To be honest, we reckon the others hurt a little bit too, reading between the lines.

- Poll kept a World Cup diary, which we're privy to here. The biggest revelation is how sincerely he took the Mars advertising slogan of that year: 'BELIEVE'. His entries are peppered with the word, always in capital letters. It's not a coincidence. He loves the slogan and was genuinely inspired by Mars bars. Do you remember the campaign? Possibly. Did you decide to live your life by it? Probably not.

- On the 2002 World Cup, Poll talks about referees who were no longer taking part consoling themselves with a karaoke party on a boat. While unfortunate Japanese referee Toru Kamikawa 'sang a Japanese folk song with tears in his eyes', Poll stepped up and 'gave a terrible rendition of "Delilah" – with special emphasis on the line "Why, why, why? …" – but it had far less effect on the room'. We would have paid good money to have seen this.

MARK HALSEY – *ADDED TIME*

Another fine refereeing pun, and one that relates to the life-threatening illness he happily beat. So good work all round.

- He's ever such good mates with Jose Mourinho, if you can imagine such a thing. Jose wrote a foreword for him, and there's a chapter titled 'Me and Jose'. Jose is quoted as saying, 'He is a good friend and top referee. He is a special one.' Special one, you see. Like he called himself that time. He really can't help making it all about himself, can he?

- In case you ever wondered, Halsey admits to being a QPR fan. That puts him in the company of Michael Gove, Toby Young and Pete Doherty, which is nobody's idea of a good night out, is it?

- Mark Halsey's missus once set them up for their house to appear on *60 Minute Makeover*. Along with Dion Dublin's stint on *Homes Under the Hammer*,[36] this can be seen as the opening salvo in football's attempts to annex daytime property TV.

HOWARD WEBB – *THE MAN IN THE MIDDLE*

The last Englishman, for a good while we imagine, to referee a World Cup Final is a complex character. The son of a miner who grew up near Orgreave and became a policeman, Webb is clearly not afraid to make the big, unpopular decisions.

- Webb is proud of his fitness levels, and equally proud of the day Gareth Southgate noticed. He recalls Southgate spotting him 'walking around in my base layer' and exclaiming 'Bloody hell, are you in good shape or what?' Well, bless you for noticing, Gareth.

- Webb titles a chapter 'If Anyone Can, Darren Cann' in praise of his long-time assistant and friend, of whom he is justifiably fond. He not only reveals that Cann is the brains of the outfit, but, in a comparison we can only applaud, also says that Cann is like Spot the Cat from *Hong Kong Phooey*, who would actually crack the case while his hapless boss took the credit. Lovely stuff.

- Still on Cann, he says that 'Darren wasn't everybody's cup of tea though. He could be a very intense, single-minded person', which manifests itself in the 'slo-mo semaphore-style routine' he would put himself through before each match. That's right,

---

36 In keeping with the theme of ex-Villa players, the German version of that show features Thomas Hitzlsperger and is called *Homes Under Der Hammer*. This may not be true.

the linesman practised putting his flag up in front of the mirror. Sheesh.

- Webb gave advice to Jeremy Hunt MP, who, as if looking for more reasons beyond overseeing the destruction of the NHS to be unpopular, 'decided to train as a referee'. Can you imagine?

- Howard once refereed a charity match at Rotherham featuring the Chuckle Brothers, and er, all the other celebrity Rotherham fans. Inevitably, they chucked a bucket of water over him after a cursory bit of 'To Me, To You'. Howard says: 'The cheeky Chuckles had quite literally wet my whistle which, in the sub-zero temperatures, totally froze up.' What we like about this story is that he says it took place in the very first minute of the match. Nobody could even keep their slapstick powder dry for 15 minutes before going for it. Cards on the table here: we preferred them when they were the Chucklehounds. There, we've said it.

YOU'VE GOT A FRIEND

Referees may be unpopular with fans, but deep down I'm sure we all concede that they do a tough job. In our hearts we'd probably all like to think that even if nobody else likes them, they have one another's back; that they form their own effective support group for the refereeing community. Unfortunately, this couldn't be more wrong, because the truth is this: they don't like each other. Well, some of them don't. It's complicated. The internecine squabbles among fellow professional referees puts *Game of Thrones* to shame.

In brief, Jeff Winter doesn't seem to like David Elleray much, while Elleray says that Clive Thomas spent a lot of time sniping at him, did Clive Thomas. Mark Halsey suspects that David Elleray wasn't keen on him, and he also couldn't stand Graham Poll (nor could Elleray). Are you with us so far? Graham Poll and Graham Barber were best buddies and were known, oddly, as 'The Tring Triads',[37] while nobody at all liked Rob Styles, it seems.

Let's get into specifics. Jeff Winter says that Elleray and Poll clashed because: 'David was the eloquent, non-drinking, well-spoken Harrow housemaster; Graham was one of the lads, rough and brash. He liked a laugh and a beer ... in fact I got on much better with David.' Fair

---

37 Surely 'Golden Grahams' would have been better?

enough. Winter does say that after early mistrust between himself and Elleray, the schoolteacher said to him, 'Do you know, Winter, you're the better for knowing.' We've no idea what he means by this, despite googling it.

If Winter's relationship with Elleray is complicated and exciting, like *Moonlighting* with whistles, his feelings on Rob Styles are less ambiguous. Complaining of 'a ruthless streak that surpassed anything I, and many others, had ever seen', Winter says 'Rob Styles had the ability to alienate nearly everybody. I have never come across a referee so roundly criticised by players, managers and supporters.' Rob Styles, then: the arsehole's arsehole.

Mark Halsey is a curious chap. We were delighted to read of his successful battle with serious health problems, but that aside, we're not sure we're buying Halsey's self-projected image of a wild card frowned upon by the authorities. You see, Halsey is under the impression that he was passed over for cup finals and bigger games in his career because he's some sort of dangerous maverick in the mould of Dirty Harry, Luther or Spender.

He claims that one of the reasons David Elleray took against him was because he showed him up in a bleep test. He goes on to say of the powers that be: 'They preferred the sticklers, the referees who obeyed edicts without question,' and he hammers home the idea that his 'face and style not fitting with certain uptight individuals' held him back from going further in his career. He's out there busting heads and taking names, guys, and if those pencil pushers at City Hall don't like the way he does it, they can go to hell. That kind of vibe.

Not even the beautiful game itself can bring these people together. Halsey tells of a referees' five-a-side game in which 'two of our number got into an argument over a penalty and a bout of pushing each other developed. One referee then pushed his head into the other's face.' Honestly, they'll copy anything they see on TV, this lot, won't they? In another game, Jeff Winter says that Peter Jones had a finger broken by a Rob Styles challenge. Grow up, eh, fellas?

It's not all bickering and whispering behind backs, though. Graham Poll credits Paul Durkin as being the funniest of the bunch during his time, which is nice to hear because we always thought he was a good ref.

Lee Mason evidently took up that baton and ran with it – binding the guys together, very much like David Brent, through the gift of laughter. You may hold a grudge against Mason because your team has been on the wrong end of a bad decision from him, but Howard Webb shows him in a different light, calling him 'the resident class joker' who was in charge of entertainment at get-togethers and Christmas dos and the like. If morale was low, Mason, 'in cahoots with Jon Moss', would pull out impressions of those in the game, or run a quiz show format complete with a Leslie Crowther or Bruce Forsyth voice up his sleeve. Plenty of scope for 'Good game' and 'So much better than last week', we'd have thought.

After a brief respite, however, the mention of game shows means that the infighting rears up once more. David Elleray tells of 'a number of colleagues' being worried that Uriah Rennie had got himself an agent to handle his burgeoning public profile, 'which might threaten our unity and strength of purpose'. Firstly, this word 'unity' – we do not think it means what they think it means. Secondly, it's having the perspicacity to get an agent that enabled Uriah Rennie, not David Elleray, to secure a spot on short-lived daytime quiz show *Freeze Out* – a programme described by *The Guardian* as: 'A game show that feels a little bit like being trapped in a coma and screaming to get out'.

If Rennie's showbiz career was something short of stellar, it did at least eclipse that of those Tring Triad lads, Grahams Barber and Poll. The pair tried to take a show on the road called 'Men in Black Evenings' (although 'Barber & Poll' seems like a perfectly serviceable double-act nickname to us – you know, like a Barber's Pole). The show, as described by GP, sounds terrific: 'We would wear black tracksuit bottoms and black polo shirts and we would talk, deliver a few well-rehearsed ad-libs and answer questions' – and we can't think why the crowds didn't flock to see it. The fact remains, however, that they didn't, and the show died a quick death. You could, cruelly, say that they had fewer bookings than that Croatian defender had at the World Cup, but that might still be too raw for Poll.

RED RED WINE

The real joy of these petty feuds among referees, though, is that it isn't just a series of isolated incidents, but rather all-out gang warfare. You think we're joking, but it isn't overstating the case to say that in the golden age of the celebrity referee (the 2000s), a schism greater than the one currently dividing UB40 opened up, with clear lines drawn on both sides. At that time, it seems, you were either with The Red Wine Club, or against them.

It's referee gang wars, and we love it. It's like the Jets and the Sharks, Montagues and Capulets, Grange Hill and Rodney Bennett. Pick your side.

The Red (Red) Wine Club, led by Graham Poll as some sort of Fonzie character, included Graham Barber (Barbs, of course), Steve Dunn (Dunny), Paul Durkin (Durks) and Rob Styles, with others like Andy D'Urso and Mike Reed holding affiliate membership without ever being part of the core, it seems (but perhaps they could be called upon if things became physical). They called themselves The Red Wine Club because, wait for it, they liked red wine. Yet from such a flimsy premise a great bond grew. Poll namechecks all of these guys as being supportive when he was passed over for Euro 2004, while he got the distinct impression the other lot were sniggering at him.

Jeff Winter apparently led the alternative group, who called them-selves, if you can believe it, 'The Good Guys'. The feeling among the Good Guys (not really good guys) clique was that the other lot always got the big games. This faction included Halsey, Mike Riley, Barry Knight, Steve Bennett and Neale Barry. Webb suggests there was a vague North–South divide to the battle lines that were drawn. He says he tried to maintain the middle ground with the likes of Dermot Gallagher and Uriah Rennie, but felt the irresistible pull of Winter's bad boys.

It's like the opposite of *Captain America: Civil War*, isn't it? In that, we're conflicted as our heroes are pitched against one another, whereas here we're witnessing a battle where nobody likes any of them.

Webb says that the 'simmering tensions' boiled over during 'an informal beer'n'barbecue night' (as opposed to one of those *formal* beer'n'barbecue nights, where people turn up in full black tie?), when Poll and Halsey went toe to toe, before Uriah Rennie stepped in and called for some order. Howard was shocked: 'Watching them trading personal insults and squaring up to each other was pretty unedifying, to say the least. These were well-regarded, well-paid Premier League referees acting like badly behaved schoolboys.' Take out the 'well-regarded' and we're with him all the way. In his book, Halsey hammers home his dislike for Poll and says he 'was not one for the trenches'. As we know, there's no greater condemnation than that.

With this damaging divide slowly tearing the brotherhood apart, things came to a head on a team-building weekend in Aldershot. An incident occurred that led to what Graham Poll calls the 'biggest act of betrayal I have ever suffered'. Dun-Dun-Daaaah! In short, Poll got himself on the outside of a few cold drinks, disgraced himself and was grassed up. Given that his company were all referees, men dedicated to letting no fun go unpunished, Poll's surprise at being undone by a tell-tale-tit is touchingly naïve. But who was it?[38]

Graham Poll, Howard Webb and Mark Halsey all devote a lot of words to this epic incident, so we can piece together a pretty good picture of what happened. Being fair, we'll go with Poll's own account first.

He claims he took part in a 'port challenge' and came off second best. He confesses to being 'inebriated as a newt', but insists: 'I wasn't shouting, or aggressive or anything. I was ill.' He confesses to being sick around the hotel corridors, then in the comfort of his own room. Contrite in the morning, he says he cleared up what he could, apologised to the duty manager and offered to pay for any further cleaning, and was told that 'there had been no complaints and that, as far as he and his staff were concerned, there was no problem'.

Halsey's version has Poll being rude to innocent bystanders and Phil Dowd alike, and describes some jumping on a car bonnet. Webb, with no particular axe to grind, backs up the car story. All three agree that it was *Freeze Out*'s own Uriah Rennie who took care of Poll.

The real drama came after that, however, as Boss Ref Keith Hackett received an anonymous (and misspelled, claims Poll) email, from the hastily registered aldershot1234@hotmail.com,[39] telling all about the drunken antics of 'Someone who lives in Tring and will be England's World Cup referee in Germany 2006' – which narrowed it down to a group of one'. Poll was promptly suspended and his story dragged through the press, and so he vowed to get to the bottom of this 'vicious act of betrayal'.

---

38 We can't help thinking that these weekends would have been amazing to film. Imagine what Louis Theroux would have done with a military barracks full of referees.

39 You can try emailing it if you like. You'll hear nothing back.

At the next referee conference at Staverton, Poll gathered everyone in one room, as if in an Agatha Christie mystery, with Detective Poll of the Yard[40] gradually dismissing those from the room that he knew hadn't sent the offending email – starting with the Red Wine Lads, naturally, though why they all sat there and took it remains a mystery to us. Webb says that Poll laid it on thick about how disappointed he was in whoever had done it, and then, 'explained how medical reasons had provoked his misbehaviour'. Chinny reckon.

Ultimately only four suspects remained – Chris Foy, Phil Dowd (who had been badly abused according to Halsey, remember), Alan Wiley and Halsey himself. The final four were left to stew in the room until one of them cracked and owned up to it, which of course, none of them did – which kind of made the whole thing pointless. Reading between the lines, Poll thought it was Halsey, while Halsey hints at Dowd and swears on his family that he didn't send any email. I guess we'll never know and the culprit will take the secret to their grave.

What we do know is that Graham Poll can handle his red wine, but not his port, and doesn't take kindly to being grassed up. It's fair to say that nobody likes a grass, but nobody likes referees either, so this affair takes on the complexity of a deep philosophical question. By all means use any free pages at the back of this book to jot down any thoughts on the matter.

The incident hastened the end of The Red Wine Club, which disbanded soon after. Poll says 'The "good old days" had started to disappear' and laments that 'the days of being relaxed and trusting were gone for ever once that email was sent'. We like to read this last bit in the voice and tone of Richard Dreyfus at the end of *Stand By Me*.

FIGHT THE POWER

If referees can't even look after each other, it's no wonder there's such friction once they actually have to take charge of players and managers – and there is no end of friction to be had. For a start, Roy Keane clearly enjoyed Poll's brush with the booze, and when he next saw Poll, the ref says he said to him, 'If you can't take it, don't drink it.'

David Elleray's take on Keane is that he 'seems scarcely able to bring himself to speak to me', and he appears put out by it. He also mentions

---

40 Miss Mar-Poll, anyone?

a time that David Batty was in a 'terribly bad mood and not his normal chirpy self' – resulting in the referee giving up on trying to natter to the midfielder. Firstly, David Batty's natural demeanour doesn't strike us as chirpy. Nor does he strike us as someone who would like a natter during a game. Has Elleray got the right person here? He wouldn't be the first ref to get the wrong player. We do like the idea of the schoolmaster running round the pitch looking for a chat, though.

Howard Webb recounts a couple of run-ins with Craig Bellamy, which will surprise no one. He says that Bellamy referred to him as 'Celebrity Ref' and shouted at him from the Liverpool bench once when he was fourth official, calling him a 'shithouse' and reminding him about his nightmare World Cup Final performance. For his part, Webb says, 'I'm not sure what I'd done to rile him' and asserts that 'there weren't many more obnoxious players around than Craig Bellamy'.

Indeed, Webb, like a significantly less hirsute Father Christmas, has a naughty-and-nice list. His good guys include Tim Howard, Brad Friedel, Joey Barton, Mark Noble and Kevin Nolan; while he's less fond of Jens Lehmann, Cesc Fabregas, Ryan Shawcross and Fernando Torres.

We were somewhat surprised by Torres, but Mark Halsey also describes him as 'another great whinger', before training his beady eye on Danny Mills, who, he says, 'could be a right prick at times'. His words, not ours. Halsey goes on to say that Ashley Cole, 'gobby' Dean Windass and Sebastian Larsson also grind his gears.

Some players have their own say on the men in the middle. The very laid-back Matt Le Tissier says that Uriah Rennie and Rob Styles were both 'up themselves' and gives a handy list of his five worst refs, which includes both Elleray and Winter, along with the flowing locks of Roger 'Should have sent Gazza off in the '91 Cup Final' Milford. For his best refs, he can only muster Paul Durkin and Dermot Gallagher, throwing in a cheeky 'Errr … That's it.'

Roy McDonough likes Graham Poll, Dean Windass doesn't and nor does Robbie Savage after all that regrettable toilet business. Savage claims that Poll 'thinks he is pretty special', in as spectacular a case of pot calling kettle black we think we've ever come across. Windass isn't keen on Phil Dowd either, while Joey Barton says of an incident in which he was elbowed in the head: 'I turned to the referee and wondered whether he had seen it. It was Phil Dowd, so he hadn't.' Phil Thompson is no fan of Clive Thomas, and Chris Sutton gets all grumpy about Hugh Dallas, who he says 'liked to be the centre of attention' – a common cause of complaint between players and referees.

Relations with managers can get a bit testy at times as well. This is particularly the case if, like Howard Webb, you send a colleague a text saying, 'Pulis? What a fucking wanker,' only to immediately realise that you've sent it to Tony Pulis by mistake. Apparently, Pulis took it well. TP also makes it on to Mark Halsey's list of favourite managers, along with Roberto Martinez, genial Harry Redknapp and, of course, lovely Chris Hughton.

He also praises 'Sir Alex', David Moyes and Sam Allardyce, though of course none can hold a candle to his mucker Jose Mourinho. His shit list is topped by a man he 'just cannot look back on with any fondness. His name: Steve Evans.'

Sam Allardyce has no hesitation in calling Barry Knight 'the worst referee in the history of the game', after he gave Ipswich three penalties in a match against Big Sam's Bolton. The manager went banging on his door after the game and Knight locked himself inside, which is perhaps for the best as 'the police would have had to take me away'. Why Allardyce couldn't call on his previous powers and smash through the door, we don't know. If you're not familiar with the play-off game in question, we urge you to take a look and decide for yourselves: an extraordinary game.

Possibly our favourite referee story, though, and one that illustrates clearly why they aren't the most popular people in the game, comes from Jimmy Greaves. Greavsie tells of a Spurs v Leicester game when he was awarded a penalty. While his England team-mate Gordon Banks was wiping his hands in preparation over by his post, Greavsie, always looking for the laugh, 'stepped up and dinked the ball with the toe end of my boot into the opposite corner of Gordon's goal. The White Hart Lane crowd saw the joke in this and as the ball crossed the line, offered an ironic cheer. To everyone's amazement, however, the referee blew his whistle and awarded the goal.' Gordon Banks was justifiably furious and told the ref he couldn't give it, only to become a part of the following exchange:

'"I played advantage," explained the referee.

'"Played advantage?" gasped Gordon. "From a penalty?"

'"Played advantage," repeated the referee, "best law there is. Allows a referee to ignore all the other rules for the good of the game."'

Now, Gordon Banks famously fell ill and his absence cost England a chance to retain the World Cup in 1970, and he later lost an eye, and yet we've never seen him do anything but smile. If this ref can make Banksy rage, he is truly a special piece of work. It's only fitting that he goes unnamed by Greavsie (never 'Greavesy', remember), for in many ways he is every ref and all refs.

SYMPATHY FOR THE DEVIL

Some of those reading this (possibly referees) may feel we've been a bit harsh. So let's devote a bit of time to empathising with the guys in the middle. After all, a job can't be easy if some managers (Dave Bassett is named as a culprit) are practising badgering the referees with their teams in training.

As a starter to this brave new way of thinking, both Robbie Savage and Graham Poll devote a lot of space in their books to 'Jobbiegate' (arguably the worst of all the 'gates): the occasion when a desperate Savage charged into the ref's room, used the toilet and left without washing his hands. We know whose side we're on there. As hard as it might be to take up with Poll on anything, the fact that the alternative is to side with Robbie Savage does make it slightly easier, although Jeff Winter inevitably takes the opposite view on Savage, that 'anyone who craps in Graham Poll's toilet can't be all bad'. We may be done with the bitchiness among colleagues now, but we do see Jeff's point about 'my enemy's enemy' and all that.

Poll also spends a lot of time telling us how Halsey's friend, Mourinho, and his henchman, John Terry, made his life a misery. While Mourinho's Chelsea were busy forging a lasting legacy as one of the most disliked teams in English football, it seems that Poll bore the brunt of it. Indeed, Poll even titles a chapter 'No Defence From John Terry', in which he relates the grief that the former England captain gave him after a red card at Tottenham. In a game soon after, when Poll 'started to have a bit of banter with Joe Cole, JT said to his team-mate, "F*** him off, Coley. Don't talk to him."' The feud between the pair of them continued and it puts us in mind of that time Jeremy Clarkson and Piers Morgan had a fight. We can't actively want either one of them to win, right?

If we're unsurprised to hear that Mourinho and Terry are capable of being less than pleasant to referees, consider our eyebrows firmly unraised at revelations about Neil Warnock. Poll sent Warnock to the stand in a Sheffield United v Leeds match after overhearing him say about Gary Kelly: 'Next time, I hope he [Kelly] breaks his f***ing leg.' Pleasant.

In the face of such provocation, we can be forgiven for enjoying the odd occasion when refs bite back, as a young Howard Webb did when running the line for a Scunthorpe v Scarborough game. He became embroiled in an argument with veteran Ian 'Snods' Snodin after disallowing a Scarborough goal for offside; Webb says Snodin 'was foaming at the mouth' and shouting everything at him to the point where the young Webb could hold back no longer: '"FUCK OFF IAN!" I shouted, as he recoiled in shock at this potty-mouthed linesman. Not only was this highly unprofessional behaviour, it was massively out of character.' This kind of thing must happen a lot, but what came next is beautiful, as Snodin made an official post-match complaint to the referee, only for Webb to maintain that he had 'simply stated "He was a foot off, Ian."' Snodin understandably lost his mind about this, and while it does prove once and for all that referees can be liars, we can't help admiring Webb for this one.

It's also possible to feel sorry for referees because, let's face it, most players are cheats. From Ballon d'Or winners to the Dog & Duck's reserve left-back (who drives a people carrier), who among us can hand on heart say we've never appealed for a throw-in that we know should be going the other way? There, feels good to admit it, doesn't it? And if we do that, we can't really grumble about players at any other level trying to cheat the referee.

Take Maradona, for example, and that handball. No, not that one, we're over that one. The other one. The handball on the line against USSR at Italia '90 to prevent a certain goal. El Diego says, 'The Russians piled on top of the ref all at once, but I'd hypnotised the guy. I'd hypnotised him!' If one of the greatest of all time can also call upon both divine intervention *and* the powers of those lads at holiday camps who can persuade people into thinking an onion is a delicious pear to trick opponents and officials alike, what chance have any of us got?

Worse even than Maradona's deity and Magic-Circle-sanctioned deception, though, is Pelé. You won't believe it, but one time, lovely, cuddly Pelé got sent off. You won't believe it because of his sweet nature on the pitch, and you won't believe it because Pelé used his star power to immediately get the decision reversed. On receiving his red card, Pelé says, 'I'm not sure who was more shocked – me or the crowd. He could have sent off anyone, but not the man everyone had come to see.' As the situation escalated, the poor referee, named Chato, needed protection from the police as the stadium was baying for his blood.

'The chants started: "Pelé! Pelé!" They had paid to see me, and weren't going to let a referee spoil their day. The only solution was the unprecedented decision to send Chato himself off. And with the referee sent off, I could be "un-sent off". I was readmitted into the game, and everyone was happy. Everyone, apart from Chato, of course.' Amid our genuine outrage about Pelé's WG Grace-style antics here, we have questions. What higher power ordered poor Chato off? Do two linesmen add up to more than one referee? Did they take the decision? How did the opposition feel? Was it at that moment they all realised they were just taking part in the Pelé show?

At least Chato got away without taking a hiding, but the late Paul Alcock was, of course, less fortunate. Alcock may have been an excellent referee, but, regrettably, what he has come to be remembered for in the game is being pushed over by Paolo Di Canio. Instead of showing any contrition or remorse for what went on, Di Canio instead pours scorn on the way he fell over, as if there was an agreed way a referee should go down when shoved by a player. Paolo says, 'Alcock kept going backwards, dragging his leg along the ground before collapsing on his buttocks. It certainly looked bizarre.' All right, mate. He does look daft, but that might be for other people to say rather than the one who pushed him over. Even Mark Halsey says of the incident that 'he had no need to fall like a sack of spuds as he did after taking five or six steps backwards. To be honest, it was a bit comical and privately as referees we had a bit of a laugh about it.' Where's the solidarity?

Elsewhere Clive Thomas tells of a time he gave a last-minute penalty against Benfica in a European tie and had a ball booted at the back of his head as he made his way back to the halfway line. 'I looked round but was unable to identify the culprit among the suddenly innocent faces, then on the following Saturday on ITV Brian Moore confirmed that it was the goalkeeper who kicked the ball.' We never had Brian Moore down as a grass.

Clive Thomas attracted all kinds of criticism and abuse, seemingly both on and off the pitch. He tells of receiving an anonymous letter from an Ipswich fan (though that narrows it down a fair amount), which claimed he would face retribution for doing wrong by the Tractor Boys: 'God don't repay his debts in money you will live to regret what you have done. There's too many crooks in sport today and we don't want any down here … You are indeed a horrible, horrible man. What did the crooks threaten to do to you? Many people here wish you the worst. So do I.'

We like this letter, as it appears to be lovingly written in the style of Wearside Jack or similar classic hoax letters. Also, people had to work harder then. When a football fan felt aggrieved they had to put pen to paper, find an envelope, buy a stamp and all that. They couldn't just go on Twitter and slag off Sir Chris Hoy every time Chris Foy gave a penalty against them.

So far, we've dealt exclusively with men, but spare a thought for that rare breed, the female official. We've all seen and heard some of the abuse that Sian Massey has famously had to endure, but Wendy Toms came before her. Can you imagine the 'banter' she had to put up with, either well intentioned or not?

Jeff Winter praises the fans ('inventive with their humour') at a Southampton v Fulham game where they sang that 'Wendy should be "doing the washing up at home". I couldn't help laughing and I glanced over towards Wendy, who was clearly suppressing a giggle,' which is, of course, another way of saying 'she wasn't laughing'.

She shouldn't have had to put up with that, much less getting the same from Winter and the rest of his team, who jokingly repeated the chant to her after the game. Winter claims that 'she knew that playing jokes on each other was part and parcel of refereeing, and kept us sane.' Difficult to agree with Winter on this one. The chant's not 'inventive', and she shouldn't have to hear sexist stuff when she's working, surely? Also, extra wrong points for using 'part and parcel', a phrase only ever uttered by people involved with football when defending something abhorrent to the rest of us.

Toms faced even worse from sexist Stan Ternent when she flagged for a penalty against his Burnley side. This is his recollection, bold as brass, from his own book:

'The ref blew and gave the penalty. We scampered down the touchline.

'"Never a penner, that!"

'She said nothing.

'"You've cost us promotion, love!"

'Still nothing.

'"Oi! Can I ask you a question? While you're here knackering our chances, who's making your husband's tea?" It was pointless abuse, but I'd be lying if I said it didn't make us feel better.'

Oh, Stan, you absolute tit.

Are you feeling sympathy for the officials yet? Feels weird, doesn't it? We've all been wronged by them and had our weekends ruined by them, but between the cheating, the verbal abuse and the physical abuse, it is possible to see cracks in their tough personae. Are they not human? If you cut them, do they not bleed? Nothing brought this home for us more starkly than poor old David Elleray's reaction to the tragic death of Diana, our Princess Queen of Hearts. His diary entry for that fateful 1997 day reads, 'I had always adored her and often dreamt about her. I was stunned and could not stop watching the TV. I am not ashamed to say that I shed tears many times that morning as I shuttled between meetings and watched the terrible story unfold.' Well, it was an emotional time for all of us, Davi… wait a minute: *often dreamt about her*?

Okay, so that might be slightly odd and creepy, but we like to think that it shows that for all our criticism, referees are human and should be treated as such. Well, apart from Mike Dean, obviously. We joke. It's a tough job for sure, and these brave men and women are out there taking charge because, well, somebody has to, or we can't have a game. Cutting through the nonsense, we all need to see that these people need our respect, and our help, in order to be the best they possibly can. Thankfully, between the catty remarks, there are some on hand to offer sound advice to their protégés. Among those to be considered as gospel are the Swiss Toni ramblings of Hugh Dallas, offering his thoughts to Howard Webb:

'Refereeing is like riding a horse you've never met before.' Stop sniggering at the back there. 'If it's a shit, and you keep your reins too loose for the first few steps, you're going to have to pull it right back. But if it's a gem, and you keep the reins too tight, you might aggravate it.'

Wise words indeed, but a bit long-winded for us. We think that Webb heard it put more succinctly and accurately by George Courtney, when he said:

'To succeed as a ref, Howard, you've got to be prepared to be a bastard, but not be a c***.'

Brings a tear to the eye, doesn't it?

12

Top Shelf
Depilated adequately

During our research into footballer autobiographies, we noticed certain patterns emerging. Many of them start not at the beginning, with birth and early memories and stuff, but by discussing a huge career moment. It might be something good (a World Cup Final in the case of someone like Jack Charlton), something harrowing (Stuart Pearce and his missed penalty at Italia '90) or something recent that seems important and topical (Kevin Keegan quitting at Newcastle (first time around – well second, if you count the earlier time he quit, but didn't quit)).

After that, it's usually the trip back to childhood, followed by nostalgic stories of their days as an apprentice – the sepia-hued bygone days when they suffered regular ritual humiliation (boot polish to the bollocks etc.) delivered by callous professionals. And then there's the real meat – the career itself. The highs, the lows, the glad times, the sad times, the managers they loved (because they picked them), the managers they hated (because they didn't).

That's the formula for a lot of autobiographies, both because it works well and because the basic building blocks of a top-level footballer's career don't vary too much. But as well as that classic structure, there were more specific elements that emerged time and again. Eventually, we came to see these as the **Golden Rules of the Football Autobiography**.

We admit, that's probably a grander title than it deserves to be, because it's not like you'll find all the golden rules adhered to in every book (although if you did, it would surely be the ultimate footballer autobiography). However, it felt like most books did feature at least one or two of the Golden Rules. We present them to you now, with a fanfare you cannot hear:

THE SIX GOLDEN RULES

1.
Always mention George Best, ideally re-telling the 'Where did it all go wrong, George?' anecdote. No one will ever get sick of hearing that one.

2.
If you mention Peter Taylor, you must also mention his brilliant impersonation of Norman Wisdom.

3.
You must tell at least one story that concerns someone's shoes or other item of clothing being cut up, burned or otherwise destroyed.

4.
If you have met Rod Stewart – and if you're a footballer, you will have met Rod Stewart – do not neglect to mention it. Bonus points if your wife/girlfriend was there too and she obviously fancied him.

5.
Always try to include a story about something daft/funny/zany/ weird/bizarre/dangerous that Gazza did. It does not matter if you were there or not – second- or even third-hand stories are perfectly acceptable.

6.
Any reference to Duncan McKenzie should be accompanied by a nod to the fact that he can jump over a Mini and that he can throw a golf ball the length of a football pitch. Bonus points for claiming to have been there when he did both.

So, there are certain things that we all expect from these books: inside info, controversial views, the reliving of great moments, plenty of funny anecdotes and, obviously, cameos from that bloke who did 'Hot Legs'. We might also expect the odd glimpse behind the net curtains of the mock-Tudor house into the private lives of our heroes – perhaps gaining a sense that away from the football they are just like us, only with more money, more cars and more time to practise playing *FIFA* on the PS4.

Many players are, however, pretty guarded about their experiences away from football. Not all – the likes of Keith Gillespie, Lee Sharpe and Tony Adams have written eye-poppingly honest books that include much about their lives off the pitch. Still, most footballers prefer to keep their books football-related – and in many cases, it's probably a decision based on there being not much else to report, rather than it being too scandalous for publication.

However.

There is one sub-genre of the footballer autobiography that fearlessly removes such sensible limitations and cheerfully offers up truckloads of personal info. And we're not talking about dates, first cars or favourite holiday destinations.

No. We're talking about sex. Genuine intercourse. Proper shagging. Not just the odd vaguely saucy titillating detail, but so much more than that; stuff that veers towards porn – but never erotica; none of this stuff is remotely erotic.

This isn't just tabloid-style sauciness, like Dave Bassett referring to the woman who would later become his wife as 'a copper-haired bombshell' who 'had a string of beauty titles to her credit'. It's more like *50 Shades of Andy Gray*. It's stuff that will make your jaw drop and your toes curl – at the same time. There are phrases from these books that we will never be able to unread and images in our minds that will never be shifted. There are anecdotes involving threesomes, vengeful husbands, mother-and-daughter romps, Swedish models, gangbangs and the icky spilling of bodily fluids.

Not that we're prudes. Don't get us wrong. Each to his or her own and all that. We're just reporting the facts. And the facts are that in several of these books – not just a couple, but around one in 12 of all the books we read – we found passages of sexy-text that made our eyes water.

Now, you may have already read one or more of these books. You may well know what we're talking about. In that case, you can go beyond the plastic curtain overleaf, confident that you have a reasonable idea of what to expect in the pages that follow. But if you haven't read the works of the likes of Frank Worthington, Frank McAvennie (the Franks love this stuff), Mick Quinn, Paul Cannell and Roy McDonough, then consider this very fair warning: here be dragons. This is not like the football literature we grew up with – the only way any of it could be described as 'Roy of the Rovers stuff' is that it's all quite Racey.

BOOKED!

Still here? Well, then. Welcome. Don't worry. It's quite safe. Ish. We're all adults. No one is judging.

So, it's true. Alongside football career highlights and lowlights, some players decided to include pretty detailed descriptions of their busy sex lives in their autobiographies. In a way, these stories can be quite compelling – not because they're particularly enjoyable (and in some cases they seem decidedly questionable) – but because they feel like stories someone might tell you over a drink. A loud drink out with the lads, admittedly, but a drink all the same.

Let's start with Teddy 'Terry' Curran, whose book often feels like it's equally divided between football and sex. Here's a line that probably could sum up Ted's tome in just a few words: 'I'd separated from my wife Kim, telling her that I needed some space – to go out and bed some more women, of course!' 'Rayyy! Lads! Lads! Lads! Lads! Lads! Classic.

Yeah, back in the day, Tel was a player in more ways than one, and very little was off-limits when it came to the ladies. Take the story about when Sheffield Wednesday played away at Wimbledon and Curran caught the eye of a girlfriend of a Dons player in the bar after the game. Secretly they swapped numbers, and when Wimbledon were due to play at Sheffield later in the season, they arranged a clandestine meeting for the Friday afternoon before the game. Curran made up an excuse to his wife about why he'd be away the night before a home game and booked a hotel room in anticipation of a great night's action. He was not let down. When he met the mysterious woman at the train station, she wore, he says, only a fur coat and suspenders. Finally, after all this build-up, he writes: 'Without writing a porno, we made love throughout the rest of the afternoon and long into the evening.'

Three odd things about this story. Firstly, why did Curran wait until Wednesday were playing Wimbledon to arrange this liaison? Makes no sense. Even if girlfriends *did* travel to away games for Division Three fixtures back in the day (which seems unlikely), wouldn't it be odd for her to be going up the night before, and staying at a hotel by herself? Wouldn't it have been simpler to arrange when Wimbledon were away somewhere else? Also, was she sitting in just suspenders and fur coat for the entire three-or-four-hour journey from London? Bravo if so – that shows great commitment to sexy times. And then there's Terry's claim he doesn't want to write a porno – an odd thing to say when he's relating a story about cheating on his wife with another player's girlfriend who arrived after a long train journey wearing only undies and a fur coat. We appreciate he hasn't given us positional details and has spared us the ins – and indeed outs – of the union, but still, if he didn't want to write a porno you have to wonder why he spends much of the book on the verge of doing exactly that.

There's the time he's in Switzerland when Everton's John 'Bales' Bailey tries to persuade him to visit a particular prostitute. Curran rejects the idea, because he 'wasn't into prostitution', but Bales persuades him. How? Well: '[He said] I should come along as well and, if I didn't agree she was worth every penny, he'd pay me back.' And that's all it took – Curran apparently succumbed to peer pressure as easily as women succumbed to his lustrous perm and well-tended moustache. He ends by assuring us that Bales 'proved to be a very good judge', so a good time had by all, then.

In the end, we were quite glad Terry didn't write a proper porno – if he had done, it might not have been that coherent. Take one tale, where he stays for a couple of days at a plush house with a married woman whose hubby is away working in Saudi Arabia: 'She ran me a bath of pink champagne and we made bubbles in the most natural of ways.' What? Wouldn't a bath of pink champagne be really cold? Or did she heat it up first in huge vats on the Aga? How many bottles would you need to fill an entire bath? At roughly 80 litres for a bath, we're talking over 100 bottles. She must have cleaned out her local Asda. And what is it with Curran and fizzy drinks? Thirty-five bottles of Coke a night and baths made of rosé champers? Wouldn't you be really sticky after that sort of bath? And, above all else, what does he mean about the bubbles? Did they sit in the bath and fart together? Not exactly DH Lawrence, is it?

There's no such coyness in the work of Paul Cannell. Of course not – this is a man, you may recall, who called one of his chapters 'One Up the Bum, No Harm Done'. And it's in that legendary chapter that we found one of the most incredible passages of prose we have ever read.

It involves Cannell and his best mate, Robert 'Stetz' Stetler, when they played together for Memphis Rogues. After one game, they're enjoying a drink as usual and Paul remembers that 'this gorgeous blonde approached us after we had both left the toilet'. Strange little detail there. But, as Tim Roth's Mr Orange would tell you, these tiny bits of extra information lend authenticity to any story. Anyway, presumably after checking they've washed their hands, she invites the pair of them back to her place for drinks and what she calls 'pure flake'. They go, they drink, they snort and afterwards she asks if they'd like to join her for a bath: 'Well as Alan Freeman would say, "Not arf!"' is Cannell's reaction to this. Have to say, Fluff would not be the first person to spring to our minds when faced with that kind of proposition, but as you were. This lady then asks if they'd like to shave her – you know, *downstairs*. And here's that paragraph:

'Shaving a woman's delicate bits when you're full of drink and toot is a bit dodgy. Anyway, she was depilated adequately and she then asked us both to "make love" to her together; you know … two's up, just like in the porn films where they make it look so fuckin' easy, one potting the pink and the other potting the brown! … Stetz was on top of her pounding away as I tried to thrust my engorged member (as they say, in the porn magazines) into her at the same time … "Argh, argh, argh" … I heard in my pissed state. "Eeee sorry pet" I apologised, "am I hurting you?" "No" replied Stetz, "but will you get your fuckin' cock out of my arse!"'

The best bit of this stupendous piece of work is not the left-field use of 'depilated' in almost the same breath as a fairly grim snooker metaphor, or even the after-dinner-speech punchline (surely that's not true – what position could they possibly have been in for that error to occur?) – it's the sign-off to this tale, which comes immediately after the word 'arse', with literally no respectful pause: 'Sadly, Stetz passed away in 1990.' Being referenced like that is surely what he would have wanted. You don't get that kind of brilliance in Sir Bobby Charlton's book, we guarantee that.

Curran and Cannell – good players, cult heroes. But not giants of the game. Surely the household names of our beloved sport wouldn't indulge in this kind of sauciness? Well, not quite.

Step forward, Frank Worthington. A bona fide legend. And his book is as stuffed with shagging stories as the average Jackie Collins novel (we assume – never actually read any Jackie Collins to be honest, but whatever – Frank has definitely written what used to be known as a 'bonkbuster').

Now, allow us a very quick diversion here. One of your authors, as a teenager, spent some time working in a factory in Kent that turned out those plastic sleeves you get on bottles of water. Anyway, there was a gentleman working there that we'll call Chas, because that was his name. And Chas was a bit of a hero among the factory boys because of his sexual exploits. The problem, at least for your author, was that a lot of these exploits sounded an awful lot like scenes from pornos. They didn't exactly involve him turning up to people's houses to do a spot of plumbing – but it wasn't far off: there was the nurse who gave him oral during a routine check-up; the teenage schoolgirl daughter of his lady friend who seduced him when her mum was out; and his liaison with a rich, married older woman who had once been the star of a TV sitcom. That's not to say these stories weren't true … it's just that they sounded more like classic jazz-mag fantasies than actual reality.

Frank Worthington's book is a little like this. Again, we have no reason to disbelieve Frank's accounts – he was a rock star footballer with, in his heyday, more than a passing resemblance to the great actor and legendary Casanova, Robert Mitchum. There's no doubt Frank had a great deal of sex with a lot of lovely ladies. But his book reads like a sort of Mills & Boon for blokes – it's jammed with typical fantasies: sex on a plane, sex with an air hostess (separate occasion, not on a plane), a threesome with two Swedish blondes, sex with celebrities and sex in a taxi.

The tale of joining the Mile High Club is arguably where Frank reaches his peak. There he is, settled into his aisle seat on a plane, when he's joined by a young, loved-up French couple. During the flight, the husband falls asleep, and at that point Frank senses the woman's interest in him stirring. They end up risking a French kiss (what other kind would it be?), before Frank mimes that they might adjourn to the bogs: 'Her G-string was off in an instant and with her pert little derriere perched on the sink, one leg on the toilet seat, the other in my right hand it was "welcome to the mile high club."' Superb recall of positional detail, there, almost like he was describing one of his great goals. He continues: 'Away the boys in blue!' Well, there you go. 'We went at each other in a frenzy of passion and I was already nearing the Sarson's when there was a rat-a-tat-tat on the door that killed our amour stone dead.'

'Nearing the Sarson's'? You can't deny the man has a turn of phrase every bit as breathtaking as *that* turn that led to *that* goal against Ipswich. Anyway, no one was at the door, but Frank sent his French paramour back to her seat regardless. No Sarson's for anyone.

As you might expect with Worthington, it's not just the stories, it's the style in which they're delivered. The aeroplane anecdote is littered with French words – you know, because the couple were French – and elsewhere he describes more than one woman as 'defying gravity', which we think means they had big boobs, but we're not quite sure how gravity comes into it.

Other players relish this sort of titillating tabloid style too. Tony Cascarino vividly transports us to the scene of one particular liaison: 'We went inside and ripped into each other like crazed animals, then dropped like crazed animals who've been shot with tranquilizing darts.' Haunting.

Frank McAvennie has a tale about how he flew to Australia for a World Cup play-off with Scotland. Struggling with a toothache, he landed and went straight to see a dentist. For most people, the result of this would be unremarkable. Not for Frank – he experienced a totally different kind of extraction, courtesy of the attractive receptionist: '[She] showed me into the waiting room and stood chatting, just being polite, or so I thought … But the language of a come on is universal and I was hearing her loud and clear. Before I knew it she was giving me an expert blow job right there in the waiting room.' That'll take your mind off a toothache.

And, had he been spotted, Mickey Thomas would have been the centre of a very juicy tabloid exposé when he spent the night at Stamford Bridge entertaining a lady friend: 'I decided to switch on the Stamford Bridge floodlights. It was the night before we were due to play a live game against Everton. I couldn't resist it. I had to christen the centre-circle spot.' Blimey – the only other time someone scored from there was when Charlie Adam pinged one over Thibaut Courtois's head for Stoke in 2015. It's worth remembering also that this was 1980s Chelsea – a very different club to the moneyed global brand we know and love (only kidding) today. No pristine pitch back then – it was a rutted mud bath, second in awfulness only to the annual quagmire at Derby's Baseball Ground. This whole idea must have held much more allure for Thomas than his beau. It's quite odd they didn't get caught, too – it's not as if you can secretly turn on the floodlights at a major football ground in the middle of London without anyone noticing – and why did he need the lights on anyway? Or perhaps he did get caught. Maybe when Ken Bates threatened electric fencing, it wasn't to keep the fans off the pitch – it was to stop his players from fulfilling their fantasies on the muddy centre spot with their womenfolk.

When it comes to cheeky, seaside-postcard sauciness, no one holds a candle to Mick Quinn. The sex he describes is usually 'drunken' or 'mind-blowing', and, like Cannell, he's not afraid of a sporting metaphor – when he spies an attractive female, he's usually 'under starter's orders' and when intercourse occurs, he's 'weighed in'.

Mick's many, many sexploits often feel like letters ripped from *The Sun*'s 'Dear Deidre' letters column. As you may know, 'Dear Deidre' follows a trusted and rigid formula: a brief explanation of the 'problem' and details on the age of the people involved are followed by a titillating story where the 'correspondent' basically asks permission from Deidre to do something a bit wrong. Quinny is very much into this style of reportage. Considering the number of women he has slept with, his recall of exactly what they were wearing when he first laid eyes on them is nothing short of astonishing – he's like the Memory Man from *The 39 Steps*. Here's a real classic of his racy output – we join it in a nightclub:

'She had a stunning figure and was wearing a black skimpy dress that I couldn't wait to see her out of. I bought her a couple of bevvies and I was under starter's orders. I'd only gone and scored with an injury. The lads shouldered me to a cab waiting outside the club, and it felt like I had scored the winner at Wembley. Back at her gaff we didn't waste any time and went straight to the bedroom, but I was in such pain with my leg that I couldn't give her one in the missionary position. She had to get on top and ride me – and very nice it was too.'

Incredible, isn't it? A masterpiece of lean, tight-as-a-drum prose. A single paragraph has got the lot: sporting metaphor – check; team-mates there to witness the successful pull – check; reference to Wembley – check; reference to an injury – check. The actual sex bit has been whittled down to a trim 49 words – not an ounce of fat on it, and yet you can see it all so clearly, can't you? Phenomenal work.

But right at the top of the Top Shelf, so high you may need a stepladder to reach it, is the stupendous oeuvre of Roy McDonough. It's his descriptions of women that really earn him the tag (awarded by us) of the male Barbara Cartland: 'their tits were pointing through their tops in all directions', he gallantly writes at one point. Or, arguably an even greater compliment, he says they 'must have been a plastic surgeon's dream, as they had matching pairs of perfectly sculpted knockers, which were browning off just nicely'. Impressively, Roy's managed to make a description of naked breasts sound like it's been nicked from a Delia Smith recipe for roast chicken.

The book is full of his sexual adventures, thankfully not with all 400 women he says he acquired carnal knowledge of – but it's in the section where he explains his pulling technique that he reaches his zenith. It's a passage of text that gave us sleepless nights (not in a good way), and left one of your authors scrubbing themselves with a Brillo pad under a cold shower muttering 'It won't come off' over and over again:

'I would patrol the club like a kid in a candy store, picking out whatever sweet little thing I fancied tasting, before ruthlessly moving in for the kill.' The 'kill' involved that classic chat-up line we've all heard a million times: 'When we get in luv, I'm going to look after you downstairs, then all hell is going to break loose.' The silver-tongued lothario. It goes on. Brace yourselves:

'Most of them were decent-looking girls, but I had my fair share of howlers too when the beer goggles were strapped on at the end of a night out; the fat pig-ugly ones. I was getting so blitzed at that time I sometimes didn't know if I'd been with a girl or not, so I used to give my moustache a quick lick in the morning to find out if I'd done the deed.'

The final sentence of that tour de force is one that will haunt us, and now you, probably, forever. Some of you may need counselling, and if anyone is interested in setting up some kind of support group, by all means get in touch. The worst thing we can do here is to try to forget it, because this kind of trauma is simply not forgettable. It'll always be there. It has to be confronted and dealt with over a number of years.

Phew. Still with us? Because there's a little more to go. Some players are brave enough to divulge the circumstances of losing their virginity, for example. Pelé doesn't mind telling us it was with a prostitute when he was just 14: 'All I could think about was the worry of catching a venereal disease. Thankfully I didn't.'[41]

Mick Quinn, meanwhile, achieved his milestone in an alleyway outside a house party. After a brief description of the act, which involves his standard horse racing metaphors, he adds: 'On the way back we stopped for a pee, and I noticed that my knob had blood all over it.' Thanks, Mick. There's really no need to write down all the details of every memory, mate.

John Burridge got his rocks off with something soft and welcoming: 'Within seconds, I told her I'd finished, but it wasn't her I'd been gyrating against – I'd been having my first sexual encounter with the cushion of the settee.' Could've been worse, Budgie – Garrincha (another little bird!) famously did it with a goat first time out.

We also discovered plenty of stories of footballers getting involved with women already in another relationship, which resulted in several instances where they've had to use all their athlete's agility and ingenuity to avoid the attentions of a miffed husband or boyfriend.

Keith Gillespie relates an enjoyable anecdote of how he was once having some fun with a woman in her home when he heard the front door close downstairs. Realising it was the husband, he legged it into a kids' bedroom, which just happened to be covered with posters of Newcastle players, including one of Gillespie himself. Keith's plan was to jump into the top bunk and … pretend to be asleep. Foolproof. The husband, unsurprisingly not falling for it, walked in and uttered the immortal line: 'Fucking 'ell, it's Keith Gillespie … Have you been shagging wor lass?' There followed a scrap, where Gillespie claims they rolled 'down the stairs in a ball, raining punches at each other', and it only ended when Keith managed to peg it out the open front door to safety. Good work there – the modern player tends to go down at the slightest contact, but Gillespie, being a bit old school, rode the heavy challenge and raced through the opening towards goal. Dele Alli would have been floundering about on the landing appealing for a penalty. Wilfried Zaha would've been holding his shin before the husband had even thrown the first punch.

---

41 Another example there of Pelé's anodyne memoirs. Yes, you won three World Cups, mate, but there's nothing interesting about VD.

Paul Cannell had a similar experience in Memphis, where he did what all men throughout time have done if the husband comes home early – he hid naked in a closet. He was bricking it too, because, as if this wasn't already enough like a scene from a *Carry On* movie, his lady friend, picking an unusual moment to indulge in a bit of clever word play, had told him: 'He's a baggage handler at Memphis airport so he's used to throwing things around and damaging them.' Paul stood in the cupboard, possibly cupping his jewels, and listened to a fight break out: 'Eventually, I heard footsteps coming up the stairs. Fuckin' hell I thought, was it him or was it her? The door slowly opened and thank God it was her, a bit dishevelled with a bloody nose but I didn't care, it wasn't him and there was no gun.' Charming – she puts her body on the line, but he 'doesn't care' about the domestic violence, such was his relief at avoiding a pasting of his own.

Terry Curran possibly got too cocky as he involved a team-mate in what he describes as a 'rare one-two – a mother and daughter', meaning, of course, that the potentially angry husband was also the potentially furious father.

'We were in separate bedrooms with our partners and, after a while, decided to change ends! This was the type of two legged tie I liked. But what was that noise I could hear at the height of our passion? Shit, it was a car pulling up near the garage. That could only mean one thing – husband alert!' The pair of them ended up escaping by jumping out of a window and fleeing via the next-door neighbour's garden. It's another story that sounds like a softcore porn plot, but what's that line about two-legged ties all about? Did he have something against Milk Cup semi-finals?

Poor Mickey Thomas wasn't so lucky and was famously stabbed in the arse with a screwdriver after being caught with someone's missus in a lover's lane tryst. Thomas being Thomas, he reckons that after the windows of the car had been smashed in, he still had the wherewithal to offer up a one-liner: '"Gentlemen," I half laughed, "Please let me finish."'

Frank McAvennie never had husbands come after him – mainly because they seemed to tacitly approve of the whole idea. He recalls one night out with Charlie Nicholas when he (Frank) was propositioned by a woman, so off they toddled to a back room for a bit of fun: 'When we returned I discovered that Charlie had been sitting chatting with the woman's husband while I was fucking with his wife through the back. Now whether or not the guy knew what we were up to I'm not certain but this scenario repeated itself so often with different people I began to wonder what kind of relationships these people had.' We might also wonder what kind of life Frank had, where married couples were continually offering him sex. And was it always Charlie Nicholas left making small talk with possibly aroused husbands? Or were other Scottish strikers involved too?

Group sex is also a fairly common scenario within these books. For example, Frank Worthington failed a medical at Liverpool because his blood pressure was high, so he went on holiday to calm down a bit before trying again. While he was there, though, he ended up as the meat in a sandwich with two Swedish ladies (that wasn't his only liaison on the 'relaxing' trip either), and when he came back he failed the medical again and missed out on loads of potential trophies. Still, the shagging, though, eh?

McAvennie also recalls a tabloid-tastic 'three in a bed romp with blonde twins', while Stan Collymore is brazenly indiscreet about his relationship with TV presenter Kirsty Gallacher, telling us that he once enjoyed a 'wild, wild night' with her and her friend.

Group sex doesn't appear to be unusual among footballers – or at least sex while team-mates look on approvingly isn't. We stress that the incidents we read about all involved consenting adults, of course, but the act seems so common and normalised that it might even be worthy of some kind of study: just why do footballers enjoy having sex in close proximity to each other? Is it just footballers? Or is it typical in all team sports played by men? If it is just footballers, when and where did it start, and why? If it's prevalent in other sports, what's the psychology behind it?

But that's not what we're here for – we don't have those kind of qualifications. Instead, we can only report the facts from our research, and, you won't be surprised to learn, Roy McDonough is bang up for this kind of caper. He writes about one occasion where he and a team-mate had a threesome with a barmaid: 'I stood there watching, before he shot his bolt and ordered me to take over.' Bridget Jones this is not. He says the other players mocked him the next morning 'for kissing the barmaid after she had given my partner in crime a blowjob – "Morning

238

cock lips'", because of course the whole story had been well told even before they'd begun doing their stretches.

Micky Quinn details a stay at a hotel in Norwich where Coventry room-mate Robert Rosario invited a local woman he knew from his Norwich City days to entertain himself and six more players with her considerable skills. 'She was like a well-oiled and finely tuned machine,' says Quinny, but he insists: 'I didn't get involved – honestly, it wasn't really my scene.' Yep, it was in Mick's room, he watched the whole thing, but he 'didn't get involved'. 'Nah, you're all right, don't mind me,' he probably said, opening the *Racing Post* while this orgy took place next to his bed.

Pat Van Den Hauwe has a sticky tale of his own that took place in another hotel (these instances are always in hotels). It started when he noticed a team-mate's door slightly open, and he spied one slumbering Everton player surrounded by three naked women. He went straight in (warning: gruesome ending): 'One woke up and immediately set about pulling my shorts down … but I refused to go too far as I knew she had already been seen to and had not showered, so I settled for a lower massage and eventually shot my load. The girl had a good grip on me but my teammate ended up getting something across his head that he was not too happy about when he came down for breakfast the following morning.'

Wow. We'd say that was the least sexy story we've ever read, but there's that McDonough moustache thing, isn't there? But who was that Everton player whose night ended so well, but whose morning started so awfully? Was Curran around then? With all due respect, it wasn't Big Nev, was it? Sharpy? Definitely not Reidy. Surely not lovely old Trevor Steven? You probably could narrow it down if you wanted to, but for legal reasons we probably shouldn't.

Even when players do go for some vanilla one-on-one action, it doesn't stop them from reporting back to their team-mates the next day – however ill-advised that might be. Lee Sharpe, who doesn't really go top shelf in his book[42] despite admitting that 'my mates used to say there should be a red light outside my house because it was like a brothel.

---

42 No, Sharpey's book is much more about how he played better when he had a smile on his face. He goes on about the smile on his face thing a lot, which only makes it even weirder that he was best mates with Keaney. Surely if Keaney saw *anyone* smiling on a football pitch he'd want to slice their lips off?

Every Sunday morning there'd be girls draped everywhere, asleep in our beds, on the floor downstairs, the settee, everywhere,' is nevertheless not afraid to tell the world (or, at least, everyone who bought his book) a great story about his Leeds team-mate Mark Ford. Fordy fancied one of the employees at Leeds and eventually asked her out for a date. She agreed, and much to his delight, one thing led to another: 'She cried out, on the brink of ecstasy: "Talk to me Mark! Talk to me!" Mark Ford was a straightforward Yorkshire lad; he wasn't quite sure what she meant. But she cried out again: "Talk to me, Mark! Talk to me!" So Fordy, struggling to think of anything to say at this point, said: "Why is there no Vimto in the drinks machine?"'

Typical footballers – even making love to the woman of their dreams isn't enough – they want bloody Vimto on bloody tap, too. What's great about this story was that while you could maybe understand an inexperienced young man struggling with the demands for 'talk' during sex, it's less understandable that he later realised what she meant, noted that what he said was ill-judged, and then still thought it would be a story worth sharing with his team-mates, who, he possibly assumed, would surely be nothing but supportive and understanding and wouldn't, under any circumstances, later publish the tale in some kind of book, like, say, an autobiography.

Okay, after all that mucky muck muck perhaps we need an antidote, or at least some sort of palate cleanser. And there's only one place to go for that – Pirlo. Does Pirlo have stories of crusty moustaches, murderous husbands or flying spunk? No, he does not. He's Pirlo, for Pirlo's sake. He has this:

'Take someone like Antonio Cassano. He says he's slept with 700 women in his time, but he doesn't get picked for Italy any more. Deep down, can he really be happy? I certainly wouldn't be. That second skin, with its smurf-like blue, gives you a whole new image across the world. It makes you better, takes you to a higher level. Much better to be a soldier on the pitch than in the bedroom.'

Oh, Andrea, you dreamboat, you're perfect.

Umm … fancy a threesome?

13

Why Can't We All Just Get Along?

Watford Mole Syndrome

We all like to think that we're nice people, with nice families and nice friends, and that, on the whole, people like us. We like to think that we don't pre-judge, that we give everyone a fair chance and that we get on with just about anybody, really. Easy-going, that's us.

That's not true, though, is it? Think of the resentment you feel when you're queuing in traffic and a Range Rover comes bombing up the outside and some idiot lets them in. The patience snaps, the swearing carries forth and maybe we're not so nice after all. In the right, you say? Well, we all think that, pal.

So why should we expect footballers to be any different? We may put them on a pedestal, but they have feet of clay. They hurt and they hate too. What we're saying is: they can't all be St Trevor Francis of Assisi. In this chapter we'll lift the lid on the dream factory and examine the furnace of boiling pus at the black heart of our so-called beautiful game.

As the great Taylor Swift correctly observed, players gonna play and haters gonna hate, and, we might add, that often times players are gonna … sorry, going to, hate. Yet not all of them dive straight in with their studs dripping with vitriol; some fall back on those lovely quaint British euphemisms about cups of tea and Christmas cards to hint subtly at an undercurrent of malice. And so we learn that Chic Charnley has never received a Christmas card from Alex Miller because he threw his boots at him, while John Burridge claims a falling-out at Newcastle saw him crossed off the Christmas card lists of both Arthur

Cox and Terry McDermott when they were assistants to Kevin Keegan. Of Keegan himself, Mick Quinn says, 'We are never going to be on each other's Christmas card list.' At least by suggesting he's been crossed off, Burridge thought he was on the list to begin with. That's something, we suppose. Southampton team-mates Jimmy Case and Peter Shilton once fell out and almost came to blows, but while things did calm down, Case concedes that 'I haven't got Shilts on my Christmas card list and judging by the fact that I never receive one from him, I guess the feeling is mutual'. Well, it saves on stamps, doesn't it?

Alan Ball suggests that Tommy Docherty is 'not everybody's cup of tea', and indeed Archie Gemmill confirms this news by having an entire chapter called 'Tommy's Not My Cup of Tea'. He really does. Elsewhere, in a series of sly digs by Harry Redknapp aimed at Trevor Brooking (he hints that he didn't champion him for the England job, and that Trev took Billy Bonds's side in a dispute that honestly could fill this chapter, but that we're not touching with a bargepole), he laments the fact that Brooking became Sir Tricky Trev while his friend and World Cup-winning captain Bobby Moore stayed as the resolutely un-knighted plain old Bobby. What does Harry put this down to? 'Sir Trevor Brooking is the Football Association's cup of tea. He's their type of person. Bobby was a player's player.'

Of course. It pays to be someone's cup of tea.

Craig Bellamy goes one further than a petty one-to-one squabble by labelling an entire club – Chelsea, naturally – as 'not my cup of tea'. He elaborates a little by saying, 'They're not the type of fans I'd want to play for.' Given that he was more than happy to play for the fans of at least nine other clubs, that's quite the slam. Not as harsh as Jamie Carragher, though. In an inspired rant about Chelsea he says that for Liverpool supporters they 'characterized everything they despised'. He bandies around words like 'smug', and 'divine right', and says they 'represented the opposite of all I believed in', leaving us in no doubt that they are not his cup of ... well, you know.

We will come to some more serious disagreements, by the way, and some pretty famous people saying some ruddy rotten things about colleagues – but, in the interests of building a bit of tension, let's deal with some at the pettier end of the scale. And boy, these people are petty. Not just petty: they're football petty.

John Aldridge kicks us off by leaving Fernando Torres out of his Top 8 (always a Top 8, remember) Liverpool strikers because he's still smarting, like a wounded lover, from Nando's defection to Chelsea. Admittedly the book is a few years old and the wound was still raw when he wrote it, but his icy tone ('he's made his choice') suggests that he's not getting over it any time soon.

Speaking of put-out moustachioed Liverpool legends, Jimmy Case is cross with Matt Le Tissier because Tiss claimed in his autobiography that Jimmy still owed him £200 from a card game. Case refutes this and says that he never played cards on the coach because 'I was too busy cooking and serving up the meals and drinks for all the players on the trips back to Southampton'. We're on Jimmy's side on this one, firstly because what's £200 between footballers, and secondly because he conjures a nice image of himself on the bus there. How much cooking did he have to do? What did he cook on? Did Southampton travel to away games in a Winnebago? It sounds to us like there's a recipe book in this for Jimmy if he plays his cards right. Our suggested title would be: *Meals on Wheels: Away Day Cooking with Jimmy Case*.

Case is proof positive that big hard men can be rattled by small-time arguments, and Stuart Pearce is the same. He takes umbrage at Forest team-mate Tommy Gaynor both for nicking his complimentary tickets and for quibbling over the bill at a team meal out. He's right on both counts, mind, particularly the meal. There's nothing worse than that person who starts going over who had a starter and who drank what, is there?

Gary Lineker provokes the following diatribe from his own hero Frank Worthington, in the never dull *One Hump or Two*: 'Never mind Mr Nice Guy, Gary is a product of the money-mad modern game who, I believe, too often finds it convenient to hide behind his agent.' Blimey. Lineker must have done something terrible to Frank to invoke that level of anger, right? Well, we've read it, and we've read it again, and it seems that all he did was pull out of Frank's testimonial to care for his very sick young son. The nerve of the man. Frank can't let it drop, though, and claims it 'soured' his special evening.

Robbie Savage is another pretty thin-skinned one, especially when it comes to Barry Horne and the day he 'lost all respect' for him. What was his crime? On his debut for Wales, Bobby Gould praised Savage, saying that he had shown the more established players the way to do it. In response, Horne said, 'I'm not having that,' and Sav tells us that 'I've blanked him ever since'. We're often told that dressing rooms aren't for the faint hearted and that it's dog-eat-dog in there. You have to man up and hold your own and all those other clichés – and yet here's Robbie cutting off a team-mate until his dying day because he slighted him in the slightest of ways.

Whether Barry Horne reciprocates the ill-feeling we don't know, but we can tell you that he's not the man Savage considers his nemesis. That would be a certain property presenter who kicks off our section on Grudge Matches (feel free to pick sides as we go along):

GRUDGE MATCHES
Robbie Savage v Dion Dublin

Poor old Robbie says that Dublin really doesn't like him 'and I have no idea why'. If anybody can help him with this, please write down your suggestions on any blank pages at the back of the book. Of course, there was the infamous Midlands derby incident when Dion lost his mind and headbutted Savage, who was then with Birmingham. We only have Savage's account of this, as Renaissance Man Dion is yet to put pen to paper on his memoirs, but Robbie is insistent that he was blameless in both the incident and the feud as a whole.

His best guess at why the former Villa man is angrier with him than he would be with an overpriced two-bedroom terrace house in Basingstoke with insufficient storage space, is that perhaps 'he holds a grudge because I am more popular than him in his own town of Leicester'. That is almost certainly it, Robbie, and it's why Dion also won't give house room to Gary Lineker, Willie Thorne or Kasabian – presumably.[43] In conclusion, Savage philosophically says: 'If he met me and still thought I was a wanker, fair enough.' And who among us can ask for more than that? We would like to think that this meeting has happened by now and that the two get along famously so that we can put this one to bed. The last thing an under-siege BBC needs is a beef between *Strictly Come Dancing* and *Homes Under the Hammer*.

---

43 A quick Google search of 'Famous People From Leicester' reveals that David Attenborough, Una Stubbs, Engelbert Humperdinck and Gok Wan could also be on Dion's shit list.

Peter Schmeichel v Paul Ince

Team-mates don't have to get on, of course not. We learn from the respective accounts of Ray Parlour and Jimmy Bullard that William Gallas and Cesc Fabregas didn't like each other at Arsenal, and nor did John Moncur and Paolo Di Canio at West Ham. Rodney Marsh says that Man City legends Franny Lee and Colin Bell are so at odds that Colin Bell won't autograph a City shirt if Lee's name is already on there. Andrea Pirlo refers to Zlatan Ibrahimovic as 'the only mean Swede', Jamie Carragher says that Sander Westerveld wasn't 'my type of fella', while Mick Quinn says in his apprentice days at Derby, his team-mate Colin 'Charlie' Chesters was 'very much in the arsehole category'.[44]

It therefore comes as no surprise that two such big characters as the Great Dane and the Self-Styled Guv'nor rubbed each other up the wrong way. Indeed, it was Ince's tendency to play up this big boss man attitude that really rankled with Schmeichel, who says, 'he had GUV written on his boots, and had a number plate made with L8 GUV on it'. We would question whether that number plate makes him sound like the big man, or like he's dead, but certainly there was some Big-Time Charlie behaviour going on.

We learned from Keith Gillespie's account that Ince used to answer his phone simply with the word 'Speak', and isn't that evidence enough to convict? However, we can't help thinking that Schmeichel is going a bit far when he talks about Ince's 'potentially adverse influence on young players', adding that he needed to be 'weeded out' of the club. Whatever you think of Ince, he was a great player, and I'm sure Schmeichel could have tried a bit harder to rub along for the greater good. However, it seems that Alex Ferguson felt similarly to his goalkeeper, as he was heard to say the words 'I'll show him who the fucking Guv is!' before selling him to Inter Milan – which doesn't sound that much like bringing him down a peg or two to us.

Phil Thompson v Ian Snodin

There's no row like a Scouse row, and few men are as bitter as Phil Thompson. His book *Stand Up Pinocchio* is peppered with grudges, feuds and perceived slights, as we'll see in more detail later.

---

44 Mind you, he did go around the dressing room headbutting people, apparently.

This one can be seen from both sides, as both Thommo and Snods mention it in their books. Their row stems from a Merseyside derby that Liverpool won, and Thompson went potty celebrating on the pitch, 'kissing his badge and pumping his arms'. Snodin picked him up on it and suggested that the Liverpool man might want to wait until he was back in the dressing room for all that carry-on.

Before the following derby later that year, the two met in a hotel and had what sounds like a priceless row as they travelled up in a lift. Snodin says: 'As the doors shut, he started to go on about the number of derby games I'd played in, telling me I didn't know what it meant because I wasn't born on Merseyside … it was a load of nonsense.' In a row that is corroborated by both accounts, there was effing and blinding and threats of violence before Snodin told the older man to 'do one', and in so doing both ended the argument and proved his Scouse credentials.

Phil Thompson v Graeme Souness

Yes, Phil Thompson again. This one starts as team-mates when Souness got the Liverpool captaincy from him, and continues for a long, long time after that. The Souness take on the captaincy is that manager Bob Paisley had a few run-ins with regular skipper Thompson (hard to believe, isn't it?), and that Souey reluctantly agreed to replace him when the offer came.

Thompson's take involves a bit more skulduggery, with Souness villainously twirling that moustache of his and plotting behind the scenes to usurp him. Whatever the truth of it (and we know who we believe), Thompson clearly took the decision like a pro and 'for two months I just ignored Souness'.

The rancour continued once Souness returned to Liverpool as manager in the early 1990s, when Thompson was there as a coach. Thompson was let go from the club, and it's fair to say he was a little bitter about it. The reason he was given was that he was a bit rough with the reserves and younger players. Thompson's response is, 'Yes, they got the verbals at times, but I had a great relationship with them.' We should say at this point that this is not a picture painted by Robbie Fowler. His exact words about Thompson's 'great relationship' are: 'A lot of the young lads coming through fucking despised him for it. I'm amazed he never got properly sparked out there.'

As a furious Thompson left the club, he bumped into new signing David James on his way in, and in an exchange to rival Alan Partridge charging out of the BBC armed with a wheel of cheese, said to him, 'Welcome to the football club, David, but keep your back to the wall. Make sure there is no one with a knife to stab you.'

An irate Thompson refuses to accept that he was let go because of any kind of wrongdoing on his part. Instead, he suspects that the real reason was speaking out of turn against the new Souness regime. In a spectacular round of gossiping that exposes the world of football for the school playground that it is, Thompson heard from Alan Kennedy and David Johnson that he had been let go because he had been critical of changes Souness had made since his return to Anfield as boss. Evidently he had said something to Brian Kidd after a match, and then, 'Brian is said to have told Alex Ferguson. He then told Everton coach Archie Knox, who told manager Walter Smith. Walter, of course, had been with Graeme at Rangers.'

And then Sharon said to Damian that she'd seen Steve round the back of the shops with Zoe, even though he'd told Rav that he was grounded because he'd told Lisa's mum lies about Lisa and Imran. Or something.

It would seem that there's always some kind of travesty going on with Liverpool. Maybe *Brookside* had it right.

John Aldridge v Brian Laws

Now this is a famous one for football fans of a certain age. In the rescheduled FA Cup semi-final between Liverpool and Nottingham Forest after the Hillsborough disaster, Liverpool prevailed 3–1 in an understandably subdued and respectful occasion. One sour note in a game that everyone was just happy to get out of the way came when Brian Laws scored an unfortunate own goal and John Aldridge celebrated by ruffling the Forest man's hair.

To be fair to Aldridge, he says, 'Immediately I knew I'd gone too far and felt bad. Brian was rightly angry about it. Forest were also our next opponents in the league and I tried to make amends but Brian refused to accept my apology.'

Laws says that what Aldridge did was 'unforgivable', but does agree that Aldridge at least tried to apologise.

Stuart Pearce, who was Forest captain, says that after Aldridge tried to apologise at the league game, Laws conceded a penalty and that 'unbelievably, Aldridge rubbed him on the head again after apologising only a couple of hours earlier. I told Laws that I wouldn't have accepted that. I would have chinned him there and then on the pitch.'

What Stuart Pearce would or wouldn't have done is none of his business, quite frankly. This is a grudge between Aldridge and Laws, and these are clearly not men of (much) violence. Laws says that the pair have sort of patched things up over time, telling us that 'although we're not exactly mates, we can get on with each other. The years of hatred are behind us – and it really was hatred on my part.' Aldridge feels that he made it up to Laws eventually when he wrote to the FA in support of the then Grimsby manager, who was in trouble for assaulting his player Ivano Bonetti. 'I managed the player at Tranmere so knew how infuriating he could be.' So, they made up over a letter to the FA along the lines of:

> Dear Sirs,
> Go on, let Brian off. I know the player he whacked in the face and I can confirm that he deserved a whack in the face.
> Yours,
> Aldo.

Maybe Pearce was right after all.

Graeme Le Saux v Chris Sutton

We're surprised to see Chris Sutton in here, because he specifically says in his book, 'I've never been one for holding grudges.' Except, of course, he does hold grudges. The man who makes a living on TV and radio these days as a professional grump seems to have a problem with a number of people (of which more later), including a falling-out with Blackburn and Chelsea team-mate Graeme Le Saux. Le Saux himself can be quite a contrary character, of course. At one point you'll recall he came to blows on the pitch with another Blackburn team-mate, David Batty – so perhaps a Sutton–Le Saux disagreement was inevitable. But when it came, it was a daft one.

In the build-up to the 2000 FA Cup Final between Chelsea and Aston Villa, Le Saux did a piece in *The Sun*, itself a curious decision for an avowed *Guardian* reader perhaps, but there you go. In the piece Le Saux made 'a harmless joke, a throwaway comment' about the way Sutton dressed. He said that although he was good-looking, 'he wasn't the best dresser and even if you put him in an Armani suit, he'd still look like a tramp'. Usually this might be chalked up to banter and everybody can move on, but '*The Sun* did this huge caricature of Chris dressed as a tramp and made it the main feature of the whole page. Chris's wife went nuts.'

If you recall Chris Sutton's time at Chelsea, it was a struggle. A very good striker everywhere else joined a very good team and, for some reason, it didn't happen for him. Clearly the Suttons were feeling the pressure a bit. Chris concedes that he was 'touchy at the time and I had been battered all season', so Le Saux calling him a bit trampy was, it seems, the final straw.

Le Saux seems to think that things calmed down, but says 'there was a distance between us after that'. Sutton, though, goes further, saying of the second-best Channel Islands footballer of all time: 'he is very self-centred and had a high opinion of himself'; although he does at least soften enough to concede that 'he was a good player and had a good career'. So that's something.

Lawrie McMenemy v Kevin Keegan

Lawrie McMenemy doesn't spend time in his book on any row with Kevin Keegan at Southampton, but Mick Channon certainly sees fit to. Channon says that after a game against Wolves, Lawrie accused the team of not trying. Now, as we know, accusing someone of 'cheating' or not trying is second only to spitting at someone in football, and Channon says that Keegan took it personally and that 'they never spoke to each other after that'.

Keegan's own account isn't quite so dramatic. He says of the row that 'things were said which I'm sure Lawrie regretted later'. He doesn't say they never spoke again, but he clearly wasn't happy, and he left for Newcastle not long after. So, even if he's not quite his Lawrie McMenemy, it certainly seems that he wasn't his Lawrie McM-friend. No, you shut up.

* * *

The McMenemy–Keegan row brings us to the number one cause of unrest in football, according to our sources. And that is a player disliking his gaffer because he won't pick him. We can all understand that. Many of us may feel under-appreciated by our boss and slag them off when we get home, in private, and who knows, given the chance, maybe we'd do it in print too. Ronnie Whelan sums it up succinctly: 'When a manager is putting you in the team, you're happy with him. When he's not, it's a different story.' He says this of Jack Charlton, who he suspects never trusted him despite Whelan scoring that mad volleyed goal from Mick McCarthy's throw-in at the Euros that time. But while the sentiment of turning against a boss that won't pick you stands to reason, the sheer scope of it quite took our breath away.

We could have filled this book just with the bile that players we've read about spit in the direction of a gaffer who's slighted them – but, in the interests of our own sanity, and of keeping the mood light, we'll keep it as brief as possible. Here then, is a breakdown of some of the disputes we came across, which are either about a manager not picking a player, or pretending to be about something else, but really being about a manager not picking a player.

Player	Manager	Team	Choice cut
Frank McAvennie	Lou Macari	Celtic	Frank says Macari treated him 'like a spare prick in a brothel' and calls him a 'vindictive wee shit' for scuppering a move to Man City.
John Aldridge	Kenny Dalglish	Liverpool	Aldo is torn throughout his book between loving Kenny because he's a Liverpool legend, and being bitter about him dropping/selling him. At one point he says they fell out because 'I'd injured my arm by elbowing an opponent in a friendly in Sweden'.
Keith Gillespie	Kevin Blackwell	Sheffield United	Keith used to anonymously drunk-text Blackwell for the way he treated him at The Blades. Anonymous no more.
Keith Gillespie	Nigel Worthington	Northern Ireland	Nigel asked him to retire so that he didn't have to explain why he'd dropped him, then described his career as 'a fling'. Keith says: 'For that comment, I can never forgive him.'

Robbie Fowler	Gerard Houllier	Liverpool	There's a lot of anti-Houllier sentiment in Robbie's book, and it's 97 per cent based on the manager not picking him. When Bradford beat a Fowler-less Liverpool on the last day to deny them a Champions League spot, Robbie made the unwise move of leaving the following message on his gaffer's phone:
			'I'm gutted you cost me the Champions' League. I hope you're fucking satisfied in leaving me out now.'
			He concedes it 'wasn't necessarily my wisest move' in a book full of not-very-wise moves, if we're all honest with each other.
Stuart Pearce	Ruud Gullit	Newcastle United	Pearce insists that he tried to remain 'the complete professional' during tough times at The Toon but admits that he used to whack Gullit whenever he joined in training, even suggesting that Rob Lee 'offered to leave his pass short to give me another crack at him'.
			Sam Allardyce adds to the legend by suggesting the grudge continued when the pair became pundits together at ITV Sport – suggesting that Pearce refused to sit next to Gullit. Sam loves the gossip.
John Barnes	Ruud Gullit	Newcastle United	Pearce wasn't the only elder statesman that Gullit inherited from Kenny Dalglish at Newcastle, and he wasn't the only one he upset either.
			Barnes calls Gullit 'cold, almost dismissive towards me', but insists the reason they fell out 'was only partly because I was being overlooked'.
			It didn't help, though, did it, John?
Alan Ball	Don Revie	England	Ball is furious because The Revs sent him an unsigned letter to tell him he no longer needed him as a captain, or indeed as a player, for England. He didn't speak to him in person. This is the football equivalent of Phil Collins divorcing his wife by fax.

Mick Channon	Ron Greenwood	England	Mick says of Ron that he 'didn't radiate any feeling of great enthusiasm. He was methodical, yes, but there was no warmth. You didn't feel he had any passion about him.' It will shock precisely no one to learn that Greenwood dropped Channon and ended his England career.
Alan Brazil	Keith Burkinshaw	Tottenham	Lots of players like Burkinshaw. Not Brazil – guess why? During an away game at QPR when Burkinshaw tried to put sub Brazil on as an afterthought, an irate Alan spat his chewing gum at his gaffer and accused him of not knowing 'how to handle good players'.
Robbie Savage	John Toshack	Wales	Savage took a phone call from then Wales manager John Toshack, expecting to be given the captaincy of his country. A proud day. Except Toshack was dropping Robbie on the grounds of trying 'something different'. Sav's calm, measured reply? '"You can stick it up your arse," I told Toshack. "I'm retiring now."' Massive overreaction, no?
Dean Windass	Neil Warnock	Sheffield United	Windass is furious with Warnock for dropping him for a play-off final, after Warnock, against his usual practice, named a sub keeper on the bench because of the magnitude of the match. 'I wanted Sheffield United to win for the lads but I didn't for Warnock. As far as I was concerned, he could go and get f*****.' Windass confronted his gaffer: 'I called him a c*** and he agreed with me.' So if nothing else good has come out of this episode, at least we have Warnock's agreement on record.

Terry Curran	Lawrie McMenemy	Southampton	Bad blood all round here. Curran claims that the experienced players like Alan Ball did the managing for Lawrie at Southampton.
			For his part, McMenemy describes Curran as 'a persistent little moaner', says he decided to get rid of him pretty quickly, and recalls with disgust the time he arrived for a game 'wearing a John Travolta outfit'.
			Going by the dates, this probably means merely a white suit rather than a costume from *Battlefield Earth* or *Hairspray*, disappointingly.
Peter Shilton	Don Revie	England	Shilton made a mistake for Stoke that led to a goal in a match against Newcastle one weekend and joined up with the England squad immediately after. The lads all had *The Big Match* on and understandably gave him some 'good-natured stick' when his error came on screen.
			Shilts takes that in good spirit, but he was less keen on seeing Revie 'laughing gleefully. I was convinced then that Don had insisted everyone should watch the game for the sole purpose of seeing my howler.'
			Either this is genuinely mean or Shilton is being paranoid. Isn't it possible that Revie was laughing at the stick he was getting? Enjoying the craic and banter?
			Also worth remembering that Revie didn't pick Peter Shilton much, preferring Ray Clemence instead. Back in the days when England were spoilt for choice in goal.

Ian Wright	Graham Taylor	England	Without a doubt, Ian Wright didn't get as many England caps as a striker of his quality should have. In theory, Bobby Robson could have taken him to Italia '90, and then Graham Taylor didn't pick him as much as he could have done. Wright says that Taylor had his favourites in the squad and Wrighty wasn't one of them. As a result, the Golden Boot winner was also left out of the Euro '92 squad (and that was a terrible squad[3]). When our Graham broke the news, Wright went crazy at him, sounding off in what the tabloids would call an expletive-filled tirade, while a passive Taylor found no reasons to give, and no swearing to give back. And if we know anything about Graham Taylor, it's that he could swear. We've all seen the documentary.
Andy Gray	Graham Taylor	Aston Villa	Another striker not too impressed with Taylor: 'My second spell at Villa ended in the summer of 1987 with the arrival of Graham Taylor. You could say it resulted from a clash of personalities – I had one and he didn't.' Miaow!
Steve Claridge	Barry Fry	Birmingham City	Fry says that Claridge called him 'the worst tactician in the game' after he froze him out and sold him to Leicester.
Graham Roberts	David Pleat	Tottenham	Many years after he felt Pleat forced him out of Spurs, Roberts says he bumped into his old gaffer at a petrol station: '"Hello, Graham. How are you?" he said with a big smile on his face, although you could tell by the tone of his voice that there was nothing sincere about his greeting. I turned round and told him to be careful parking next to the kerb as you never know what you might pick up. It was a reference to his penchant for driving around the seedy red-light districts of London.' Yeah, Graham – we got it.

3   By our reckoning, all things being equal without injury problems, and with different managerial preferences, we could have gone to the eminently winnable Euro '92 with the following squad: Seaman, Martyn, Woods, Dixon, Adams, Bould, Winterburn, Walker, Parker, Pearce, Batty, Ince, Gascoigne, Platt, Rocastle, Le Tissier, Merson, Waddle, Beardsley, Lineker, Wright, Shearer. It could all have been so different. We'd have lost in the final to Germany.

Paolo Di Canio	David Pleat	Sheffield Wednesday	'I know that in England he's regarded as some sort of sophisticated footballing genius, but that's not the impression I got.' This is because David Pleat preferred to play Andy Booth up front to Di Canio. Actually, this one might be fair enough.
Neil Ruddock	David Pleat	Tottenham	The final word on Pleat: 'He's a total prat and the biggest arsehole I ever had the misfortune to meet.'

TECHNICAL AREA

David Pleat took a bit of a hammering towards the end of the last section there from some of his players, but he fares a lot better among his fellow managers. Not a bad word said about him. At least, not in the ones we read. That's not true of everyone, however. As discussed in our chapter on gaffers, the management side of the game is a kill-or-be-killed bear pit where you live by your wits and die by your decision to sub the wrong player when things aren't working.

In such an environment, you certainly forge a few firm friendships among your peers, but you also make a few enemies along the way. Managers might fall out about anything from deep divides in their philosophy on the game, to differences of opinion over decisions on the field, or whether to be a tracksuit guy or a suit guy on the sideline – though in recent years Pep Guardiola has taken us away from what was once a binary choice on that score, with his deck shoes, slacks and jackets full of zips; in many ways, that may be his lasting legacy to the game.

You would have to ask Sam Allardyce his main criteria for not getting on with some managers, but on the face of it, managing a bigger club seems to go a long way, and, of course, being foreign. Allardyce admits that he loved winding Arsene Wenger up, and says that Rafa Benitez had a superior attitude that he loved deflating: 'Here was a trendy foreign manager with all his smart ideas getting beat by some oik from the Midlands.' It's lucky that Sam has such broad shoulders to bear the weight of that chip, isn't it? One thing he laments is the passing of the tradition of getting together with his opposite number for a post-match drink. Apparently: 'The foreign bosses aren't keen on it, and there are so many duties after the match that there isn't the time.' Pardon us for pointing this out, but if there isn't the time for it any more, then it doesn't really matter whether the foreign bosses are keen on it or not, does it? It could be the new flavour of the month from the continent's lifelong dream to share a post-match pint of wine with Sam Allardyce, but if duties don't give them the time, it can't be helped, can it?

Post-match etiquette has always been a minefield. Think of the arcane rules of shaking hands that Mark Hughes lives by. He's forever upset that somebody has shaken his hand too early, too late or not at all. It seems that Don Revie was equally fussy. Geoff Hurst tells us that The Revs bore a grudge against Ron Greenwood for several years because of some objectionable Greenwood behaviour after West Ham once gave Leeds a good hiding: 'Years later when Revie was England manager he visited Ron at Upton Park. "Remember that night you beat us 7–0?" said Revie. "I went into your dressing room and congratulated you all and all you could say to me was 'Thank you very much.' I found your attitude hurtful and went back to our dressing room and told the players, 'You'll never lose to that man's team again.'"'

What was Don hoping for here? 'Thank you very much' seems a reasonable response to somebody saying 'well done', doesn't it? Poor old Ron was probably torn between celebrating a big win and not wanting to rub it in, little knowing that his polite response was going to get him in Revie's bad dossiers for years to come.

Occasionally, managers bear a simmering resentment for the gaffer who replaces them in a role, and to an extent we can understand that. Nobody wants to see a rival instantly doing a better job than them, any more than we want to see an ex-partner marry their very next lover. For two good examples of this we need look no further than Old Trafford. Ron Atkinson says of Sir Alex Ferguson that 'I tended to get on OK with Fergie, although there was one occasion where I threatened to knock his head off'. This was over a proposed move for Gordon Strachan, apparently.

Tommy 'The Doc' Docherty is a bit bitchier towards his successor, Dave Sexton, who he says 'was appointed because he was a nice man'. That doesn't seem such a bad thing, does it? Well, according to Tommy it is: 'He was well-liked because he's soft. Some players don't like a firm man.' Bitter Docherty continues: 'They got what they appointed and they deserved what they got.' Just to confirm, Tommy Docherty didn't get sacked from Manchester United for being a firm manager, he got sacked because he had an affair with the physio's wife. If what he means is they wouldn't get that sort of thing with Dave Sexton, well, then he's right. The Doc also seems to be glossing over the fact that Sexton had forged a good reputation by recently taking QPR – *QPR* – to within a whisker of winning the First Division championship. It's not like he didn't have other credentials than being a nice man.

There exists also the lesser-spotted example of falling out with the guy who was in the job before you. Step forward Brian Laws once more, who upset his predecessor at Grimsby, Alan Buckley, over a family matter. Buckley's son was on the books and Laws refused to let him sign for his dad's new club for nothing, instead demanding a fee for the lad and truly testing a father's love for his son. You can't put a value on that. Or maybe you can. Laws insists, 'There was nothing personal, it was simply a sound business decision.' Bit tight, though, Lawsy.

For a much more high profile, and less fishy, case we can look to two knights of the realm in Sir Bobby Robson and Sir Alf Ramsey. Bobby Robson's book is, quite frankly, a bit dull. For the most part it reads like a police report – just the facts – apart from one spectacular chapter when he gets even with everyone who has ever slagged him off, and top of the shop in a chapter titled 'Thanks a Lot, Sir Alf' is, you guessed it, Sir Alf Ramsey.

He questions why Ramsey criticised him in newspaper articles and insists that of all the abuse he received as England manager (several truck loads, if we remember correctly), the stick he got from the World Cup-winning boss hurt him the most. He suggests that Ramsey's motivation for writing scathing articles must have been the money, because he didn't see enough of him for the pair to be on *any* terms, let alone bad terms, despite being near neighbours in Ipswich. Bobby does recount one particularly funny snub, though, when they were both at a Chelsea game. 'I greeted him and conversationally asked how he had travelled to Stamford Bridge. "I came by train," he answered. "Oh," I responded, "I drove up and you are very welcome to come back with me." In the light of his experience in Mexico, I thought that there was a great deal we could discuss before I took my team out. But he stunned me when he replied: "I came by train – I shall return by train."'

We certainly feel for Bobby here, who was merely looking for advice about the trip to Monterrey – how many suitcases of baked beans should he take for the lads? Are Mars bars available out there? When's the worst time to take off your best player in a quarter-final? That sort of thing, but we can also see Ramsey's point – travelling with other people can be a nightmare, can't it? Given the choice of sitting on a lovely train with a nice book or a newspaper or having stilted conversation up the A12 with someone you barely know, we'd ask for a lift to the station at the most. Robson says that Ramsey would answer questions with a 'monosyllabic "yes" and "no" to everything'. He was lucky to get that. If we'd won the World Cup we'd answer every single question we were asked from 'Have you got the time?' to 'Who's your favourite Doctor Who?'[45] with a cheery 'I won the World Cup, you know.'

Robson's problems are very Ramsey-specific when it comes to fellow managers. Lawrie McMenemy, however, who we now realise is coming up a lot in this chapter, spreads it a bit thinner with a series of petty tiffs. In his two entertaining books he references issues and clashes he had with a circle of managers who clearly all had a bit of rivalry going on.

Somewhat inevitably, he fell out with Tommy Docherty over a potential transfer for Colin Todd. He accuses The Doc, in a phrase that our grandparents would have enjoyed, of 'playing silly buggers'. And yet Lawrie and Tommy are able to, well, bond, over a shared disdain for John Bond. It seems that Docherty outright couldn't stand 'Bondy', while Lawrie just engaged in a bit of concerted one-upmanship with him, for example: 'In the summer he was saying he was about to go to Torremolinos on holiday and I spoilt it for him by saying I'd just come back from Portugal.' Evidently Portugal beat Torremolinos in 70s holiday destination trumps.

McMenemy has a similarly prickly relationship with Ron Atkinson. They're clearly mates on some level, but there's petty rivalry there too, and they try to outdo each other whenever they can – a bit like Del Boy and Boycie, but with more jewellery. It's complicated.

The constant cropping up of Lawrie McMenemy in this chapter got us thinking about who might be the most abrasive characters in the

---

45 There are, of course, now enough Doctors to make a football team with. For the record, we'd have them line up as follows: GK Hartnell; RB Troughton, CB Capaldi, CB Baker T., LB McGann; RM Pertwee, DM Eccleston, CM Smith, LM Whittaker; CF Tennant, CF Davidson. Subs: Hurt (GK), McCoy, Baker C. Paul McGann having licence to bomb forward on the overlap, of course.

game. Who gets the hackles up among the other proper football men? Lawrie goes close and has clearly upset a few people, but he's not the most prolific. One of his former players might be, though. Step forward (but not so far that you won't be able to get back on your line in time if a ball ricochets up off of Paul Parker) Peter Leslie Shilton.

Shilts had a long and famous rivalry with Ray Clemence when it came to winning precious England caps. Two of the very greatest England goalkeepers of all time couldn't play together, obviously, so they spent many years fighting for one place, or taking it in turns to play for their country. The reason for pointing this out is to show that in spite of this tussle, the pair got on famously, to the point where they posed topless together (a 70s staple – see our pictures section for their racy snap) and even released a single – a cover of 'Side by Side' (well worth a listen if you can find it). So, given this, why did Shilton upset so many other people?

What we learn from Frank Worthington, his team-mate at Leicester, is both that 'he can be hard to know unless he's had a drink', and 'after a couple of glasses or three could be a bit Jekyll and Hyde'. So basically what he's saying is that for Peter Shilton to be in any way tolerable you have to catch him on one drink. No more, no less. Margins.

Worthington insists that on the whole they have got on over the years, but he does say they had a dressing-room row once after Shilton accused him of not trying. As we know, this accusation will always induce a sharp intake of breath around the room. On this occasion Frank threatened to take Shilts 'outside right now and break your nose for you'.

Shilton backed down when Worthington challenged him to a fight, just as he did when Jimmy Case did likewise, but clearly there's something about Shilts that team-mates find difficult. We were sorry to read that the keeper fell out with fellow Forest legend John McGovern over money, and we won't dwell on that, but we can talk about Mick Channon's complicated relationship with him. The pair never came to blows, but the Southampton team-mates clearly didn't get on. Channon devotes a bit of space to saying things like 'Nothing gives me greater pleasure in the game than to stuff Peter Shilton.' He says that Shilton was tremendously self-confident, was insistent that he would one day be a great manager, probably of England ('fraid not, Shilts), and damns him with that greatest of insults among footballers of a particular vintage – he was a boring card player.

Ron Atkinson found Shilton arrogant. Yes, you read that right. Big Ron recalls an encounter where Shilton asked him why he had never signed him for United, insisting that he was the best goalkeeper in the world and that 'you would have won everything in sight'. Now let us just say that at this point Shilton arguably *was* the best goalkeeper in the world, but it's probably for others to say. In response, Atkinson pointed to United's excellent defensive record (perhaps while throwing a protective arm around incumbent keeper Gary Bailey), called Shilton a 'nugget' and suggested that the best goalkeeper in the world might have got to Maradona's 'Hand of God' goal before he did. I said good day, sir.

The Hand of God is certainly a touchy subject for Shilton. Of course it is. But here's some succour: Diego Maradona himself finishes his book with a list of players he considers greats of the game, and Shilton makes the cut. Hurrah! Having said that, this is the entry:

'94. Peter Shilton: the thermos-head got cross because of my hand-goal. What about the other one, Shilton, didn't you see that one? He didn't invite me to his testimonial … oh my heart bleeds! How many people go to a goalkeeper's testimonial anyway? A goalkeeper's!'

It might have been better just to leave him out, Diego. What does 'thermos-head' even mean?

Kevin Dillon isn't a player that makes Diego's greatest list, which does at least save him from the sort of pasting Shilton got; but he certainly seems an odd sort. Truth be told, he's not a player we thought about much before this book, beyond a vague recollection of him at Portsmouth as a player and Reading as a coach, but it seems he's left an indelible mark on many of our subjects. There was that time Roy Keane slammed his head on a desk (see 'Hard, Harder, Hardest' chapter), but there are other instances of him leaving people cold. In two separate examples, this Eeyore-type character told Jim Smith and Alan Ball that he was 'only happy when I'm sad'. Ball says they had a 'love-hate relationship' as player and manager. Once, when Dillon had scored a cracking 'Beckham-esque' goal (which everyone will tell you he was capable of), Ball tried to congratulate him 'and asked him what he was thinking when he went for the shot. He said: "I saw your face on the ball and hit it as hard as I could.'" All right, mate, calm down. Ball describes Dillon as an 'oddball' and that just about covers it.

From the Oddball to the Hoddball himself – Glenn Hoddle. Hoddle has his devotees for sure; Harry Redknapp can't speak highly enough of him, Paul Merson approves of his methods (even the crackers ones) and Uwe Rosler likes him, along with a legion of Spurs fans who revere him. However, let's just say that within the game, the meeting room for the pro-Hoddle camp could perhaps be a scout hut, while the anti-Hod meetings might need somewhere bigger – like the Albert Hall.

What comes up a lot is that Hoddle could get exasperated with players who couldn't do what he could do, as admittedly he was an incredibly talented player. Tony Cascarino and Stan Collymore are among those who complain of this, and Stan goes further to mention something else he found irritating: 'He would still run around the training pitch, tapping the ground as he ran with the point of his boot like a fucking dick. That just lost him the respect of the players.' It doesn't take much, does it?

Chris Sutton and Glenn Hoddle fell out for a specific reason, as most of us know. Sutton was called up for a B international (remember them?) and refused to play. Sutton felt short-changed by the call, and Hoddle felt that was disloyal to the country and had no more to do with him, chiefly because he had a wealth of other mid-90s striker options. Apart from Shearer and Sheringham, there were plenty of good forwards from that era that can claim not to have got a fair rub of the green: Robbie Fowler, Andy Cole, Ian Marshall – the list is endless. Sutton's not alone. It was a great time for English goalscorers. You can debate the merits of the argument, but it certainly appears to have lingered, with Hoddle refusing to be interviewed for Sutton's book.

Stuart Pearce is another one who resents Hoddle for not picking him for England, and feels that he could have made an impact against Argentina at the World Cup in 1998. Hoddle seems to be under the impression in his World Cup diary that consummate professional Pearce took the decision well, but having read the books of both men, we're here to tell you that he really didn't: Pearce complains at length about being discarded.

Perhaps nobody has more reason to be bitter on these grounds than Matt Le Tissier. Le God lit up the 90s and was rewarded with a paltry number of caps by a succession of England managers. Hoddle was supposed to be the man who changed all that, because he was a flair player who, in his day, had himself perhaps been undervalued by the national team. But no. As a result, Le Tiss is not a big fan of Glenn, labelling him 'incredibly arrogant and extremely stubborn', and saying that 'if he could get a semblance of man management he'd be a huge asset to any club'.

Joey Barton is another one who questions Hoddle's man-management, saying that he 'had evidently done little work on his people skills. I took an instant dislike to him because of his aloof manner.' It's fair to say that there are several people Joey doesn't like much, but that doesn't make his opinion on Hoddle any less valid; Joey knows what he likes and he definitely knows what he doesn't.[46]

The flip side of those people who are disliked across the board are those, like Barton, who use their books to settle some scores. That's where the real juice is. Dave Bassett actually called his entire book *Settling the Score*, but he's disappointingly light on airing his grievances, even stopping short of naming names when he complains of being undermined during his time at Vicarage Road. He writes bitterly of what he charmingly calls the 'Watford mole syndrome' but says, 'I know very well who were involved but they are completely unworthy of any mention in this book.' That's not the sort of thing we're after, Dave … Harry … Dave – whatever your name is.

Zlatan Ibrahimovic is also strangely coy when it comes to naming names. When he talks about the Swedish national side he says that everyone got on well, a great bunch of lads, apart from one prima donna. He says, 'The prima donna was all like, "At Arsenal, you know, this is how we do it. That's how you ought to do it. Because they know about that stuff at Arsenal, and I play for them." Pretty much like that.' You know, and we know, and he knows that he's talking about Freddie Ljungberg, but he doesn't name him, which is disappointing … unless this is expert trolling in a different way and he thinks that by being

---

46 Can we add our own voice to this chorus of disapproval? One of your authors, as a teenager, once saw Glenn play in a testimonial game at Dartford. At the end, kids streamed onto the pitch to get some big-name autographs. Mark Bright signed loads, but when we asked Glenn he didn't even look down. Maybe he hadn't heard the first time: 'Glenn, may I have your autograph, please?' He was walking towards the tunnel. He was tall, it was noisy. Maybe he genuinely still hadn't heard. 'Glenn? Glenn? GLENN?' Not a sausage. Off he popped, not stopping to squiggle his name even once. But, like Chris Sutton, we don't hold grudges.

coy and only hinting at what he thinks of people he's getting at them in a more subtle manner. And we might even believe that if elsewhere he wasn't quite so forthright about how he thinks Louis van Gaal is a 'pompous arse'.

Carlton Palmer is another one not quite right for this section. Palmer certainly has a list of people who have upset him that's as long as one of his telescopic, ground-covering legs – but, being a better person than us, he always tries to point out that he subsequently made up with everybody he's fallen out with. Palmer has things to say about managers Trevor Francis and George Graham, who he refers to as a 'swaggering bully of a man, his debonair appearance never quite able to obscure the jutting, single-minded chin and resolute, unbending jaw'. We've always said it about George Graham – look at him there, with his unbending jaw.

In terms of team-mates, Palmer's biggest beef seems to be with Matt Le Tissier (again) when he arrived at Southampton, and we can't help thinking it was Carlton's fault: 'When I first arrived at Southampton, the kit man had put my kit out and I began to change. Le Tissier arrived a few minutes later and told me to move, saying that he "always" changed there. It was his place.

'"Well, you aren't getting changed here today," I said.

'"You what?" he replied.

'"You aren't getting changed here today," I repeated. "I am."'

Carlton says that Le Tissier should have asked him nicely and that Guernsey's finest 'made it into a thing. He challenged me and I rarely back down in those situations.' It seems to us that you made it into a thing, Carlton.

We had to dig through Palmer's book (*It Is What It Is*) to find the people he didn't like much – sort of pick them up as we went through. More handily for us, some people will devote a chapter to their shit lists and have done with it. As documented, Bobby Robson is one such person. Apart from Sir Alf Ramsey, other people that have upset him include Kevin Keegan, Emlyn Hughes, Malcolm Macdonald and Alan Ball – for the most part, former England players who were critical of him and his England team.

Not content with saying that these people were disloyal by giving his England teams a pasting in the papers, Sir Bobby can't help having a pop at the lacklustre management careers of Messrs Hughes, Macdonald and

Ball. Ball in particular comes in for some stick as Bobby calls him a 'joke' and says, 'Perhaps he couldn't live with what I achieved at Ipswich.' Yes, Bobby, that will be it. Among his own players he slates Steve Perryman for taking him to task in his book, and Terry Fenwick, who he calls a traitor for sticking his oar in. Who knew Uncle Bobby could be as vicious as this?

Referee Clive Thomas is another one who puts aside a chapter to list the people he doesn't like, giving himself a brief respite from telling us how great he is to do so. Top of his list is Sir Bobby Robson himself. Quite why it's any of his business as a Welshman is unclear, but he seems in part upset by the 'gutless displays' of Robson's England side. 'It gave me no satisfaction that the man in charge was one of the very few managers in the league I could not stand. Nor could I understand him: any man who airs his complaints to the press rather than talking man to man lacks courage in my view.' Says Clive Thomas as he airs his complaint in print.

The problem with Robson evidently goes back to a couple of disputed decisions in Robson's Ipswich days, and his ill-feeling towards that club goes deeper. He insists that neither Russell Osman nor Terry Butcher should have been anywhere near the England team, hinting at favouritism by Robson. He also says that Ipswich captain Mick Mills is on his list because 'the way he looks at me when a decision goes against him is sufficient to ensure that our relationship has never been good'. We think as long as he doesn't say anything, Clive, you shouldn't take against him – it seems unfair.

Graham Taylor is another surprising name on Thomas's roll call of people he couldn't get along with. He talks of 'two major altercations' with GT after Taylor criticised him in the newspapers, and describes him as 'not senior management material' – a claim that's plainly wrong. Others he doesn't like include John Bond (again), Don Revie (again), Billy Bremner, Gordon Milne and Ossie Ardiles (again).

Thomas reserves the special 'H' word, though, for a certain someone else who criticised him on TV: 'With respect to the BBC, there are two people I hate at the moment and Jimmy Hill is both of them.' Marvellous. Yet not even the grudges that Thomas kept notes on in his little black book can see him into our TOP FIVE PEOPLE WHO HATE PEOPLE.

These are the Premier League, tippermost toppermost, world-class grudge-bearers, with barely a nice word to say about anyone. Here are the guys you wouldn't want to get on the wrong side of.

PEOPLE WHO HATE PEOPLE
5. Craig Bellamy

Glenn Roeder once described his West Ham striker David Connolly as 'an angry ant'. We don't really know what he means, but we reckon Craig Bellamy is one too. Bellamy always cultivated an image as something of a troublemaker throughout his much-travelled career. Opinions have probably mellowed about him in recent years, as he undeniably put a shift in for most of the clubs he played for, we now know about the significant amount of charity work he does, and we all liked it when he had a go at John Terry that time around the Wayne Bridge incident. His book, *Goodfella*, is thoroughly entertaining and honest, but besides a lengthy telling of his tale of whacking John Arne Riise with a golf club, a good many others come up as Bellamy enemies.

Considering he played for so many different clubs, what's remarkable is the concentration of aggro around his spell at Newcastle. He didn't get on with Dean Saunders, for example, either as a team-mate for Wales, where he felt Deano would stir up trouble and then watch it explode under Bobby Gould, or as a coach under Graeme Souness at St James' Park.

With Bellamy sharing a dressing room with Souness, of course, a row was as inevitable as one at the Queen Vic if Pat and Peggy were sharing a shift behind the bar. The verbal clash came when Bellamy said something and Souness took offence. Craig claims Souey ranted about the trophies he'd won and threatened to knock him out. Whether Souness was naked at this point or not is unclear, but 'he was absolutely raging, he came over to where I was sitting and tried to grab me. I pushed his hand away and he lost his balance slightly and stumbled. That made a couple of the other boys laugh which made Souness even more furious than he was anyway.' With his dander up, Souness invited Bellamy to the gym for a Ronnie Pickering-style bare-knuckle, which Bellamy declined.

Probably a good decision. He did, however, have an actual fight with coach John Carver after conceding to being 'mischievous really. A little provocative perhaps.' This mischief took the form of parking in Carver's parking space one morning, then teasing him about it as the team were preparing to travel to Majorca. Carver finally snapped at the airport and confronted Bellamy, and the pair fought. Well, it is tricky to know how to pass the time before a flight, isn't it? Bellers denies reports that he threw a chair at Carver, instead insisting that he threw a chair out of the way to get to Carver. So that's all right, then. He adds, 'We ended up wrestling stupidly on the floor. I didn't know at the time but Bobby was giving a press conference on the other side of the screens from where we were grappling and the press could hear that a kerfuffle was going on.' Good use of 'kerfuffle' there.

Also on Tyneside, Bellamy famously fell out with the Prince of the City, Alan Shearer – a clash of personalities that, after Bellamy had moved to Celtic on loan, continued via the medium of text messaging, which all the kids used to do before they started WhatsApping, Instagramming or Snapchatting, or whatever it is now. After seeing Shearer on TV mentioning 'shortcomings in defence', Bellamy wielded his phone to tell him: '"You need to look at yourself instead. Your legs are fucking shot. Concentrate on yourself and let the team take care of itself." I got one back from him straight away.

'"If I ever see you in Newcastle again," he wrote, "I'll knock you out."

'"I'm back in Newcastle next week," I texted back. "Pop round and say hello."'

As far as we know, this rumble never quite took place, but we would have paid good money to see it if it had done. It's fair to say that Bellamy burned his bridges in Newcastle, which is a shame because they've got some nice bridges in Newcastle.

4. Joey Barton

Joey Barton is another man you won't be surprised to see here. An equally abrasive character as Bellamy, he has certainly made his share of enemies. Whether you think he's a misunderstood victim of circumstance, or entirely at fault for his own problems (and after reading his excellent book *No Nonsense*, we'll admit we're none the wiser), what is clear is that there are several people that he isn't very keen on.

We'll leave aside the big, famous flashpoints that have seen him put behind bars, and instead focus on the fun stuff, shall we? Petty squabbles, disagreements and catty remarks only.

There are several team-mates that Barton doesn't care for, usually rival midfielders who he saw off to first get, and then keep, his own place in the team. Eyal Berkovic is given short shrift as Barton calls him 'just another body, a diva who dared to dwell on the ball'. We enjoy this Raymond Chandler-esque tone, and the hard-bitten detective vibe continues with the icy 'Don't waste your compassion on him.' Barton showed Berkovic up in training with a few robust challenges, and the Israeli was soon on his way.

Just as Bellamy has his Newcastle issues, so too did Barton (another who fell out with Shearer); but his highest concentration of aggro came at QPR, where, despite embracing the move, visiting the museums and generally trying to use his time in London to improve himself, he fell out with a succession of managers. He says of Neil Warnock that 'we were destined never to see eye to eye', and likens him to Mike Bassett. But he really goes to town on Warnock's successor, Mark Hughes. After checking up with mates who had played under Hughes and received less-than-flattering reviews,[47] he feared the worst. Sure enough, the pair ended up squaring up in Hughes's tiny office: 'I could see in his eyes, and his flared nostrils, that he was desperate to get it on. He was aggressive as a player, but as a manager knew he had more to lose.'

Eventually Hughes was gone, to be replaced by Harry Redknapp, a man who took Rangers down, then up then pretty much down again before bailing out with that bad knee. Evidently things weren't right during the promotion season and the air needed to be cleared, and clear it spectacularly Joey did. Poor old Harry was just sitting watching the Racing Channel in his office, apparently, when Joey entered and delivered the following home truths: 'Gaffer, I need to speak with you. I don't know how you've managed to do this, but everyone hates you. I've known managers polarise a dressing room, but I have never been in this situation, where no one has a positive word to say about you. That's difficult to do, because even if a fella is a cunt there will be people who like him for his arrogance.'

Wow. None of us would like to hear something like that, but it appeared to do the trick, as QPR went up.

---

47 Maybe all football teams and clubs should air such reviews publicly, like a TripAdvisor for football managers or players. A Kieran Trippier Advisor, if you will.

3. Phil Thompson

Phil Thompson was a very good footballer and enjoyed an extremely successful and trophy-laden career as a defender for Liverpool. You would think he would be content with that and that his book would be a giddy whirl of drinking champagne from all the different cups he'd won. The fact that we have already heard about one or two of his grudges, and that he is so high up on this list, tells you that it isn't. Instead, *Stand Up Pinocchio* is the spectacular roll call of score-settling that Dave Bassett's *Settling the Score* can only dream of.

For starters, Thompson expresses his displeasure with (in addition to Graeme Souness, of course) Don Hutchison, Robbie Fowler, Paul Ince and Ian Wright. His problem with Wright dates back to a Liverpool v West Ham game in 1999 when Thompson was Liverpool coach and Wright was on the bench for the Hammers. Wrighty decided to amuse himself by throwing chewing gum and paper at Thommo's head without him realising, making the standard 'big nose' gesture behind his back and, just for good measure, giving the wanker sign. Tellingly, three-fifths of the Liverpool subs found it funny, with only Riedle and Friedel toeing the party line and keeping straight faces.

Childish, yes, but hardly a diplomatic incident, you might think – yet Thompson took action. First he pulled the subs, including Ince, aside at training the following day, 'screaming blue murder about what was expected from the players', then he rang Harry Redknapp and demanded satisfaction. Redknapp said Wright was denying it, even though the manager himself knew he had done it. Thompson is unforgiving, saying, 'I just thought it showed a total lack of respect. It shows him in a different light to the friendly, chirpy face we see on TV. He thinks he's a funny, good guy but he lacks something in my book.' One thing Thompson's book certainly doesn't lack is people he moans about. Joining those previously mentioned are Ian St John, Terry McDermott, Roy Evans, Larry Lloyd and Joe Fagan. That's an awful lot of Liverpool legends. Maybe Thompson had it wrong all those years and if he'd played across the park at Everton he'd have loved every minute of it.

2. Stan Collymore

Stan Collymore is another player who ran into problems at Liverpool, but at least he didn't hang around too long before realising the place might not be for him. For a glorious couple of years there, Collymore led the attack alongside Robbie Fowler for a stylish, but ultimately fragile, Liverpool team. It should have been a 90s Mersey paradise – all Britpop and Cool Britannia – but instead of that, the pair didn't get on, and the partnership soon broke up.

Stan likens their relationship to that of Andy Cole and Teddy Sheringham: they kept it civil, but no more than that. He says their dispute dated back to a pre-season friendly against Ajax when Fowler should have passed to him and he complained. Stan thought it was run-of-the-mill stuff, but Fowler just swore at him and that was it: 'We never spoke again in my two years at Liverpool.' It's worth saying at this point that Robbie Fowler says he doesn't know what Collymore is talking about and insists that 'I reckon that I spoke to him every day – when he actually turned up'. Mixed messages on this one, then – but, at the very least, the conversation can't have been up to much. For good measure Stan also says that Steve McManaman didn't like him either.

Way beyond these minor disagreements, however, comes Collymore's real villain at Liverpool: Steve Harkness. Harkness doesn't have his own book, so we should say that all we have to go on is what Collymore says, but what Collymore says is very worrying. He describes Harkness as a 'neanderthal from Carlisle with a very, very small brain', and 'a nasty, horrible, mean, racist little prick'. Stan claims Harkness racially abused him and delights in telling us he caught up with him once he'd left for Villa in an incident that saw Harkness carried off, and Stan only booked, something he sees as a win-win.

Back on safer, more trivial ground, Collymore moans about team-mates Geoff Thomas and Ian Woan, agent Frank McLintock and manager John Gregory ('one of the biggest pricks I have ever had the misfortune to come across'). For good measure he adds that Martin O'Neill thought Gregory was an even worse word (the very worst) as well.

But above all others it would seem that Stan reserves his greatest anger and bile for lovely Gareth Southgate, which came as something of a surprise. He has several pops at Southgate, who was a team-mate of Collymore at both Crystal Palace and Aston Villa, and sneers at his professionalism and ability to do the more mundane aspects of training without complaining – which doesn't seem like the greatest crime to us.

Stan says 'he comes across as a sweet-tempered, affable, wonderful middle-class guy', but suggests that he's two-faced. He's confident that the feeling was mutual and says that Southgate came looking for him in the 1996 FA Cup semi-final, when Collymore was still with Robbie Fowler at Liverpool and Southgate was already at Villa: 'I was glad all that seething enmity we felt for each other was out in the open at last.' Better out than in, we suppose.

Imagine how Collymore felt during the 2018 World Cup, as Gareth took England to the semis and became a national treasure and a firm housewives' favourite along the way. Stan must have been absolutely fuming as the adulation, waistcoat-wearing and hashtags escalated the further England got. And there was nothing he could say or do, because Saint Gareth somehow united the country and any criticism would have sounded churlish and bitter. Stan'll bide his time, though. Eventually Southgate will do something wrong and Stan will be ready. Just you wait.

1. Chris Sutton

And so we arrive at our number one, and it's grumpy Chris Sutton, a man who has earned a place in our hearts in recent years as a pundit with a disdainful take on everything and everybody. It wasn't always this way, of course, for once upon a time Sutton was also a very good footballer – with a disdainful take on everything and everybody. The real reason that Sutton makes it as Grumpster No. 1 is because of his insistence that he doesn't hold a grudge. If he said that to your face, you'd expect him to stare deep into your eyes with a cold glare for a moment before breaking up and jokingly clarifying that 'I don't hold *A* grudge, I hold many grudges'.

Honestly, the list of people that have upset him is longer than the credits sequence on a Marvel film.

Sutton will always chiefly be remembered for the amazing SAS partnership he struck up with Alan Shearer that propelled unfashionable but newly minted Blackburn Rovers to the Premier League title in 1995, but we're sad to report that there was no love lost between the two of them. Chris says that 'there wasn't any warmth towards me from Alan', because, he suspects, Shearer was close with Mike Newell, who Sutton replaced in the side. Sutton bemoans the fact that when he scored,

Shearer sometimes 'didn't come over to celebrate with me and this left me very unsure about what he thought about me'. This makes us feel a bit for Chris: he's clearly a sensitive soul, but it's not long before he's making people uncomfortable himself with his forthright views. He's a man who doesn't pull his punches:

On Blackburn manager Ray Harford: 'I didn't like him as a person. I think it's fair to say the feeling was mutual.' BIFF!

On Chelsea team-mate Dan Petrescu: 'I thought he was a bit snide,' and: 'I wouldn't trust him as far as I could throw him.' ZAP!

On Norwich manager Nigel Worthington: 'Maybe if he'd signed me, he would have kept his job.' KAPOW!

On Blackburn coach Derek Fazackerley: 'I told Derek to shut up, that his opinion didn't mean anything to me and that he was a budgerigar.' Wait, what?

A budgerigar? Now perhaps this means that Fazackerley liked looking at himself in a mirror, like budgies do, but there's no further evidence for that; or possibly it means something along the lines of repeating everything the manager says, but wouldn't that be a parrot? Maybe Fazackerley just really liked cuttlefish.

It's not Sutton's only odd turn of phrase when criticising people. Inevitably, he's fallen out with that other professional controversialist Robbie Savage, and he says of him that 'it was part of his game to noise people on the pitch'. Noising people? Is that a thing? We think we get the idea, based on what we know of Savage and how annoying he must be to play against, but we've just never heard 'noising people' as a slur before.

There came a time when Chris Sutton grew discontent with merely being the grumpiest footballer in England, and marched north of the border to take his rightful crown as the grumpiest man in Scotland too. During his successful spell with Celtic, predominantly under Martin O'Neill, he made a series of enemies, both in the camp and outside of it in the more traditional areas.

Within the camp, he fell out with Olivier Tebily, who continually went through him in training up to the point where Sutton did what any reasonable grumpy bugger would do and 'swung my elbow at him, and he ended up on the floor'. Sutton never mentions him again. Tebily made it out of there alive and went to Birmingham City, possibly just to get away from Sutton, so he must have been cock-a-hoop to see Chrissy turn up at St Andrews a few years later.

Chris Sutton in an Old Firm environment was always going to be ripe for a bit of friction. He refers to Ibrox as Castle Grayskull,[48] and picks in particular on Nacho Novo, who he says he couldn't stand 'because of his antics'. His biggest problem with Novo seems to be that he 'strutted around' as if he was as important to the team as some of Rangers' very best players. Maybe in the eyes of some, he was, Chris. 'On the park he'd clap the fans at every opportunity and I couldn't be bothered with that type of player. It used to annoy me.' Yeah, those bloody players who have a rapport with the fans – who needs them, right? Of all the people and things about Rangers that could have upset a mardy Celtic player, this seems among the very slightest that Suts could have picked on. Elsewhere, he took against Hearts player Steven Pressley for shouting in the tunnel and geeing his players up. For having the temerity to do this, he gets called 'a buffoon'.

We all fear change, but not many of us fear it as much as Scottish referee Hugh Dallas, who regularly used to have the stuff chucked at him in Old Firm matches – they even hit him once. But beyond the visceral thrill of pound coins whizzing by your earhole, we'll wager that not many things rattled Dallas more than locking horns with Sutton. Chris reckons that Dallas liked the focus to be on him, and he got it with the way he not only followed the rules but 'applied them to my playing style'. This translates as Dallas giving a lot of free kicks against him for roughing people up, doesn't it? The referee's biggest crime, however, was to ignore an injured Sutton when he was calling for help after tearing knee ligaments in a game against Aberdeen. If Chris didn't like him already, then Dallas urging him to get up would not have helped.

You can be in no doubt by now that Chris Sutton is right up there when it comes to footballers moaning about others. You might argue with us about picking him as a number one, but frankly, after all this negative energy, we'd be too exhausted to argue back. Let's just bring the curtain down on Sutton's enemies by dealing with his relationship with

---

48 Common error this, pedantic *Masters of the Universe* fans. Don't be fooled by the spooky name: Castle Grayskull was the goodies' castle. If you want to convey an image of breaching the enemy walls, it's Snake Mountain you want.

Gordon Strachan. Oh, look – it's a player being cross with a manager who didn't play him and eventually sold him.

Sutton's gripe isn't just that, of course, it's that the manager didn't speak to him much while he was out injured: 'In my opinion, he treated me appallingly and, to be honest, that hurt.' Sutton recounts a comical exchange in the Celtic canteen in which Sutton insists that Strachan hadn't left him a voicemail message about his injury and Strachan insists that he had.

We'll never know the truth, but the impression we get is that had Strachan not sold Sutton on, the pair would still be there having the same conversation. To sum up, Sutton says of Strachan, 'I didn't think too much of him, really. I was glad to get away from him, to be honest.' A suitably negative note to leave Big Chris on.

* * *

After all this bile and enmity, we're sure you'll agree that a bit of a palette cleanser is what's wanted, so that we don't let the dark side win out. Here, then, are a couple of lovely nuggets of goodwill that will restore your faith in human nature, put the hope back in your heart and maybe even cheer you up. Firstly, Graham Roberts tells us that when he arrived at Tottenham, Gerry Armstrong 'came to the rescue and bailed me out with a huge favour. His mate had a furniture and fittings shop and he arranged to carpet my whole house for nothing.'

There we are – that's better already, isn't it? Imagine that! All that lovely free carpet for Graham Roberts. It's bringing us back from the brink, if we're honest. If we have a happy place – an oasis of calm and inner peace; a mind palace if you will – then we want it done out in carpet by Gerry Armstrong's kind mate.

Secondly, all of these players and managers featured within this chapter should really take a leaf out of Jimmy Case's book. Case had his fair share of run-ins, but talks warmly of getting a bit of perspective and leaving grievances behind on the pitch. For example, he fondly recalls bumping into Terry Phelan, a player he had definitely kicked up the arse on the pitch at least once. The two got chatting and drinking and the hard feelings dissipated, 'then Terry invited me to his kid's christening party the next day. I couldn't make it, but I appreciated the offer.'

It's the detail we love here. What kind of anecdote finishes with being invited somewhere but being unable to make it? And yet the love and respect within the story is palpable. It's not the anecdote we necessarily wanted for the end of a barbaric and traumatic chapter, but it's the anecdote we need right now.

Postscript

There's probably an apposite Kenneth Wolstenholme quote to use here to mark the end of things, but right now it escapes us – we're all quoted out.

Hopefully you've enjoyed reading this as much as we've enjoyed writing it, and hopefully we've all learned something along the way. Even if we all now have certain images seared on to our brains forever, at least we're sharing them together.

This book would, of course, be nothing without the source material. We've sought to gain an insight into how footballers live, as well as enjoying the very best of their weird, funny and sometimes unbelievable stories, but we would urge further reading and encourage you to go out and get some of the original works and enjoy them in full for yourselves.

To that end, we wanted to leave you with a few recommendations of our favourites. If we had to narrow it down, we'd point you in the direction of the following.

For sheer eye-opening candidness, debauchery and entertainment we'd recommend Roy McDonough's *Red Card Roy*, Mick Quinn's *Who Ate All the Pies?* and Pat Van Den Hauwe's autobiography.

For genuinely good reading for those with even a cursory interest in football, we would suggest Joey Barton's *No Nonsense*, Roy Keane's *Second Half* and Ian Wright's *A Life in Football*.

Special mentions too for the life stories of Gary Neville, Andrea Pirlo, Neville Southall, Leroy Rosenior, Tony Cascarino and Craig Bellamy.

Hopefully, however, we've shown that there is something in all of them for somebody.

Acknowledgements

John would like to thank ...

Jo for her love and support throughout, and Archie, Evie and Martha for understanding what I've been trying to do when I've been too busy for them. Hopefully they will all read it at some point once I've censored out the rude bits.

My mum for always encouraging me to write and tolerating a football obsession through childhood, whether I was nagging to get the Subbuteo pitch out or knocking the heads off her flowers in the garden. Unfortunately, my dad is no longer around to see this, but I would like to thank him (along with my Uncle Stan) for taking us to countless West Ham games while we were growing up. The ones under floodlights were always the best.

Dan would like to thank ...

Carmen for all her love, encouragement and understanding while I spent quite a lot of spare time that should have been family time reading and writing about football.

Dad, for taking me to see my beloved Stones (not the band, obviously) at two years old and thereby infecting me with the disease that meant I had to keep going to the football most weekends for the rest of my life. This book would not have been written had we not shared hundreds, even thousands, of games together – whether they were joyous thrashings, soul-destroying 0–0 draws or heartbreaking defeats. From London Road to Loftus Road. And the sofa in 1990. Never been a silence like it. Thanks also to Mum for putting up with it all.

And Leo, who I hope one day might like football and football history enough to read and enjoy this thing.

ACKNOWLEDGEMENTS

Both authors would like to thank …

Paul and Jane Camillin at Pitch Publishing for having faith in the idea and allowing us to fulfil a long-cherished ambition.

Lee Dixon, Frank Skinner, Tom Davis and Paul Hawksbee for their very kind words.

Zebedee for his spot-on illustrations.

Mark Lucey for being a great champion of the idea and a top, top, top sounding board throughout. If Mark doesn't like it, nobody will.

Anyone who donates unwanted books to charity shops. One person's waste is another's treasure, and finding gold on the second-hand shelves was part of the thrill.

Above all though, the authors would like to thank the footballers themselves for what they've done on the pitch and off the pitch, for what they've been happy to share in their own books, and for being thoroughly entertaining across all three. None of us would be here if we didn't like football.

Bibliography

Adams, Tony with Ian Ridley, *Sober: Football. My Story. My Life* (Simon & Schuster UK, 2017).

Aldridge, John with John Hynes, *Alright Aldo: Sound as a Pound. On the Road with Everybody's Favourite Irish Scouser* (Trinity Mirror Sport Media, 2010).

Allardyce, Sam, *Big Sam: My Autobiography* (Headline, 2015).

Ardiles, Ossie, *Ossie's Dream: My Autobiography* (Transworld Digital, 2010).

Atkinson, Ron, *The Manager* (deCoubertin Books, 2016).

Ball, Alan, *Playing Extra Time* (Sidgwick & Jackson, 2004).

Barnes, John, *The Autobiography* (Headline Book Publishing, 1999).

Barton, Joey, *No Nonsense* (Simon & Schuster UK, 2017).

Bassett, Dave, *Settling the Score* (John Blake, 2002).

Bassett, Dave and Downes, Wally, *The Crazy Gang* (Bantam, 2016).

Bellamy, Craig with Oliver Holt, *Goodfella* (Trinity Sport Media, 2013).

Bergkamp, Dennis, *Stillness and Speed: My Story* (Simon & Schuster UK, 2014).

Best, Clyde, *The Acid Test* (deCoubertin Books, 2016).

Bonds, Billy, *Bonzo* (Arthur Barker, 1988).

Brazil, Alan with Mike Parry, *There's an Awful Lot of Bubbly in Brazil: The Life and Times of a Bon Viveur* (Highdown, 2007).

BIBLIOGRAPHY

Brooking, Trevor, *My Life in Football* (Simon & Schuster Ltd, 2014).

Bullard, Jimmy, *Bend it Like Bullard* (Headline, 2014).

Burridge, John, *Budgie: The Autobiography of Goalkeeping Legend John Burridge* (John Blake, 2011).

Cahill, Tim, *Legacy* (HarperSport, 2015).

Cannell, Paul, *Fuckin' Hell It's Paul Cannell* (Createspace Independent Publishing Platform, 2012).

Cantona, Eric, *Cantona on Cantona* (Andre Deutsch, 1996).

Carragher, Jamie, *Carra: My Autobiography* (Corgi, 2009).

Case, Jimmy, *Hard Case: The Autobiography of Jimmy Case* (John Blake Publishing Ltd, 2014).

Channon, Mick, *Man on the Run: An Autobiography* (Littlehampton Book Services Ltd, 1986).

Charlton, Bobby, *1966: My World Cup Story* (Yellow Jersey, 2017).

Charlton, Jack, *The Autobiography* (Partridge Press, 1966).

Charnley, Chic with Alex Gordon, *Seeing Red: The Chic Charnley Story* (Black and White Publishing, 2009).

Clough, Brian, *Cloughie: Walking on Water – My Life* (Headline, 2002).

Cole, Ashley, *My Defence: Winning, Losing, Scandals and the Drama of Germany 2006* (Headline Publishing Group, 2006).

Collymore, Stan, *Tackling My Demons* (Willow, 2013).

Cottee, Tony, *West Ham: The Inside Story* (Philip Evans Media Ltd, 2012).

Cruyff, Johan, *My Turn: The Autobiography* (Macmillan, 2017).

Curran, Terry with John Brindley, *Regrets of a Football Maverick: The Terry Curran Autobiography* (Vertical Editions, 2013).

Dalglish, Kenny with Henry Winter, *My Autobiography* (Hodder & Stoughton, 1996).

Di Canio, Paolo with Gabriele Marcotti, *The Autobiography* (Willow, 2001).

Dixon, Kerry with Harry Harris, *Up Front: My Autobiography* (John Blake Publishing, 2016).

Docherty, Tommy, *Call the Doc* (Littlehampton Book Services Ltd, 1981).

Drinkell, Kevin, *Drinks All Round: The Autobiography* (Black and White Publishing, 2010).

Drogba, Didier, *Commitment: My Autobiography* (Hodder & Stoughton, 2016).

Dunphy, Eamon, *Only a Game?* (Penguin, 1987).

Duxbury, Mick with Wayne Barton, *It's Mick Not Mike: The Autobiography of Mick Duxbury* (Pitch Publishing, 2015).

Elleray, David, *Referee! A Year in the Life of David Elleray* (Bloomsbury Publishing, 1998).

Eriksson, Sven-Göran, *Sven: My Story* (Headline, 2014).

Ferdinand, Les, *Sir Les: The Autobiography of Les Ferdinand* (Headline Book Publishing, 1997).

Ferdinand, Rio, *#2Sides: My Autobiography* (Blink Publishing, 2014).

Ferguson, Alex, *My Autobiography* (Hodder & Stoughton, 2013).

Fowler, Robbie, *Fowler: My Autobiography* (Pan, 2009).

Francis, Trevor with David Miller, *The World to Play For: A Great Footballer's Own Story* (Granada Publishing Limited, 1983).

Fry, Barry, *Big Fry: Barry Fry – The Autobiography* (Willow, 2011).

Gemmill, Archie, *Both Sides of the Border: My Autobiography* (Hodder & Stoughton, 2005).

Gillespie, Keith with Daniel McDonnell, *How Not to Be a Football Millionaire: Keith Gillespie – My Autobiography* (Trinity Mirror Sport Media, 2013).

Gray, Andy, *Gray Matters: Andy Gray – The Autobiography* (Pan Books, 2005).

BIBLIOGRAPHY

Greaves, Jimmy, *Greavsie: The Autobiography* (Time Warner, 2003).

Halsey, Mark with Ian Ridley, *Added Time: Surviving Cancer, Death Threats and the Premier League* (Floodlit Dreams Ltd, 2013).

Hasselbaink, Jimmy Floyd, *Jimmy: The Autobiography of Jimmy Floyd Hasselbaink* (HarperSport, 2011).

Hoddle, Glenn with Harry Harris, *Spurred to Success: The Autobiography of Glenn Hoddle* (Queen Anne Press, 1987).

Holloway, Ian with David Clayton, *Ollie: The Autobiography of Ian Holloway* (Green Umbrella Publishing, 2009).

Hunter, Norman, *Biting Talk: My Autobiography* (Hodder & Stoughton, 2004).

Hurst, Geoff with Michael Hart, *1966 And All That: My Autobiography* (Headline, 2001).

Ibrahimovic, Zlatan, *I Am Zlatan Ibrahimovic* (Penguin, 2013).

Jones, Vinnie, *It's Been Emotional: My Story* (Simon & Schuster, 2013).

Jordan, Joe, *Behind the Dream: The Story of a Scottish Footballer* (Hodder & Stoughton, 2004).

Jordan, Simon, *Be Careful What You Wish For* (Yellow Jersey, 2013).

Keane, Roy with Roddy Doyle, *The Second Half* (W&N, 2015).

Keegan, Kevin, *Kevin Keegan* (Readers Union, 1978).

Keegan, Kevin, *My Autobiography* (Warner Books, 1998).

Kimmage, Paul, *Full Time: The Secret Life of Tony Cascarino* (Simon & Schuster Ltd, 2000).

Laws, Brian with Alan Biggs, *Laws of the Jungle: Surviving Football's Monkey Business* (Vertical Editions, 2012).

Le Saux, Graeme, *Left Field: A Footballer Apart* (HarperSport, 2010).

Le Tissier, Matt, *Taking Le Tiss: My Autobiography* (HarperSport, 2009).

Lyall, John, *Just Like My Dreams: My Life with West Ham* (Penguin, 1990).

Macari, Lou, *Football, My Life* (Bantam Press, 2008).

Maradona, Diego Armando, *El Diego: The Autobiography of the World's Greatest Footballer* (Yellow Jersey, 2005).

Marsh, Rodney with Brian Woolnough, *I Was Born a Loose Cannon* (Optimum Publishing Solutions, 2010).

McAteer, Jason, *Blood, Sweat and McAteer: A Footballer's Story* (Hachette Books Ireland, 2016).

McAvennie, Frank, *Scoring: An Expert's Guide* (Canongate Books, 2003).

McCulloch, Lee, *Simp-Lee the Best: My Autobiography* (Black & White Publishing, 2013).

McDonough, Roy with Bernie Friend, *Red Card Roy: Sex, Booze and Early Baths: The Life of Britain's Wildest Ever Footballer* (Vision Sports Publishing, 2015).

McGovern, John, *From Bo'ness to the Bernabeu: My Story* (Vision Sports Publishing, 2015).

McKenzie, Duncan with David Saffer, *The Last Fancy Dan: The Duncan McKenzie Story* (Vertical Editions, 2009).

McMenemy, Lawrie, *The Diary of a Season* (Arthur Barker, 1979).

McMenemy, Lawrie, *A Lifetime's Obsession: My Autobiography* (Trinity Mirror Sports Media, 2017).

Merson, Paul with Ian Ridley, *Hero and Villain: A Year in the Life of Paul Merson* (Willow, 1999).

Merson, Paul, *How Not to Be a Professional Footballer* (HarperSport, 2012).

Nelson, Garry, *Left Foot Forward: A Year in the Life of a Journeyman Footballer* (Headline, 1996).

Neville, Gary, *Red: My Autobiography* (Transworld Digital, 2011).

Palmer, Carlton with Steve Jacobi, *It Is What It Is: The Carlton Palmer Story* (Vertical Editions, 2017).

Parlour, Ray, *The Romford Pelé: It's Only Ray Parlour's Autobiography* (Cornerstone Digital, 2016).

Pearce, Stuart, *Psycho: The Autobiography* (Headline, 2014).

Pelé, *Pelé: The Autobiography* (Simon & Schuster, 2007).

Pirlo, Andrea with Alessandro Alciato, *I Think Therefore I Play* (Backpage Press, 2014).

Poll, Graham, *Seeing Red* (HarperSport, 2018).

Quinn, Mick with Oliver Harvey, *Who Ate All the Pies? The Life and Times of Mick Quinn* (Virgin Digital, 2011).

Redknapp, Harry, *A Man Walks On To a Pitch: Stories from a Life in Football* (Ebury Press, 2014).

Redknapp, Harry with Martin Samuel, *Always Managing: My Autobiography* (Ebury Press, 2013).

Redknapp, Harry, *My Autobiography* (CollinsWillow, 1998).

Regis, Cyrille with Chris Green, *Cyrille Regis: My Story* (Andre Deutsch, 2010).

Roberts, Graham with Colin Duncan, *Hard as Nails: The Graham Roberts Story* (Black and White Publishing, 2008).

Robertson, John with John Lawson, *Super Tramp: My Autobiography* (Mainstream Publishing, 2011).

Robson, Bobby with Bob Harris, *Against the Odds: An Autobiography* (Hutchinson, 1990).

Rosenior, Leroy with Leo Moynihan, *'It's Only Banter': The Autobiography of Leroy Rosenior* (Pitch Publishing, 2017).

Rosler, Uwe, *My Autobiography: Knocking Down Walls* (Trinity Mirror Sport Media, 2013).

Ruddock, Neil, *Hell Razor: The Autobiography of Neil Ruddock* (Willow, 1999).

Savage, Robbie with Janine Self, *Savage! The Robbie Savage Autobiography* (Mainstream Publishing, 2010).

Schmeichel, Peter with Egon Balsby, *Schmeichel: The Autobiography* (Virgin Publishing, 2000).

Sharpe, Lee with David Conn, *My Idea of Fun: The Autobiography* (Orion Books Ltd, 2006).

Shilton, Peter, *The Autobiography* (Orion, 2004).

Smith, Kelly, *Footballer: My Story* (Corgi, 2013).

Snodin, Ian with Alan Jewell, *Snod This for a Laugh* (Trinity Mirror Digital Media, 2013).

Souness, Graeme with Ken Gallacher, *Graeme Souness: A Manager's Diary* (Mainstream Publishing, 1989).

Souness, Graeme, *Football: My Life, My Passion* (Headline, 2017).

Southall, Neville, *The Binman Chronicles* (deCoubertin Books, 2012).

Stewart, Ray, *Spot on with 'Tonka'* (West Ham United Football Club, 1991).

Storey, Peter, *True Storey: My Life and Crimes as a Football Hatchet Man* (Mainstream Digital, 2011).

Sturrock, Paul with Charlie Dudby and Peter Rondo, *Forward Thinking: The Paul Sturrock Story* (Mainstream, 1989).

Suarez, Luis, *Crossing the Line: My Story* (Headline, 2014).

Sutton, Chris with Mark Guidi, *Paradise and Beyond: My Autobiography* (Black & White Publishing, 2011).

Ternent, Stan with Tony Livesey, *Stan the Man: A Hard Life in Football* (Blake Publishing, 2003).

Thomas, Clive, *By the Book* (HarperCollins, 1984).

Thomas, Mickey, *Kickups, Hiccups, Lockups: The Autobiography* (Century, 2008).

Thompson, Phil, *Stand Up Pinocchio: Thommo from the Kop to the Top – My Life Inside Anfield* (Trinity Mirror Sport Media, 2013).

Van Den Hauwe, Pat, *The Autobiography of the Everton Legend* (John Blake Publishing Ltd, 2015).

Vardy, Jamie, *From Nowhere: My Story* (Ebury Press, 2017).

Venables, Terry, *Born to Manage: The Autobiography* (Simon & Schuster UK, 2015).

BIBLIOGRAPHY

Wark, John, *Wark On: The Autobiography of John Wark* (Know the Score Books, 2009).

Webb, Howard, *The Man in the Middle: The Autobiography of the World Cup Final Referee* (Simon & Schuster UK, 2017).

Whelan, Ronnie, *Walk On: My Life in Red – My Autobiography* (Simon & Schuster UK, 2011).

Windass, Dean, *Deano: From Gipsyville to the Premiership* (Great Northern Books, 2011).

Winter, Jeff, *Who's the B*****d in the Black? Confessions of a Premiership Referee* (Ebury Press, 2006).

Worthington, Frank with Steve Wells, Nick Cooper and Ian Worthington, *One Hump or Two? The Frank Worthington Story* (ACL & Polar Publishing, 1994).

Wright, Ian, *A Life in Football: My Autobiography* (Constable, 2016).